Understanding
Things Fall Apart

The Greenwood Press "Literature in Context" Series
Student Casebooks to Issues, Sources, and Historical Documents

UNDERSTANDING
Things Fall Apart

A STUDENT CASEBOOK TO ISSUES, SOURCES, AND HISTORICAL DOCUMENTS

Kalu Ogbaa

The Greenwood Press
"Literature in Context" Series
Claudia Durst Johnson, Series Editor

GREENWOOD PRESS
Westport, Connecticut • London

Library of Congress Cataloging-in-Publication Data

Ogbaa, Kalu.
    Understanding Things fall apart : a student casebook to issues,
sources, and historical documents / Kalu Ogbaa.
        p.   cm.—(The Greenwood Press "Literature in context"
series, ISSN 1074–598X)
    Includes bibliographical references and index.
    ISBN 0–313–30294–4 (alk. paper)
    1. Achebe, Chinua. Things fall apart.   2. Achebe, Chinua—
Contemporary Nigeria.   3. Igbo (African people) in literature.
4. Nigeria—Civilization.   5. Igbo (African people).   I. Title.
II. Series.
PR9387.9.A3T5365   1999
823—dc21   98–22902

British Library Cataloguing in Publication Data is available.

Library of Congress Catalog Card Number: 98–22902
ISBN: 0–313–30294–4
ISSN: 1074–598X

First published in 1999

Greenwood Press, 88 Post Road West, Westport, CT 06881
An imprint of Greenwood Publishing Group, Inc.

Printed in the United States of America

∞™

The paper used in this book complies with the
Permanent Paper Standard issued by the National
Information Standards Organization (Z39.48–1984).

10 9 8 7 6 5 4 3 2

To my **Glory** and **Uchenna**
for coming . . . at noonday

Contents

Acknowledgments

I am indebted to Professor Claudia Durst Johnson, Series Editor of Greenwood Press's "Literature in Context" series, for inviting me to participate in the project; to the Connecticut State University System, for giving me a grant to do research for the book; to the faculty development unit of the Office of the Vice President for Academic Affairs of Southern Connecticut State University, for providing secretarial support; to my colleague and friend, Professor George A. Rosso of the English department at Southern, for proofreading the typescript; and to my son Ikenna (Iyke), for getting me research material from his college library at Yale University. For all their individual help, I remain eternally grateful.

—Kalu Ogbaa

Chinua Achebe. Courtesy of Anchor Books.

Introduction

Published in 1958 to great critical acclaim at the height of African political independence movements, Chinua Achebe's *Things Fall Apart* is a watershed novel in which artistic achievement and cultural reeducation form a perfect balance. When it appeared in world markets and academic institutions, the novel was immediately recognized as a blueprint for budding novelists by African writers and critics, as a literary classic by Canadian and American critics, and (not unexpectedly) as a novel of protest by British critics and press. In spite of these divergent critical evaluations of the novel, the common point of agreement is that, in developing the character of his hero Okonkwo Unoka, Achebe combined the techniques of literary modernism, the socio-literary philosophy of naturalism, and Igbo story-telling devices to recapitulate the history and consequences of the late nineteenth-century African encounter with European colonialism, which marked the end of the sovereignty of African nation-states.

Having sold to date over 8 million copies in fifty languages worldwide, *Things Fall Apart* is unquestionably the most widely read, best-selling, and influential book in modern African literature. According to Bernth Lindfors, "Indeed, it has outsold all the rest of the three hundred titles in Heinemann's African Writers Series combined. One reason this novel became such a runaway bestseller is that it was quickly adopted for use as a textbook in high school and university English classes, particularly in Africa and most notably in Nigeria" (*Conversations with Chinua Achebe* [Jackson: University Press of Mississippi, 1997] ix). Also, the novel has made a difference in the lives of its African readers, who have since begun to appreciate Achebe's message: "One big message, of the many that I try to put across, is that Africa was not a vacuum before the coming of Europe, that culture was not unknown in Africa, that culture was not brought to Africa by the white world" (*Conversations*, blurb). The message has helped to create in Africans a sense of pride in their past (however imperfect it was), as well as modifying to some extent the cultural bigotry of Europeans, whom the novel forces to acknowledge the viability of African culture.

Part of the immediate appeal of *Things Fall Apart* lay in the fact that until its publication, no other African novel contained such a wide range of both literary and historical references; nor had any other African novelist yet displayed the kind of craftsmanship Achebe exhibits in this novel, where he holistically interweaves Igbo customary activities, the people's worldview and beliefs, and their material possessions into a rich tapestry, thereby helping to demolish the cultural presumptions of European writers of novels about Africa. Instead of offering a stereotypical depiction of Africa as the "heart of darkness" and its peoples as "primitives" and "savages," Achebe delineates Umuofia as a human community of nine villages, and his characters as human beings who possess minds, a language, a religion, and a culture, with vices and virtues like other groups of people in the world. In that human community, readers find clan leaders such as the level-headed Obierika and his friend Okonkwo, who, although not as level-headed, is nonetheless as pious and nationalistic. In other words, despite Okonkwo's tragic flaws, the two men are able to work together for the common good of their community, their differences in character, temperament, and conduct notwithstanding.

Born in Ogidi, an Igbo community in Nigeria, Achebe grew up in an oral culture in which story-telling was the major means of transmitting culture and civilization. Story-telling sessions served (and still serve today) as an Igbo traditional education forum in which the story-tellers became teachers and their listeners students. Having attended such sessions in which his mother and elder sister served as "teachers," Achebe, the "graduate," asserts that "stories are the very center, the very heart of our civilization and culture," for "it is the story that conveys all our gains, all our failure, all we hold dear and all we condemn. To convey this to the next generation is the only way we can keep going and keep alive as a people. Therefore the story is like the genes that are transferred to create the new being. It is far more important than anything else" (*Conversations* x–xi).

Despite his obsessive ambition to tell the African stories because of what they mean to him and his fellow Africans, Achebe would not have become the renowned raconteur he is today if he had not learned to write with his right hand and with his left hand, so to speak: the right hand representing the Igbo story-telling skill he acquired while growing up in Ogidi, and the left hand the formal Western creative writing skill he developed while studying at the University College in Ibadan, Nigeria. The successful combination of these two apparently divergent but necessary skills resulted in the narrative techniques and craftsmanship that characterize *Things Fall Apart* (and other modern African novels patterned after it) as a hybrid genre. Also, Achebe's achievements in this first novel helped to extend the possibilities of the novel as a potent medium of expressing the people's folklore, oral history, and folk entertainment while simultaneously allowing the novelist to serve as teacher and social critic.

Those Igbo folkways (most of which are shared by other West Africans) that Achebe romanticizes make *Things Fall Apart* an enduringly pertinent novel for study by Africans and foreigners who are interested in learning about pre-colonial African cultures and civilizations through literature. That is why anthropologists and sociologists, as well as students and teachers of literature, comparative religion, and oral history, approach *Things Fall Apart* as an authentic information source on the nineteenth-century Igbo and their neighbors. Achebe's compendious treatment of Igbo folkways makes it easy for his readers to learn much from this relatively short work. However, some of the information it contains, especially Igbo metaphors and symbols, requires explication.

The novel can be studied as a self-contained unit if readers choose to limit their appreciation of it within the literary confines. But as Achebe himself has demonstrated in public lectures, interviews, and critical essays, extra-textual information sources can help deepen readers' understanding of the novel, helping them to appreciate its message more fully. Also, aware that the Igbo did not construct a rigid and closely argued system of thought to explain the universe and the place of humans in it, preferring the metaphor of myth and poetry, Achebe asserts that anyone seeking insight into their world must seek it along the Igbo way, through folktales, proverbs, proper names, rituals, and festivals (*Morning Yet on Creation Day* 132–33). As any reader of *Things Fall Apart* knows, Achebe uses folkways very effectively as thematic material and metaphor to explain the Igbo world and culture to those unfamiliar with them. Like the apostles of Christ explaining in the Bible their heavenly Father's "way to man," Achebe's narrative is sometimes straightforward, but at other times it becomes esoteric, especially when he speaks of spirit beings and esoteric organizations, rituals, and ceremonies. Such exotic Igbo cultural cruxes require explication by Igbo scholars who, in addition to their critical training, are equipped with insiders' knowledge of the culture about which Achebe writes.

The objective of this study is to elucidate unfamiliar literary and historical references, as well as Igbo cultural elements that Achebe has succinctly appropriated as thematic material, and out of which the fiction has emerged. Such elucidation necessitates Igbo cultural exegesis as well as careful examination and analysis of contemporary nineteenth-century historical, socio-cultural, and political issues that affected the conception and purpose of *Things Fall Apart*.

Things Fall Apart has as much to say about culture conflicts between the Igbo (indeed Nigerians) and the Europeans of Achebe's own time as about the nineteenth century of his Igbo ancestors. Such conflicts are rooted in British colonial history, the people's traditional religion, educational system, rituals and ceremonies, worldview and beliefs, social institutions, social control and values, as well as political authority.

The first whites to visit West Africa, the Portuguese navigators, had free commercial interests in mind, but soon those interests degenerated into slave raid and trade. However, those who thought that the Africans, whom the navigators branded "primitives" and "savages," could be Christianized sent missionaries to save the "benighted" African souls. On arrival, the missionaries found fault with African traditional religions, which they made little or no effort to understand. Instead, they condemned unconditionally all aspects of those religions, while making great efforts to convert the people to Christianity. Among the Africans—especially the Igbo, in the case of the novel—many pious and patriotic leaders and warriors resisted the alien religion. Unfortunately the fight was won by the missionaries, who requested and received the assistance of armed forces from their home countries, especially Britain.

Once the missionaries gained a foothold, they built churches and schools in which they preached against anything African. Above all, the missionaries used the converts they made among the outcasts, the poor, the diseased, and twins and their mothers to fight their fellow Africans who could not fight back because it was an abomination to spill the blood of fellow clansmen and women. The established churches and schools necessitated the employment of foreign teachers and government agents such as district commissioners, courts, prisons, the police, and army garrisons. That development also created paid native manpower pools including court messengers, interpreters, catechists, and warrant chiefs. They teamed up with the Christian converts to fight on the side of the whites. Soon they became a formidable economic and social class.

In romanticizing all aspects and ramifications of the conflicts in *Things Fall Apart*, Achebe maintained a historical approach and perspective, in the belief that an awareness of the weaknesses of their past can help the people of Africa to avoid such weaknesses in the future, provided they have the will and determination to change. A similar historical approach and perspective have been adopted in this examination and explication of the issues raised in *Things Fall Apart*.

Chapter 1, a literary analysis of *Things Fall Apart*, examines similarities and dissimilarities in the use of elements of fiction by Western writers and modern African novelists. Such an analysis is necessary to explain why critics characterize the modern African novel as a hybrid genre.

Chapters 2 and 3 focus on the novel's historical context and related issues: the scramble for and partition of Africa by European powers, and the creation and colonization of Nigeria by Britain. Both chapters delineate how the coming of Europeans destroyed the sovereignty of African nation-states, leading to the intrusion of Western ways of life into the continent.

Chapters 4 through 6 focus on the novel's cultural context: Igboland as the world of man and the world of spirits; Igbo language and narrative customs; and traditional Igbo religion and material customs. In these chapters the viability of Igbo culture vis-à-vis the British is carefully evaluated.

Chapter 7 examines the elements of fiction that characterize *Things Fall Apart* as "the African novelists' novel."

Chapter 8 examines the debate on writing African novels in ex-colonizers' languages.

Excerpts from a variety of documents, all bearing on issues related to or raised by *Things Fall Apart*, are included here:

- critical volumes
- journal and magazine articles
- historical articles
- maps
- diagrams
- photographs
- passages from novels
- interviews
- a slave narrative

In addition to the documents, each section of the study contains an introductory discussion, study questions, topics for written or oral exploration, and a list of suggested readings.

The translation of Igbo words and expressions in the text is based on the Igbo orthography recommended by the 1961 Onwu Committee Report. Unfortunately, punctuation and tone-marking of Igbo words and sounds are limited by typographical technology. Nevertheless, the overall exegesis of the Igbo cultural elements that Achebe appropriates in *Things Fall Apart* is standard.

1

Literary Analysis: Unifying Elements of *Things Fall Apart*

HISTORICAL VALIDITY OF THE NOVEL

One of the major attractions of *Things Fall Apart*, the most widely read African novel both in continental Africa and abroad, is its historical validity. The novel contains a literary re-evaluation of the historical past of Chinua Achebe's people and their ways of life, which, to Achebe, constitutes an important creative exercise, for (as the author tells his audience in a magazine article titled "The Role of the Writer in a New Nation") "there is a saying in Ibo that a man who can't tell where the rain began to beat him cannot know where he dried his body. The writer can tell the people where the rain began to beat them" (*Nigeria Magazine* 81 [1964]: 157–60). It is in that sense that *Things Fall Apart* is a casebook that makes the point that contemporary Igbo, Nigerian, and African social and political problems derive from the historical past of their societies—a past that was intact before the advent of the white men in Africa.

Achebe's investigation of that past reveals that Africans and Europeans contributed equally to the tragic encounter between Europe and Africa that ultimately weakened the African societies; so both parties must be held responsible for scotching Africa. For their part, however, Africans must also be prepared to face that

past, however ugly, and to acknowledge the mistakes of their ancestors so as to avoid similar mistakes and their consequences in
the future. Achebe's literary revelation is in sharp contrast to the
erroneous but popular belief of some Africans that Africa was an
Edenic continent until the white men came to colonize it. Instead,
an objective evaluation of the folkways that constitute Igbo life,
culture, and civilization, as enunciated in *Things Fall Apart*, clearly
demonstrates that some social and religious institutional practices—such as killing twins and ostracizing their mothers because
they were considered religiously unwholesome to live with the rest
of society, as well as the outcasting of the *osu* (those dedicated to
gods and not allowed to mix with the freeborn in any way) and
dropsy patients—embraced by the Igbo characters, especially the
hero Okonkwo, made it all too easy for the white men to gain a
foothold in Igboland. In this sense, the narrator appears to blame
Africans more than whites for causing things to fall apart in Umuofia.

In his writing style, Achebe assumes the role of the writer as
teacher. He teaches his African, indeed Igbo, readers and budding
writers to seek and maintain the truth even when it hurts. That is
why he has stressed how important it was for him to maintain the
truth while adopting a historical approach in his novel-writing:

> The question is how does a writer re-create the past? Quite clearly
> there is a strong temptation to idealize it—to extol its good points
> and pretend that the bad never existed. This is where the writer's
> integrity comes in. Will he be strong enough to overcome the temp-
> tation to select only those facts which flatter him? If he succumbs
> he will have branded himself as an unworthy witness. But it is not
> only his personal integrity as an artist which is involved. The cred-
> ibility of the world he is attempting to re-create will be called [in]to
> question and he will defeat his own purpose if he is suspected of
> glossing over inconvenient facts. We cannot pretend that our past
> was one long, technicolor idyll. We have to admit that like other
> people's pasts ours had its good as well as its bad side. (*Nigeria
> Magazine* 59–60)

The authentic and balanced view of an African society that Achebe recreates in *Things Fall Apart* surely gives the lie to the one-
sided and murky images of Africa that the British novelists Joyce
Cary and Joseph Conrad created in their novels *Mister Johnson*

and *Heart of Darkness*, respectively. Thus, even as British critics and readers (who were hitherto contented with the available novels of Africa by British writers) labeled *Things Fall Apart* a protest novel, they could not completely resist the fascination of the new image of Africa as portrayed by a native African writer. Soon, other European, American, and Canadian readers were drawn to the unique qualities of *Things Fall Apart*, a novel that was branded quaint by some, hybrid by others, and classic by more open-minded and sophisticated critics and readers.

In fact, this third group of readers recommended the adoption of the novel as an essential text for study in English, African, Igbo, and Black Studies programs in African and foreign universities. *Things Fall Apart* has remained, since its publication, the African literary text that most people turn to for a balanced view of nineteenth-century Africa.

ELEMENTS OF MODERN AFRICAN FICTION

Unlike the African novels that preceded it, *Things Fall Apart* is not a mere appendage to the British novels that inspired its publication. While using the usual elements of fiction—plot structure, point of view and language, tone and voice, setting, characters, and symbols and imagery—to convey its themes, Achebe gave them a unique quality of "Africanness," which makes the novel a hybrid genre in terms of verbal art, cultural elements, and overall contents—a quality that separates it from the British corpus. Hence the novel can be aptly interpreted as a realization in fiction of the same spirit that expressed itself politically in the struggle for independence by African politicians. In other words, with the publication of this modern African novel in 1958, Achebe not only won literary independence for Nigeria, but also inspired other African writers to write in the same fictional mode, just as Kwame Nkrumah won political independence for Ghana in 1957 and inspired other West African political leaders to do so for their countries, including Nnamdi Azikiwe, whose political leadership won independence for Nigeria in 1960.

The first element of fiction that delineates the major issues of *Things Fall Apart* is *plot structure*. Plot is constituted by the events and actions (verbal discourse as well as physical actions) which are performed by particular characters as rendered, ordered, and or-

ganized by the author towards achieving some emotional and artistic effects (Abrams 159). In *Things Fall Apart*, the effects are
achieved as the narrator weaves the story, developed out of the
plot around Okonkwo, on whom the interest of the author and
his readers centers. Okonkwo is in conflict against fate, against the
circumstances that stand between him and his goal of becoming
the lord of the clan, and against the opposing desires in his temperament. Hence, the novel is divided into three parts that reflect
the making of the hero, his triumphs, and his downfall: his emergence from relatively obscure and poor parentage to become one
of the lords of the clan; his exile from Umuofia to Mbanta; and his
return from exile to Umuofia, where he faces his final conflicts and
eventual tragic death. Each part consists of distinct episodes.

Part One contains thirteen short chapters in which the following
episodes take place:

1. Okonkwo is introduced as a wrestler who is obsessively fighting the
   effeminacy of his father, Unoka; in the process he establishes solid
   personal achievements, which make him both a rich man and one of
   the lords of the clan.

2. Based on his prior military successes, Okonkwo is appointed leader
   of the emissaries of war to Mbano and given custody of Ikemefuna,
   as restitution for the murdered Umuofia woman.

3. Okonkwo asks for seed-yams from Nwakibie to sharecrop, and the
   yams he receives make him a rich farmer.

4. Okonkwo beats up one of his three wives during the Week of Peace,
   which is his first abominable act against the earth goddess, Ani.

5. His polygamous family members are introduced as an example of the
   traditional Igbo family structure.

6. The great wrestling matches, which foreshadow Okonkwo's wrestling
   with his *chi*, are described.

7. Okonkwo helps to kill Ikemefuna, his adopted son, which is his second abominable act against Ani.

8. Obierika's son's (Maduka's) engagement ceremony to his bride Akueke is presented as a model Igbo engagement ceremony. It makes
   Okonkwo envious of Obierika.

9. Ezinma is ill with *iba*, and the concern and attention that Okonkwo
   shows reveal his softer emotional side.

10. The Uzowulu-Mgbafo family case, tried by the *egwugwu* as the Umu-ofia Supreme Court, is described.

11. Ezinma's second illness is an opportunity for the narrator to describe the concept of *ogbanje* and the role of the priestess Chielo, and to reveal the romantic side of Okonkwo.

12. Akueke's wedding is described as a model Igbo traditional wedding ceremony.

13. Okonkwo inadvertently kills Ezeudu's sixteen-year-old son in a funeral dance. It is the third abominable act against Ani, and it earns him and his family instant exile to Mbanta.

Part Two contains six chapters and fewer episodes:

1. Okonkwo and his family are well received at Mbanta by his maternal uncle Uchendu. The reception showcases the famous Igbo extended family system.

2. Obierika visits Okonkwo in Mbanta, bringing him money from the sale of some of his yams, but he also tells him about the massacre of Abaeme people by the occupying British forces.

3. Obierika visits Okonkwo again in his fifth year in exile, this time bringing him the bad news of the coming of the missionaries to Umuofia and the conversion of their own people, especially the *efulefu*, into Christians.

4. The missionaries are given land, "the evil forest," to build their church in Mbanta, and Okonkwo's son Nwoye is converted; he later abandons his father to join other Igbo Christian converts in Umuofia, where such converts are already learning to read and write in school.

5. The white man's religion and government have not only set the outcasts free but also emboldened them to challenge the native religion and government. Okonkwo is incensed by this and wants to lead the fight against the Christians, but Mbanta's citizens do not let him; however, Okoli, who kills their sacred python out of his new religious overzealousness, dies overnight, and the people feel vindicated by their gods.

6. Okonkwo's time in exile is up. He hurriedly prepares to return to Umuofia in a big way. He feasts his host family, that is, his uncle Uchendu and family, and leaves Mbanta for his home clan, Umuofia, with his family.

Part Three also contains six chapters, but with more power-packed and bloodier episodes:

1. Upon his return, Okonkwo soon discovers that Umuofia has become a more open society: some titled men have converted to Christianity, and a church, a school, and a court have been built to buttress the alien culture. When Okonkwo asks why the elders allowed the white men to settle in Umuofia without a fight, Obierika responds by explaining the clever means by which the whites found a foothold (124–25).

2. A conversation between Akunna and Mr. Brown reveals in a comparative manner the viable tenets of both the traditional Igbo religion and Christianity. Mr. Brown has just sent Okonkwo's son Nwoye, now called Isaac, to the Teacher Training College at Umuru, and that, coupled with the little attention his people pay him, makes Okonkwo mourn for himself and the clan, which is now breaking up and "unaccountably becoming soft like women" (129).

3. Mr. Brown is succeeded by Mr. James Smith, who reverses Mr. Brown's policy of compromise and accommodation. However, Mr. Smith's new policy creates greater conflicts between the natives and the church, and between individual natives—a situation that offers Okonkwo a good opportunity to lead the band of *egwugwu* that destroys Mr. Smith's church; and "for the moment the spirit of the clan was pacified" (135).

4. Two days after the church is destroyed, Okonkwo has become the leader of the *egwugwu* again, and he goes with the rest, armed with machetes, to answer the call by the District Commissioner (D.C.). Without warning, they are disarmed, arrested, and detained until they are able to pay restitution fines to the court. The court episode reveals the corrupt role of the *kotma* in the Indirect Rule of Nigeria by the British.

5. Okonkwo and his fellow prisoners are set free as soon as the fines are paid, but they come home broken-hearted. Okonkwo chooses to fight alone if the clan fails to go to war with the British forces. The clan is summoned to deliberate the issue, but while they are still listening to their orator, a messenger approaches from the District Commissioner to stop the meeting. He is accosted by Okonkwo. When he refuses Okonkwo's order to go back, Okonkwo draws his machete in a flash and cuts off the messenger's head. However, when he looks around and finds that nobody supports his rash action, he wipes his machete on the sand and goes away to commit suicide (145).

6. The District Commissioner arrives at Okonkwo's house with armed soldiers and messengers. Okonkwo is not there, but his friend Obierika leads them to the tree from which Okonkwo's body is dangling. Obierika pleads with the D.C. to ask his men to cut down the dangling

body for ritual burial and pays a glowing tribute to Okonkwo as "one of the greatest men in Umuofia. You drove him to kill himself; and now he will be buried like a dog . . ." (147). After the episode, the D.C. learns enough of the Igbo culture to enable him to write a book whose tentative title is *The Pacification of the Primitive Tribes of the Lower Niger*.

The action of the novel is unified by the fact that it opens with Okonkwo in a community activity, wrestling, and closes with Okonkwo in another community action, deliberating about an adequate response to the British humiliation of their elders in jail, which eventuates in the deaths of both Okonkwo, the leader of his people, and the head messenger of the British authority. Also, by means of Okonkwo's exile in Mbanta, readers learn about and understand the coordinated activities of the missionaries and the British administrators in the three principal Igbo communities, Umuofia, Umuru, and Mbanta. In all three places, Okonkwo is either absent from the scene or not in charge of the opposition; and when he makes a belated effort to organize the people against the whites, the social order and the temperament of the people have undergone such tremendous changes that it is impossible for the people to follow his leadership. But as a professional wrestler, he continues to change his tactics, so as to overcome adversities.

Regarding the elements of *point of view* and *language*, it is very clear to a careful reader that Achebe intended his narrator to be an omniscient reporter, one who is very familiar with the primordial customs and traditions of his Igbo people and whose point of view reflects the feelings of the Igbo folk, who are very proud and protective of their cherished culture and civilization, which are currently under alien attack. That is why the hero, Okonkwo, in spite of his character flaws, is highly admired for playing a messianic role throughout the novel. The narrator, however, has a sophisticated knowledge of the invading alien culture as well.

The admiration for the Umuofia heroic characters such as Okonkwo and Obierika, who are fighting to protect their people, their land, and their culture, comes as result of a complex, yet identifiable *narrative technique*: as the narrator recalls past events, he seductively elicits the sympathy of the listeners, who are subliminally drawn to take sides in the black-white encounter; when the narrator vividly describes the folk chants, dances, and celebrations, the audience is drawn to dance with the people; and when he painfully tells of the deaths of the strongman Okonkwo and the village patriarch Ezeudu, the audience also vicariously mourns with the people, who now feel like defenseless fatherless children in the face of imminent British and tribal attacks. In a word, the participatory role readers and listeners are compelled to play as a result of Achebe's unique narrative technique makes them pseudo-characters, known as narratees.

Achebe uses the following types of *figurative language*:

Proverbs, which Achebe described as "the palm-oil with which [Igbo] words are eaten," often used by elders of the clan: "As the elders said, if a child washed his hands he could eat with kings. Okonkwo had clearly washed his hands and so he ate with kings and elders" (6). The contextual interpretation is that although Okonkwo was a young man, he became rich through hard work and personal achievements, and so he became one of the lords of the clan by taking some of the titles that the older and greater men had taken.

Folk songs and chants, which the people sing during rituals and ceremonies:

> Who will wrestle for our village?
>   Okafo will wrestle for our village.
> Has he thrown a hundred men?
>   He has thrown four hundred men.
> Has he thrown a hundred Cats?
>   He has thrown four hundred Cats.
> Then send him word to fight for us. (36)

This praise song, popular during inter-village wrestling matches, mentions two standard denominations in Igbo counting—*ogu ise* (100) and *nnu* (400)—which were also the traditional numbers of men sent to fight other villages in inter-tribal wars. Military officers in charge of 100 or 400 men had special honors conferred on them at the end of campaigns. That is why the women urge the "faceless" elders in charge of war logistics to "send [Okafo] word to fight for us" (36). Okafo has demonstrated wrestling prowess that can enable him to lead their men successfully through any war.

Esoteric language and imagery, used by the priests and diviners, as well as titled men:

When a handshake passes the elbow it becomes another thing. The sleep that lasts from one market day to another has become death. The man who likes the meat of the funeral ram, why does he recover when sickness visits him? The mighty tree falls and the little birds scatter in the bush. (*Arrow of God* 226)

In context, these sentences are spoken by a masked spirit, Ogbazulobodo, who after running across the village (*obodo*), dies of fever or heart attack. The narrator utters the proverbial sentences to presage the untimely death of the masked spirit. The elders and titled men understand them easily; but readers and ordinary people can only understand them if the sentences are interpreted. For example, a handshake (symbolizing an expression of friendship) that passes the elbow becomes something else—an attack or fight. The man who likes the meat of the funeral ram (in other words, one who enjoys entertainment at other people's funerals) recovers when sickness visits him because he fears his own death. And when a mighty tree falls—when a great man dies—the little birds scatter in the bush, meaning that lesser people wander in various directions for lack of care and protection.

Ordinary vernacular utterances of women and children:

Ezinma was always surprised that her mother could lift a pot from the fire with her bare hands.

"Ekwefi," she said, "is it true that when people are grown up, fire does not burn them?" Ezinma, unlike most children, called her mother by her name.

"Yes," replied Ekwefi, too busy to argue. Her daughter was only ten years old but she was wiser than her years.

"But Nwoye's mother dropped her pot of hot soup the other day and it broke on the floor."

Ekwefi turned the hen over in the mortar and began to pluck the feathers.

"Ekwefi," said Ezinma, who had joined in plucking the feathers, "my eyelid is twitching."

"It means you are going to cry," said her mother.

"No," Ezinma said, "it is this eyelid, the top one."

"That means you will see something."

"What will I see?" she asked.

"How can I know?" Ekwefi wanted her to work it out herself.

"Oho," said Ezinma at last. "I know what it is—the wrestling match." (*Things Fall Apart* 29)

Unlike the passage from *Arrow of God*, nothing in this conversation between Ezinma and Ekwefi requires interpretation or explanation. The language is prosaic and vernacular because it is spoken by ordinary people, unlike the elders and titled men, who are taught the use and meaning of esoteric language and rituals.

All these types of language are dexterously used as essential elements of the Igbo oral tradition and lore, which Achebe romanticizes in his rural novels, *Things Fall Apart* and *Arrow of God*. By themselves, the verbal elements are not easily understood by the non-initiated, non-Igbo reader; however, Achebe has appropriated them in all his novels in a style that is both easy to understand and attractively engaging.

Tone and *voice* are so interrelated in *Things Fall Apart* that they are treated together here. For, according to M. H. Abrams, these terms, frequent in recent criticism, reflect the tendency to think of all narrative and lyric works of literature as a mode of speech, or what is now a favored term, "discourse." To conceive a work as an utterance suggests that there is a speaker who has determinate personal qualities, and expresses attitudes both toward the characters and materials within the work and toward the audience to whom the work is addressed. Thus *tone* expresses a literary speaker's "attitude to his listener;" it also reflects his stance toward those he is addressing. *Voice*, however, in its recently evolved usage in literary criticism, points to the fact that readers are aware of a voice beyond the fictitious characters who speak in a work, as well as a person behind all the dramatis personae, including even the first-person narrator. We have a sense of a pervasive authorial presence, a determinate intelligence and moral sensibility, which has invented, ordered, rendered, and expressed these literary characters and material in just this way (Abrams 155–56).

The following passage exemplifies Achebe's use of tone and voice in *Things Fall Apart*:

"You say that there is one supreme God who made heaven and earth," said Akunna on one of Mr. Brown's visits. "We also believe in Him and call Him Chukwu. He made all the world and the other gods."

"There are no other gods," said Mr. Brown. "Chukwu is the only God and all others are false. You carve a piece of wood—like that one" (he pointed at the rafters from which Akunna's carved *Ikenga* hung), "and you call it a god. But it is still a piece of wood."

"Yes," said Akunna. "It is indeed a piece of wood. The tree from which it came was made by Chukwu, as indeed all minor gods were. But He made them for His messengers so that we could approach Him through them. It is like yourself. You are the head of your church."

"No," protested Mr. Brown. "The head of my church is God Himself."

"I know," said Akunna, "but there must be a head in this world among men. Somebody like yourself must be the head here."

"The head of my church in that sense is in England."

"That is exactly what I am saying. The head of your church is in your country. He has sent you here as his messenger. And you have also appointed your own messengers and servants. Or let me take another example, the District Commissioner. He is sent by your king."

"They have a queen," said the interpreter on his own account.

"Your queen sends her messenger, the District Commissioner. He finds that he cannot do the work alone and so he appoints *kotma* to help him. It is the same with God, or Chukwu. He appoints the smaller gods to help Him because His work is too great for one person."

"You should not think of him as a person," said Mr. Brown. "It is because you do so that you imagine He must need helpers. And the worst thing about it is that you give all the worship to the false gods you have created."

"That is not so. We make sacrifices to the little gods, but when they fail and there is no one else to turn to we go to Chukwu. It is right to do so. We approach a great man through his servants. But when his servants fail to help us, then we go to the last source of hope. We appear to pay greater attention to the little gods but that is not so. We worry them more because we are afraid to worry their Master. Our fathers knew that Chukwu was the Overlord and that is why many of them gave their children the name Chukwuka— 'Chukwu is Supreme.' "

"You said one interesting thing," said Mr. Brown. "You are afraid of Chukwu. In my religion Chukwu is a loving Father and need not be feared by those who do His will."

"But we must fear Him when we are not doing His will," said

Akunna. "And who is to tell His will? It is too great to be known."
(126–28)

Ostensibly, the argument is between the white missionary, Mr.
Brown, and the Igbo religious leader, Akunna, over their different
religious beliefs. But in actuality, the argument is between Achebe
the author, who represents the Igbo people in the guise of Akunna,
and Mr. Brown, who represents one of Achebe's Bible instructors
at the University College, Ibadan, where Achebe studied English
and religion. Achebe creates not only the two characters but also
the unusually friendly atmosphere in which both the white missionary and the Igbo religious leader are given an equal opportunity to explain their religious tenets to each other and, by
indirection, to the audience. The end result is that Achebe, "the
novelist as teacher," teaches his audience that the traditional Igbo
religion is in no way inferior to the new invading dispensation,
Christianity. He could not come to this conclusion if he were ig-
norant of either of the two religions. The whites, however, because
of their ignorance of African culture and civilization, which they
termed barbaric, pagan, and evil, failed to grasp the true nature of
the traditional African religions.

In other areas of confrontation between black and white characters, the black characters are able to stand their ground in terms
of logical arguments because Achebe, whose voice they represent,
is knowledgeable about both cultures and civilizations. That is
why, at the end of the novel, there seem to be no victors and no
vanquished, although the Igbo society is brutally maimed.

The fourth important element of the novel is the *setting*. It is a
literary term which refers to the general locale, historical time, and
social circumstances in which its action occurs. The locale of
Things Fall Apart is Umuofia, an Igbo country in southeastern Nigeria; the time is the 1860s, when various European countries,
including Britain, were scrambling to establish colonies in Africa;
and the coming of the British to Igboland is the social circumstance
in which the action of the novel occurs.

Initially, the encounter between the whites and the natives was
peaceful because the white missionaries were making ostensibly
harmless efforts to establish churches and mission schools. However, things changed when the Christian converts became more
confrontational and some of the policies of the missionaries

changed. Also, when the Igbo fathers and elders realized that the alien institutions taught their children religious beliefs and educational ideals totally at variance with the Igbo ones, they attempted to withdraw their children from the white institutions, some of whose buildings they burned down—not only a violent and confrontational act, but also the crime of arson punishable by the white man's law. When it was reported to the white judge (the District Commissioner), the Igbo elders, the *egwugwu*, were arrested, detained, humiliated, and fined as restitution for the destroyed church and school properties. That became the first and toughest challenge that the strongman Okonkwo faced and lost; and for the first and last time, Umuofia local authority was flagrantly violated by an alien power without Okonkwo coming out of the battle a winner.

Generally, in the face of the ever-present and formidable British army and police, who were commanded by the dreaded District Commissioner (D.C.), himself aided and abetted by the notoriously corrupt court messengers (*kotma*), some Igbo elders counseled caution in their dealings with the whites. But others, more headstrong and vocal, preferred armed confrontation, and so died in the process. In the end, however, it was not the white men's superior weapons that weakened Igbo society. Instead, it was the local assistance the whites got from the Igbo social underclass—namely, the *osu*, who were forbidden from having any social interaction with the free citizens; twins, some of whom were killed at birth, along with their mothers, who were usually ostracized, and those with dreadful diseases like dropsy, who were cast out of the villages and abandoned in the "evil forests" to die. In a word, the survivors from among the dregs of society, the *efulefu*, not only left their own people's customs, traditions, and religion to join the alien institutions of church and school, but also fought on the side of the whites against their own Igbo kith and kin. In time, the *efulefu* were the first to embrace all aspects of Western education and, ironically, became the ruling class of civil servants and administrators in colonial and post-colonial Eastern Nigeria.

Although the overall action of *Things Fall Apart* is about the conflict between the Igbo and the intruding white representatives of foreign religion, schools, and administration, Achebe devotes much space, time, and emphasis to the description of the rich culture and civilization of his people for a purpose: to give his readers a unique opportunity to compare and contrast the Igbo culture with the intruding British culture. For Achebe and his fellow Africans, this is an important issue because, up until the publication of *Things Fall Apart*, the British had claimed that their culture was superior to the African, and offered that claim as a reason for the unwarranted, if indefensible, colonization of Igboland, Nigeria, and other African societies from the 1860s to the 1960s, when many of those countries fought and regained their sovereignty.

The *characters*, the fifth element of the novel, represent the two parties to the conflicts in Umuofia—the Igbo villagers on the one hand and the incoming white missionaries and administrators on the other. The major Igbo characters include the Okonkwo family (Okonkwo the father, Nwoye the son, Ezinma the beloved daughter, and Nwoye's mother, the senior wife). Equally important is the Obierika family (Obierika the father, who is Okonkwo's alter ego, and his wrestler-son Maduka, whom Okonkwo feels should have been his son in place of his own effeminate son, Nwoye). Among the whites are Mr. Brown and his successor, Rev. James Smith, as missionaries, and the District Commissioner (D.C.) and the court messengers (*kotma*) as representatives of the British administration.

Of all the characters from both sides, however, Okonkwo is the most important, for his private and public life, as well as the personal and communal roles he plays, affect every other Igbo villager and white man. The German edition of *Things Fall Apart* is simply titled *Okonkwo*, acknowledging the hero's towering position in the novel.

Because *Things Fall Apart* is a novel of conflicts (a fact embedded in the title), its characters are divided into opposing camps according to race, religion, age, and gender, as well as economic and social groups. That is, the major conflicts occur between African natives, who are black, and Europeans, who are white; between Igbo traditional religious leaders and white missionaries; between elders of the clan, called *ndichie*, and youth who are now being converted into Christians and educated formally in mission schools; between males (who dominate the females and challenge the incoming alien authority) and females (who are expected to be seen but not heard); and between rich and titled men and poor and untitled ones. But the most vicious of the social divisions is that between the free citizens and the outcasts or *efulefu* collectively.

Three things hold the society together, though, despite the social divisions: the traditional Igbo religion, which pervades all aspects of the citizens' lives; their social philosophy, known as communitarianism, in which the community is more important than any individual or groups of individuals; and the extended family system, which provides a social and economic safety net for anyone in need of help. That is why the strongman Okonkwo, in spite of his wealth and military successes, has to offer the propitiation sacrifice when he desecrates the Week of Peace; that is why Ikemefuna is forcefully taken from his mother and sacrificed in Umuofia as restitution for the murder of an Umuofia woman by a man from his clan, Mbaino, an act that saves his clan from being wiped out in a war with Umuofia-obodo-dike!; and that is why Okonkwo is given some seed-yams to sharecrop, thereby overcoming his poor parentage. Above all, the rituals and ceremonies, as well as gods, goddesses, oracles, and divination (which sanction the general behavior of clansmen), are occasions and agencies that create opportunities for exhibition of communal unity as well as the temporary appearance of social classlessness.

Finally, readers are enabled to picture Okonkwo's struggles vividly because of the author's use of the sixth element of fiction, *imagery* and *symbolism*. The recurrent image or leitmotif in *Things Fall Apart* is wrestling. Literally, Okonkwo wrestles fiercely with Amalinze the Cat and throws him; but metaphorically he wrestles with the whites, with his people and family members, with his two selves—his softer inner side and his more aggressive, outward side—and with his *chi*. Sometimes his *chi* says yes when he himself says yes, but in most cases his *chi* says no, even when he wants it to say yes, because he is ill-fated. When he wrestles well and successfully throws Amalinze, he becomes the clan's Cat. But when he wrestles poorly by desecrating the Week of Peace, or behaves arrogantly by showing no patience with less successful men, he is referred to as "the little bird *nza* who so far forgot himself after a heavy meal that he challenged his *chi*" (22).

In addition, the author uses lesser symbols and images like foils alongside the dominant ones to weave the textual web so as to produce emotional and artistic effects. For example, Okonkwo's successful transformation through personal achievements, from the son of an *agbala* (poor and wretched man) to one of the lords of the clan is praised proverbially thus: "Age was respected among his people, but achievement was revered. As the elders said, if a child washed his hands he could eat with kings. Okonkwo had clearly washed his hands and so he ate with kings and elders" (6). And his obsessive desire to fight and conquer whenever the talking drums are beaten is metaphorically described: "Okonkwo cleared his throat and moved his feet to the beat of the drums. It filled him with fire as it had always done from his youth. He trembled with the desire to conquer and subdue. It was like the desire for women" (30).

All told, both major and minor symbols and imagery are expressed, in the main, through proverbs: "Among the Igbo the art of conversation is regarded highly, and proverbs are the palm-oil with which words are eaten" (5).

The literary analysis of *Things Fall Apart* reveals one of the novel's attractions: Chinua Achebe's technical style. While using the usual elements of fiction to unify all aspects of this first novel, Achebe gave them a unique quality of "Africanness" which makes his fiction a hybrid genre. He expertly combines Western narrative techniques with Igbo story-telling habits to put his message across to readers. The outcome of the style is that non-African readers can approach a seemingly "quaint" culture with relative ease, and the African readers are equally enabled to appreciate their culture and civilization with much enthusiasm, even though *Things Fall Apart* is written in a language foreign to them.

TOPICS FOR WRITTEN OR ORAL EXPLORATION

1. Name the six elements of fiction that unify *Things Fall Apart*, and discuss any two of them.

2. Discuss the point of view of the narrator.

3. Discuss the author's narrative techniques.

4. Discuss wrestling as both an essential Igbo ceremony and a recurrent symbol in the novel.

5. Using the conversation between Akunna and Brown as a guide, compare and contrast the tenets of Igbo traditional religion and Christianity.

6. Compare and contrast the missionary work of Mr. Brown and Mr. James Smith. How do their individual styles help to maintain peace or create chaos in Umuofia society?

7. Discuss the Igbo socio-cultural philosophy known as communitarianism and the ways in which it helps or harms some families in Igboland.

8. What is the Igbo extended family system? How did it help Okonkwo to survive his exile in Mbanta?

9. Discuss the role of gods, oracles, and divination in all aspects of traditional Igbo life.

10. Discuss the concept of *chi* and its role in Igbo life.

11. Comment on the social stratification of people into the haves and have-nots, the free and *efulefu*.

12. Discuss the makeup of a typical Igbo family structure in the context of the novel.

13. Discuss the roles that women play in Umuofia society, paying particular attention to Nwoye's mother, Chielo, and Ezinma.

14. Describe and comment on traditional Igbo marriage, engagement, and wedding ceremonies.

15. What is the attitude of Umuofia society toward the battering of women?

16. Who is an *ogbanje*? How is he or she healed when they become ill?

17. Discuss the tragic dimensions of *Things Fall Apart*.

18. Write a character analysis of Okonkwo as a tragic hero.

19. Write a character analysis of Obierika as Okonkwo's alter ego.

20. Define and discuss the proverb as an essential Igbo verbal art.

21. Identify and discuss two Igbo folktales from the novel that you enjoy.

22. Who are the *egwugwu*? What are their principal roles in Umuofia?

23. Discuss the roles of the district commissioners and the court messengers (*kotma*) in the governance of traditional Igbo society.

24. Based on your reading of the novel, discuss aspects of Igbo culture you admire and aspects you dislike. Give persuasive reasons for your choices.

25. Taking into consideration the use of language, themes, and elements of fiction, compare *Things Fall Apart* with other novels you have read.

SUGGESTED READINGS

Abrams, M. H. *A Glossary of Literary Terms*, 6th Edition. New York: Holt, Rinehart and Winston, Inc., 1993.

Achebe, Chinua. *Arrow of God*. New York: Anchor/Doubleday, 1989.

———. *Morning Yet on Creation Day*. New York: Anchor/Doubleday, 1976.

Arinze, Francis A. *Sacrifice in Ibo Religion*. Ibadan, Nigeria: Ibadan University Press, 1970.

Brown, Lloyd W. "Cultural Norms and Modes of Perception in Chinua Achebe's Fiction." In *Critical Perspectives on Nigerian Literatures*, ed. Bernth Lindfors. Washington, D.C.: Three Continents, 1976, 131–45.

Carroll, David. *Chinua Achebe*. New York: Twayne, 1970.

Fraser, Robert. "A Note on Okonkwo's Suicide." *Kunapipi* 1, no. 1 (1980): 108–13.

Griffiths, Gareth. "Language and Action in the Novels of Chinua Achebe." *African Literature Today* 5 (1971): 88–105.

Innes, C. L., and Bernth Lindfors, eds. *Critical Perspectives on Chinua Achebe*. Washington, D.C.: Three Continents, 1978.

Jones, Eldred. "Language and Theme in *Things Fall Apart*." *Review of English Literature* 4, no. 4 (1984): 39–43.

Killam, G. D. *The Novels of Chinua Achebe*. London: Heinemann Educational Books, 1971.

Mbiti, John S. *African Religions and Philosophy*. New York: Frederick A. Praeger, 1969.

Njaka, Mazi Elechukwu Nnadibuagha. *Igbo Political Culture*. Evanston, Ill.: Northwestern University Press, 1974.

Nwoga, Donatus I. "The *Chi* Offended." *Transition* 15 (1964): 5.

Ogbaa, Kalu. "A Cultural Note on Okonkwo's Suicide." *Kunapipi* 3, no. 2 (1981): 126–34.

————. *Gods, Oracles and Divination: Folkways in Chinua Achebe's Novels*. Trenton, N.J.: Africa World, 1992.

————, ed. *The Gong and the Flute: African Literary Development and Celebration*. Westport, Conn.: Greenwood Press, 1994.

Seitel, Peter. "Proverbs: A Social Use of Metaphor." *Genre* 2 (1969): 43–61.

Trench, Richard C. *Proverbs and Their Lessons*. London: Paul Kegan Associates, 1965.

Winters, Marjorie. "An Objective Approach to Achebe's Style." *Research in African Literatures* 12, no. 1 (1981): 55.

2

Historical Context I: The Scramble for and Partition of Africa

CHRONOLOGY

c. 7th century   Muslim Arab invasion of North Africa ends the Roman presence in Africa

1441   Gonsalves, a Portuguese explorer, captures West Africans and makes them the first West African slaves in Europe

1450–60   The Portuguese raid Senegal and Gambia (West Africa) for slaves

1492   The "discovery" of America by Columbus leads to the use of African slaves there; on average 13,000 slaves per year are taken to Spanish holdings in America

1494   European "scramble for Africa" begins

1607   English settlement at Jamestown, Virginia

1619   Black Africans come to Jamestown, Virginia

1660–72   Great Britain, represented by the Company of Royal Adventurers to Africa, joins the scramble for Africa

1701   The English Industrial Revolution begins

1750   The Company of Royal Adventurers to Africa renamed the Company of Merchants Trading in Africa

1830s	The Industrial Revolution creates the need for more African slaves, and Britain ships away 135,000 slaves per year from Africa
1874	British expedition against the Asante (Ghana) in West Africa
1884–85	The partition of Africa by European powers
1885	The beginning of the official colonization of various African nation-states by Europeans

EARLY EUROPEAN CONTACTS WITH AFRICA

Things Fall Apart dramatizes the encounter between Africa and Europe during the mid-nineteenth century. Achebe localizes that encounter in Igboland with the fictive Umuofia clan, so as not to overgeneralize what happened in the entire continental Africa. In spite of Achebe's creative caution though, whenever critics discuss issues concerning Africa, one picture that persists in people's minds is Africa branded as a "dark continent." The nations that compose it are generally referred to as "third world countries"— meaning that they are primitive, undeveloped, and ungovernable, regardless of the developments that have taken place in individual countries. However, even if the murky, stereotypical picture were accurate, the fact remains that it is a picture only of the Africa invaded and carved up from the late nineteenth century to the present, a picture created by the scramble for and partition of Africa by Europe. Thus, in order to have a comprehensive and balanced view of Africa (just as Achebe gives a balanced view of Igboland in *Things Fall Apart*), one must know what uninvaded Africa looked like before European colonial rule.

The early contacts Europeans made with pre-colonial Africa stemmed from the importance of that continent to the world, which George C. Bond describes as follows:

Africa is a rich continent that has for centuries provided the world with art, culture, labor, wealth, and natural resources. It has vast mineral deposits, fossil fuels, and commercial crops. But perhaps most important is the fact that fossil evidence indicates that human beings originated in Africa. The earliest traces of human beings and their tools are almost two million years old. Their descendants have migrated throughout the world. To be human is to be of African descent. (Ogbaa 6)

Early explorers and navigators in search of African wealth and natural resources made contacts with ancient northern Africa long before the birth of Jesus Christ.

History further records that ancient Africa had been in contact with people beyond the continent, especially in Europe and Asia, long before European colonialism. The closest of such contacts were between Europe and Africa north of the Sahara Desert. Egypt (with Mesopotamia), for example, is referred to in ancient history as the "cradle of civilization." Through its pyramids, it taught the world architecture and engineering; through its irrigation technology, it taught the world agronomy and provided food for southern Europe and Israel; and through its art, culture, and military powers, it attracted the Romans to its shores. The Egyptian queen Cleopatra put the Roman general Marc Antony under her feet, as it were. Morocco, in northwestern Africa, ruled Spain between the eighth and tenth centuries.

At the Horn of Africa, Ethiopians discussed religion and trade and vied for power with their Middle Eastern neighbors. The Ethiopian matriarch, the Queen of Sheba, so enthralled King Solomon of Israel that their cohabitation produced a lineage of Ethiopian Jews including the twentieth-century Emperor Haile Selassie. In addition, through the conversion of the Biblical "Ethiopian eunuch" by Philip, Ethiopia became the "cradle of Christianity" outside the Holy Land.

The African-based empire of Carthage developed an awesome army under General Hannibal that challenged and successfully repelled the encroaching Roman armies. The Carthaginian region of ancient Africa produced the renowned fifth century Catholic Bishop of Hippo, St. Augustine, who became one of the most revered theologians in Church history.

While northern Africa, southern Europe, and the Middle East were sparring commercially, militarily, and religiously, and as European commercial interests shifted toward Asia (especially to China and India) because of the Muslim Arab invasion of North Africa A.D. 709, Africa south of the Sahara (or Black Africa) was very much a closed world of its own, dealing with the rise and fall of its own empires without the assistance or interference of Europe

or Asia. The freedom and sovereignty of the area were not challenged by outside forces until the fifteenth century, when the first
Portuguese navigators visited the Atlantic shores of Africa and
opened its formerly closed societies to other European explorers
and navigators. That initial visit of the Portuguese to Black Africa
marked the historic beginning of the catastrophic loss of sovereignty by African nation-states.

THE SCRAMBLE FOR AFRICA

The Muslim Arab invasion of North Africa in the seventh century
replaced Roman rule and discouraged European interest in the
region. After the Romans, Prince Henry of Portugal fought to gain
control over the Moors, but he was conquered by the Kingdom of
Morocco in 1440. He withdrew to Cape Verde in Northwest Africa
from where his men began the African gold trade. He and his Portuguese forces navigated the Atlantic coasts of West and Southwest
Africa, establishing trading posts in the Gold Coast (now Ghana),
Lagos (now Nigeria), the Congo Valley (now Congo and Zaire),
and Southwest Africa (now Angola, Mozambique, and Benin).
Some of the kings of the region became Christians and encouraged
the establishment of churches and mission schools in their countries.

What began as a friendly and equal trade partnership between
the Portuguese and the Africans led to one of the world's cruelest
historic developments, the Slave Trade. Prince Henry, also known
as Henry the Navigator, had taken a group of Africans to Lisbon to
educate, intending to use them to further "civilize" their brethren
back home in Africa. However, Gonsalves, a Portuguese explorer,
captured a small group of Africans in 1441 and turned the Africans
into slaves. This practice increased following the death of Prince
Henry. The trade in West African slaves was so lucrative for the
Portuguese that they exported on the average 13,000 slaves per
year to Spanish holdings in the Americas following the "discovery"
of America in 1492.

The scramble for Africa began seriously when other European
countries, seeing the commercial gains of the Portuguese in Africa,
began their expedition efforts in 1494. Among the European powers were the Spanish, French, Dutch, Swedes, Danes, and Bran-
denburgers. The British, who later colonized Nigeria, joined the

scramble in the 1660s, first as the Company of Royal Adventurers to Africa, then as the Royal African Company in 1672, and finally as the Company of Merchants Trading in Africa in 1750. In 1714 the British won from the Spanish the *asiento*, or the right to sell slaves in Latin America and the Caribbean, the profits of which helped fuel the Industrial Revolution.

Thus the eighteenth-century Industrial Revolution did not make things easier for Africans, for it created the need not only for gold and heavy metals—the lures for the exploration of the Atlantic coastal shores—but also for other African natural and human resources, especially slaves. By the 1830s, Europe was carting away on the average 135,000 slaves per year from Africa to the Caribbean and South America. The gains the Europeans realized from the trade led to territorial clashes. Although they managed to suppress such clashes and settle some minor disputes privately, the problems the scramble created were so enormous that the Europeans called an international conference in Berlin to discuss the partition of the African continent into colonial pieces to be ruled by the participating powers.

THE PARTITION OF AFRICA

As every African historian knows, the coming of Europeans to various parts of Africa was occasioned by commercial motives. First, the major interest was in gold, then, as African rulers and traders sold prisoners of war, convicted criminals, and some outcasts into European slavery, Europe and the United States of America saw at close quarters the physical strength and mental capacity of Africans and so invested more capital in the trade. Other more daring Europeans went beyond peaceful slave trading and began slave raiding.

The scramble for Africa enabled the Europeans, especially the British, who started the Industrial Revolution in central England in the eighteenth century, to procure enough raw materials from Africa to make them prosperous. With prosperity came the establishment of more factories, which produced more consumer goods. And since Europe could not consume all the products of its factories, it turned its attention to Africa as a market. The new European entrepreneurs sought assistance from their governments in protecting their investments in Africa. In the end, the dual need

Map 1
Africa at the Beginning of the Nineteenth Century

Source: J. D. Omer-Cooper et al., eds., *The Making of Modern Africa: The Nineteenth Century to the Partition*, vol. 1 (London: Longman, 1968), xiv.

to protect a market for industries at home and to create new, protected markets for industrial products through seizing colonies abroad led to an unholy alliance between European capitalists and their home governments. As a result, European governments sent armed forces to the trading posts and colonies which they had seized before the 1880s in Africa to protect the assets of their citizens.

European armed forces met defeat from African forces for a number of reasons. Some were ill-equipped to put down the local resistance; some were attacked by dreadful tropical diseases like malaria; they were unfamiliar with the local terrain; and the Europeans weakened themselves as they fought each other while trying to acquire more African territories. In the end, however, most of the European commanders sent for reinforcements and more arms supplies, insisting on the newest and best weapons their factories could produce, including cannons. The British expedition against the Asante (Ghana) in 1874 was equipped with the newest rifle available, just issued to the British army at home.

The Europeans, having thus weakened Africa militarily and plundered its human and natural resources, had only one more problem to solve: namely, how to divide and rule all parts of Africa permanently without going to war with each other. From November 1884 to February 1885, Britain, France, Belgium, Spain, Italy, Germany, Portugal, Austria-Hungary, Denmark, the Netherlands, Russia, Sweden, Norway, and Turkey (with the United States as observer) met at the Conference of Berlin and divided Africa into colonies, which they handed over to the attending powers in a General Act that each of them signed. That way the map of Africa was redrawn through the historic act known as the "Partition of Africa." It remained so through most of the twentieth century, when the results of World Wars I and II and the attainment of independence by African nations changed the map of Africa again.

UNINVADED AFRICA

As the following excerpt shows, Africa was not always an invaded continent. It had kingdoms, wealth, and natural and human resources that attracted Europeans to make early contacts and even sign treaties of trade and friendship, which they later betrayed, thus opening up conflicts that led to the partition of Africa.

FROM J. D. OMER-COOPER ET AL., "INTRODUCTION," *THE MAKING OF MODERN AFRICA*, VOL. 1 (1968)

Introduction

In size the African continent, with its 11,673,000 square miles, may be compared with Asia (10,654,000 square miles), and the USSR (8,649,000 square miles). This vast land mass straddles the equator, facing the Mediterranean Sea in the north and the Antarctic in the south. Its wide variety of climates and natural conditions has greatly influenced the development of its inhabitants.

The geography of Africa

One characteristic of Africa is the striking regularity of its coastline, which has relatively few bays and inlets or promontories and peninsulas reaching out to sea. This has meant that the African peoples have not had the same opportunities and incentives for the development of navigation on the sea, whether for long- or short-range trade, as have the peoples of Europe and Asia. Thus, except for the countries bordering the Mediterranean, they have not until comparatively recent times been brought into close and frequent contact with other continents. Until the nineteenth century African development was relatively self-contained, though this does not mean that there were no contacts with other nations, nor that such contacts were unimportant.

Africa north of the Sahara

The northern part of the continent lies along the Mediterranean Sea and enjoys a climate similar to, though warmer and drier than, that of southern Europe. This Mediterranean area is a narrow coastal strip varying in width according to geographical circumstances. It is widest in the north-west corner of the continent, known as the Maghreb (Arabic word for west), where the modern states of Morocco, Algeria and Tunisia are situated. There the Atlas mountains cause winds from the Mediterranean and the Atlantic to deposit their moisture and the soil has been noted for its fertility from ancient times.

The Sahara Desert

Behind this narrow strip of fertile country with its Mediterranean climate lies the vast desert of the Sahara, greater in extent than the whole of Europe and by far the largest desert in the world. This huge area—which is now almost entirely uninhabited outside the occasional oases which provide welcome islands of green in the almost endless wastes of barren rock and burning sands—was once very different. In remote prehistoric times it enjoyed a reasonable rainfall and supported a considerable population. Gradually, for reasons which are still not well understood, it dried up and its peoples congregated around the oases or moved further afield. By the times of the ancient Greeks and Romans it was in much the same condition as today. But though the Sahara is such a vast and formidable desert it must not be thought that it separated the northern part of the continent from all contact with the center and south.

The Nile valley

On the eastern side of the continent the river Nile, starting from two sources, one in the highlands of Ethiopia (the Blue Nile) and the other in the Lake region of East Africa (the White Nile) threads its way across the desert to reach the sea through the many mouths of its delta in Egypt. Every year the rains in Ethiopia and East Africa cause the river to overflow its banks, and as the water subsides it leaves behind a layer of fertile mud which it has brought from the Ethiopian highlands. Along the banks of the Nile there is a narrow cultivable strip containing some of the richest agricultural land in the world. Though it is often no more than a few miles wide it can support a dense population and it gave rise to one of the world's most ancient and elaborate civilizations. Navigation is possible along great stretches of the river and the winding thread of water and the vivid strip of green beside it form one of the strongest links binding the history of the peoples north and south of the Sahara.

Caravan routes across the Sahara

In the central and western parts of the Sahara the mountains of Tibesti Air and the Hoggar capture sufficient rain to make agriculture possible. In other places underground water provides wells and springs to nourish oases. These provide natural staging posts on the caravan routes which from ancient times have criss-crossed the desert, bringing the peoples of West Africa and the Maghreb into contact with each other.

The Sudanic belt in West Africa

To the south of the Sahara in the west, desert conditions gradually give way to increasing vegetation nourished by the rains brought by warm equatorial winds from the Atlantic. A great belt of savannah stretches across the continent which is called the "Sudanic belt."

The West African forest belt

South of the Sudanic belt, along the coast of much of West Africa, stretching inland to varying distances, lies the great West African rain forest which, with a few gaps, meets the dense forests of the Congo to form one of the largest tropical forests in the world.

Thus the pattern of West African geography consists of a fairly regular succession of belts of vegetation, from the Sahara desert, across the grasslands of the savannah belt to the lush forests of the coastal strip. But this pattern is broken by major rivers which have had a significant influence on history, such as the complex Niger-Benue river system which might be described as the Nile of West Africa. Rising in the mountains of the Futa Jallon range in modern Guinea, the river Niger makes a great northward loop almost into the Sahara before turning south into modern Nigeria where it links up with the Benue, another mighty river which rises in the mountains of the Cameroun. The combined waters finally find their way to the sea through the maze of creeks and rivers of the Niger Delta. In its northward path the Niger runs for part of its course over level ground where it overflows its banks every year when the rains in the Futa Jallon bring down the flood waters to form what is often called the inland Delta of the Niger. A relatively dense population can be supported there and it is not surprising that the valley of the Niger should have been the centre of some of West Africa's most ancient and powerful kingdoms. Further east Lake Chad, lying on the fringes of the Sahara and fed by rivers in the Cameroun mountains, also modifies the climate and provides agricultural opportunities.

The Ethiopian highlands

On the eastern side of the continent the highlands of Ethiopia, lying within the triangular projection known as the Horn of Africa, constitute a special environment of their own. They consist largely of volcanic material which breaks down to give a rich soil of almost unlimited depth. It is this soil which washes down the Nile to provide the fertility of Egypt. Abundant rains fall every year and the climate of the cool uplands has been described as the closest to paradise on earth. No wonder the ancient Greeks regarded Ethiopia as the favourite earthly residence of the gods. Between this fertile highland area—a natural centre of civilisation—and the sea, is the dry and torrid plain of Somalia, suitable only for nomadic herdsmen and incapable of sustaining a large settled population.

East and Central Africa

Further south again the African continent consists of a vast plateau rising to its highest point in the Ruwenzori mountains, sometimes described as the spine of Africa. To the west of the Ruwenzori lies the great basin of the Congo and Kasai rivers system, much of it covered by forest which towards the south gives way to savannah and the Genguella and Katanga plateaus where the Zambesi river has its source. East of the Ruwenzori is the region of the Great Lakes, Victoria, Tanganyika, Malawi and many others that are smaller but still large and important. In spite of the presence of the Great Lakes much of this East and Central African plateau is hot and rather dry, covered with a poor tree scrub. There are important exceptions, however. The cool and fertile highlands of Kenya provide excellent farming country. The area between Lakes Victoria, Kyoga and Kivu, the so-called inter-lacustrine region which forms the heart of modern Uganda, benefits from abundant rains which make it a green and smiling land. Here was another natural centre for the development of African civilizations. The slopes of Mount Kilimanjaro and the Shire highlands of modern Malawi are other examples.

South Africa

The southernmost part of the continent constitutes a prolongation of the great African plateau, surrounded by a coastal strip of varying width, the result of age-old erosion of the plateau edge. Like most of the African plateau this is generally rather dry, open savannah country with grass or bush or thorn scrub. Its climate is strongly affected by its southerly latitude and the winter months of June and July can be bitterly cold. On the other hand the southern part of the continent is free from malaria and the tsetse fly which are plagues north of the Equator. It is ideal country for cattle keepers and mixed farmers but cannot support a dense agricultural population.

London: Longman, pp. 1–5.

PRINCE HENRY THE NAVIGATOR AND SLAVE RAID/TRADE IN WEST AFRICA

In tracing the history of the coming of white men to Igboland in *Things Fall Apart*, Chinua Achebe starts with white missionaries represented by Mr. Brown and Mr. Smith, whom he identifies as Englishmen of the Victorian Age: for the interpreter refers to the District Commissioner as the messenger of their queen, Victoria (162). As the plot develops, other English governmental authorities, including prison officials, court judges and messengers, soldiers, and the police, are brought in and discussed to show readers how things turned against the Igbo.

Things Fall Apart traces the larger historic event of the coming of the Portuguese to open up West Africa during the fifteenth century under the great commission of Prince Henry the Navigator. As in the case of the English colonizers, whose harbingers were missionaries, Prince Henry sent out his men on a crusade: to go liberate the Africans from the control of Muslim Arabs, whom the Christian Portuguese branded infidels, and to save the "benighted" souls of the Africans from hell fire. The commercial and imperial ambitions of the explorations were never publicly declared.

The excerpt that follows shows how Portuguese navigators raided West Africa for their first slaves, which yielded them so much personal profit and praise from their Prince that, with the cooperation of Arab middlemen, they transformed slave raiding into international slave trading.

FROM C. RAYMOND BEAZLEY, *PRINCE HENRY THE NAVIGATOR*
(1967)

But with the year 1441 discovery begins again in earnest, and the original narratives of Henry's captains, which old Azurara has preserved in his chronicle, become full of life and interest. From this point to the year 1448, where ends the *Chronica* [chronological records of events], its tale is exceedingly picturesque, as it was written down from the remembrance of eye-witnesses and actors in the discoveries and conquests it records. And though the detail may be wearisome to a modern reader as a wordy and emotional and unscientific history, yet the story told is delightfully fresh and vivid, and it is told with a simple naiveté and truth that seems now almost lost in the self-consciousness of modern literature.

"It seems to me, says our author" (Azurara's favourite way of alluding to himself), "that the recital of this history should give as much pleasure as any other matter by which we satisfy the wish of our Prince; and the said wish became all the greater, as the things for which he had toiled so long, were more within his view. Wherefore I will now try to tell of something new," of some progress "in his wearisome seedtime to preparation."

"Now it was so that in this year 1441, as the affairs of the kingdom had now some repose, though it was not to be a long one, the Infant [the prince] caused them to arm a little ship, which he gave to Antam Gonsalvez, his chamberlain a young captain, only charging him to load a cargo of skins and oil. For because his age was so unformed, and his authority of needs so slight, he laid all the lighter his commands upon him and looked for all the less in performance."

But when Antam Gonsalvez had performed the voyage that had been ordered him he called Affonso Goterres, another stripling of the Infant's household and the men of his ship, who were in all twenty-one, and said to them, Brothers and friends, it seems to me to be [a] shame to turn back to our Lord's presence, with so little service done; just as we have received the less strict orders to do more than this, so much more ought we to try it with the greater zeal. And how noble an action would it be, if we who came here only to take a cargo of such wretched merchandise as these sea wolves, should be the first to bring a native prisoner before the presence of our Lord. In reason we ought to find some hereabout, for it is certain there are people, and that they traffic with camels and other beasts, who bear little merchandise; and the traffic of these men must be chiefly toward the sea and back again; and since they have yet no knowledge of us, they will be scattered and off their guard, so that we can seize them; with all which our Lord the Infant will be not a little content, as he will thus have knowledge of who and what sort of people are the dwellers in this land. Then what shall be our reward, you know well enough from the great expense and trouble our Prince has been at, in past years, only to this one end.

The crew shouted a hearty "Do as you please; we will follow," and in the night following Antam Gonsalvez set aside nine men, who seemed to him most fit, and went up from the shore about three miles, till they came on a path, which they followed, thinking that by this they might come up with some man or woman, whom they might catch. And going on nine miles farther they came upon a track of some forty or fifty men and boys, as they thought, who had been coming the opposite way to that our men were going. Now the heat was very great and by reason of that, as well as of the trouble they had been at, the long tramp they had on foot and the failure of water, Antam Gonsalvez saw the weariness of his men, that it was very great. So let us turn back and follow after these men said he, and turning back toward the sea, they came upon a man stark naked, walking after and driving a camel, with two spears in his hand, and of our men, as they rushed on after him, there was not one who kept any remembrance of his great weariness. As for the native, though he was quite alone, and saw so many coming down upon him, he stood on his defence, as if wishing to show that he could use those weapons of his, and making his face by far more fierce than his courage was warrant for. Affonso Goterres struck him with a dart and the Moor, frightened by his wounds, threw down his arms like a conquered thing and so was taken, not without great joy of our men. And going on a little farther they saw upon a hill the people whose track they followed. And they did not want the will to make for these also, but the sun was now very low and they were weary, and thinking that to risk more might bring them rather damage than profit, they determined to go back to their ship.

But as they were going, they came upon a blackamoor woman, a slave of the people on the hill, and some were minded to let her alone, for fear of raising a fresh skirmish, which was not convenient in the face of the people on the hill, who were still in sight and more than twice their number. But the others were not so poor-spirited as to leave the matter thus, Antam Gonsalvez crying out vehemently that they should seize her. So the woman was taken and those on the hill made a show of coming down to her rescue; but seeing our men quite ready to receive them, they first retraced their steps and then made off in the opposite direction. And so Antam Gonsalvez took the first captives. (192–95)

. . .

So, as the beginning of general interest in the Crusade of Discovery which Henry had now preached to his countrymen for thirty years, as the beginning of the career of Henry's chief captain, the head of his merchant allies, as the beginning, in fact, of a new and bright period, this first voyage of Lancarote's, this first Armada sent out to find and to conquer the Moors and Blacks of the unknown or half-known South, is worth more than a passing notice.

And this is not for its interest or importance in the story of discovery pure and simple, but as a proof that the cause of discovery itself had become popular, and as evidence that the cause of trade and of political ambition had become thoroughly identified with that of exploration. The expansion of the European nations, which had languished since the Crusades, had begun again. What was more unfortunate, from a modern standpoint, the African slave trade, as a part of European commerce, begins here too. It is useless to try to explain it away.

Henry's own motives were not those of the slave-driver; it seems true enough that the captives, when once brought home to Spain, were treated, under his orders, with all kindness; his own wish seems to have been to use this man-hunting traffic as a means to Christianise and civilize the native tribes, to win over the whole by the education of a few prisoners. But his captains did not always aim so high. The actual seizure of the captives—Moors and Negroes—along the coast of Guinea, was as barbarous and as ruthless as most slave-drivings. There was hardly a capture made without violence and bloodshed; a raid on a village, a fire and sack of butchery, was the usual course of things—the order of the day. And the natives, whatever they might gain when fairly landed in Europe, did not give themselves up very readily to be caught; as a rule, they fought desperately, and killed the men who had come to do them good whenever they had a chance.

The kidnapping, which some of the Spanish patriot writers seem to think of as simply an act of Christian charity, "a corporal work of mercy," was at the time a matter of profit and money returns. Negro bodies would sell well, Negro villages would yield plunder, and, like the killing of wild Irish in the sixteenth century, the Prince's men took a Black-Moor hunt as the best of sport. It was hardly wonderful, then, that the later sailors of Cadamosto's day (1450–60) found all the coast up in arms against them, and that so many fell victims to the deadly poisoned arrows of the Senegal and the Gambia. Every native believed, as they told one of the Portuguese captains in a parley, that the explorers carried off their people to cook and eat them.

In most of the speeches that are given us in the chronicle of the time, the masters encourage their men to these slave-raids by saying, first, what glory they will get by a victory; next, what a profit can be made sure by a good haul of captives; last, what a generous reward the Prince will give for people who can tell him about these lands. Sometimes, after reprisals had begun, the whole thing is an affair of vengeance, and thus Lancarote, in the great voyage of 1445, coolly proposes to turn back at Cape Blanco, without an attempt at discovery of any sport, "because the purpose of the voyage was not accomplished." A village had been burnt, a score of natives had been killed, and twice as many taken. Revenge was satisfied.

New York: Barnes and Noble, pp. 207–9.

THE CRUELTIES OF SLAVE TRADE

Once the Portuguese opened the floodgates of slave trade to other European powers, African slavers treated their captives with unimaginable cruelty. The stories of the horrors of slavery usually evoke painful emotions in readers of history books. Such emotions seem to be still more deeply felt, if the stories are told directly by the victims and the victimizers themselves.

In the following excerpts, Captain Theodore Canot, a trader in gold, ivory, and slaves on the coast of Guinea (West Africa), and Olaudah Equiano, an Igbo slave, write about their personal experiences.

FROM THEODORE CANOT, *ADVENTURES OF AN AFRICAN SLAVER* (1928)

At meal time they are distributed in messes of ten. Thirty years ago, when the Spanish slave trade was lawful, the captains were somewhat more ceremoniously religious than at present, and it was then a universal habit to make the gangs say grace before meals, and give thanks afterwards. In our days, they dispense with this ritual, and content themselves with a *"Viva la Habana,"* or "Hurrah for Havana," accompanied by a clapping of hands.

This over, a bucket of salt water is served to each mess, by way of "finger glasses" for the ablution of hands, after which a *kidd*—either of rice, farina, yams or beans, according to the tribal habit of the negroes—is placed before the squad. In order to prevent greediness or inequality in the appropriation of nourishment, the process is performed by signals from a monitor, whose motions indicate when the darkies shall dip and when they shall swallow.

It was the duty of a guard to report immediately whenever a slave refused to eat, in order that his abstinence may be traced to stubbornness or disease. Negroes have sometimes been found in slavers who attempted voluntary starvation; so that when the watch reports the patient to be shamming, his appetite is stimulated by the medical antidote of a *cat*. If the slave, however, is truly ill, he is forwith ticketed for the sick-list by a bead or button around his neck, and dispatched to an infirmary in the forecastle.

These meals occur twice daily—at ten in the morning and four in the afternoon—and are terminated by another ablution. Thrice in each twenty-four hours they are served with half a pint of water. Pipes and tobacco are circulated economically among both sexes; but as each negro cannot be allowed the luxury of a separate bowl, boys are sent round with an adequate supply, allowing a few whiffs to each individual. On regular days—probably three times a week—their mouths are carefully rinsed with vinegar, while, nearly every morning, a dram is given as an antidote to scurvy.

Although it is found necessary to keep the sexes apart, they are allowed to converse freely during day while on deck. Corporal punishment is never inflicted save by order of an officer, and even then, not until the culprit understands exactly why it is done. Once a week, the ship's barber scrapes their chins without assistance from soap; and on the same day their nails are closely pared, to insure security from harm in those nightly battles that occur, when the slave contests with his neighbour every inch of plank to which he is glued. During afternoons of serene weather, men, women, girls, and boys are allowed to unite in African melodies, which they always enhance by an extemporaneous tom-tom on the bottom of a tub or tin kettle.

The greatest care, compatible with safety, is taken of a negro's health and cleanliness on the voyage. In every well-conducted slaver, the captain, officers, and crew, are alert and vigilant to preserve the cargo. It is [in] their personal interests, as well as the interest of humanity, to do so. The boatswain is incessant in his patrol of purification, and disinfecting substances are plenteously distributed. The upper deck is washed and swabbed daily; the slave deck is scraped and holystoned; and, at nine o'clock each morning, the captain inspects every part of his craft, so that no vessel, except a man-of-war, can compare with a slaver in systematic order, purity, and neatness. I am not aware that the ship-fever, which sometimes decimates the emigrants from Europe, has ever prevailed in these African traders.

At sundown, the process of stowing the slaves for the night is begun. The second mate and boatswain descend into the hold, whip in hand, and range the slaves in their regular places; those on the right side of the vessel facing forward and lying in each other's lap, while those on the left are similarly stowed with their faces towards the stern. In this way each negro lies on his right side, which is considered preferable for the action of the heart. In allotting places, particular attention is paid to size, the taller being selected for the greatest breadth of the vessel, while the shorter and younger are lodged near the bows. When the cargo is large and the lower deck crammed, the supernumeraries are disposed of on deck, which is securely covered with boards to shield them from moisture. The strict discipline of nightly stowage is of the greatest importance in slavers, else every negro would accommodate himself as if he were a passenger.

In order to insure perfect silence and regularity during the night, a slave is chosen as constable from every ten, and furnished with a cat to enforce commands during his appointed watch. In remuneration for his services, which are admirably performed whenever the whip is required, he is adorned with an old shirt or tarry trowsers. Now and then, billets of wood are distributed among the sleepers, but this luxury is never granted until the good temper of the negroes is ascertained, for slaves have often been tempted to mutiny by the power of arming themselves with these pillows from the forest.

It is very probable that many of my readers will consider it barbarous to make slaves lie down naked upon a board, but let me inform them that native Africans are not familiar with the use of feather-beds, nor do any but the free and rich in their mother country indulge in the luxury even of a mat or raw-hide. Among the Mandingo chiefs—the most industrious and civilized of Africans—the beds, divans, and sofas, are heaps of mud, covered with untanned skins for cushions, while logs of wood serve for bolsters. I am of opinion, therefore, that emigrant slaves experience very slight inconvenience in lying down on the deck.

But ventilation is carefully attended to. The hatches and bulkheads of every slaver are grated, and apertures are cut about the deck for ampler circulation of air. Wind-sails, too, are constantly pouring a steady draft into the hold, except during a chase, when every comfort is temporarily sacrificed for safety. During calms or in light and baffling winds, when the suffocating air of the tropics makes ventilation impossible, the gratings are always removed, and portions of the slaves allowed to repose at night on deck, while the crew is armed to watch the sleepers.

Handcuffs are rarely used on shipboard. It is the common custom to secure slaves in the barracoons, and while shipping, by chaining ten in a gang; but as these platoons would be extremely inconvenient at sea, the manacles are immediately taken off and replaced by leg-irons, which fasten them in pairs by the feet. Shackles are never used but for full-grown men, while women and boys are set at liberty as soon as they embark. It frequently happens that when the behaviour of male slaves warrants their freedom, they are released from all fastenings long before they arrive. Irons are altogether dispensed with on many Brazilian slavers, as negroes from Anjuda, Benin, and Angola, are mild, and unaddicted to revolt, like those who dwell east of the Cape or north of the Gold Coast. Indeed, a knowing trader will never use chains but when compelled; for, the longer a slave is ironed, the more he deteriorates.

New York: Garden City Publishing, pp. 108–12.

FROM OLAUDAH EQUIANO, "THE INTERESTING NARRATIVE OF
THE LIFE OF OLAUDAH EQUIANO, OR GUSTAVUS VASSA, THE
AFRICAN, WRITTEN BY HIMSELF" (1997)

I hope the reader will not think I have trespassed on his patience in introducing myself to him with some account of the manners and customs of my country. They had been implanted in me with great care, and made an impression on my mind, which time could not erase, and which all the adversity and variety of fortune I have since experienced served only to rivet and record; for, whether the love of one's country be real or imaginary, or a lesson of reason, or an instinct of nature, I still look back with pleasure on the first scenes of my life, though that pleasure has been for the most part mingled with sorrow.

I have already acquainted the reader with the time and place of my birth. My father, besides many slaves, had a numerous family, of which seven lived to grow up, including myself and a sister, who was the only daughter. As I was the youngest of the sons, I became, of course, the greatest favourite with my mother, and was always with her; and she used to take particular pains to form my mind. I was trained up from my earliest years in the art of war; my daily exercise was shooting and throwing javelins; and my mother adorned me with emblems, after the manner of our greatest warriors. In this way I grew up till I was turned the age of eleven, when an end was put to my happiness in the following manner: —Generally when the grown people in the neighbourhood were gone far in the fields to labour, the children assembled together in some of the neighbours' premises to play; and commonly some of us used to get up a tree to look out for any assailant, or kidnapper, that might come upon us; for they sometimes took those opportunities of our parents' absence to attack and carry off as many as they could seize. One day, as I was watching at the top of a tree in our yard, I saw one of those people come into the yard of our next neighbour but one, to kidnap, there being many stout young people in it. Immediately on this I gave the alarm of the rogue, and he was surrounded by the stoutest of them, who entangled him with cords, so that he could not escape till some of the grown people came and secured him. But alas! ere long it was my fate to be thus attacked, and to be carried off, when none of the grown people were nigh. One day, when all our people were gone out to their works as usual, and only I and my dear sister were left to mind the house, two men and a woman got over our walls, and in a moment seized us both, and without giving us time to cry out, or make resistance, they stopped our mouths, and ran off with us into the nearest wood. Here they tied our hands, and continued to carry us as far as they could, till night came on, when we reached a small house, where the robbers halted for refreshment, and spent the night. We were then unbound, but were unable to take any food; and, being quite overpowered by fatigue and grief, our only relief was some sleep, which allayed our misfortune for a short time. The next morning we left the house, and continued travelling all the day. For a long time we had kept the woods, but at last we came into a road which I believed I knew. I had now some hopes of being delivered; for we had advanced but a little way before I discovered some people at a distance, on which I began to cry out for their assistance: but my cries had no other effect than to make them tie me faster and stop my mouth, and then they put me into a large sack. They also stopped my sister's mouth, and tied her hands; and in this manner we proceeded till we were out of the sight of these people. When we went to rest the following night they offered us some victuals; but we refused it; and the only comfort we had was in being in one another's arms all that night, and bathing each other with our tears. But alas! we were soon deprived of even the small comfort of weeping together. The next day proved a day of greater sorrow than I had yet experienced; for my sister and I were then separated, while we lay clasped in each other's arms. It was in vain that we besought them not to part us; she was torn from me, and immediately carried away, while I was left in a state of distraction not to be described. I cried and grieved continually; and for several days I did not eat any thing but what they forced into my mouth. At length, after many days travelling, during which I had often changed masters, I got into the hands of a chieftain, in a very pleasant country. . . . I therefore determined to seize the first opportunity of making my escape, and to shape my course for that quarter; for I was quite oppressed and weighted down by grief after my mother and friends; and my love of liberty, ever great, was strengthened by the mortifying circumstance of not daring to eat with the free-born children, although I was mostly their companion. While I was projecting my escape, one day an unlucky event happened, which quite disconcerted my plan, and put an end to my hopes. I used to be sometimes employed in assisting an elderly woman slave to cook and take care of the poultry; and one morning, while I was feeding some chickens, I happened to toss a small pebble at one of them, which hit it on the middle and directly killed it. The old slave, having soon after missed the chicken, inquired after it; and on my relating the accident (for I told her the truth, because my mother would never suffer me to tell a lie) she flew into a violent passion, threatened that I should suffer for it; and, my master being out, she immediately went and told her mistress what I had done. This alarmed me very much, and I expected an instant flogging, which to me was uncommonly dreadful; for I had seldom been beaten at home. I therefore resolved to fly; and accordingly I ran into a thicket that was hard by, and hid myself in the bushes. Soon afterwards my mistress and the slave returned, and, not seeing me, they searched all the house, but not finding me, and I not making answer when they called to me, they thought I had run away, and the whole neighbourhood was raised in the pursuit of me. In that part of the country (as in ours) the houses and villages were skirted with woods, or shrubberies, and the bushes were so thick that a man could readily conceal himself in them, so as to elude the strictest search. The neighbours continued the whole day looking for me, and several times many of them came within a few yards of the place where I lay hid. I then gave myself up for lost entirely, and expected every moment, when I heard a rustling among the trees, to be found out, and punished by my master; but they never discovered me, though they were often so near that I even heard their conjectures as they were looking about for me; and I now learned from them, that any attempt to return home would be hopeless. Most of them supposed I had fled towards home; but the distance was so great, and the way so intricate, that they thought I could never reach it, and that I should be lost in the woods. When I heard this I was seized with a violent panic, and abandoned myself to despair. Night too began to approach, and aggravated all my fears. I had before entertained hopes of getting home, and I had determined when it should be dark to make the attempt; but I was now convinced it was fruitless, and I began to consider that, if possibly I could escape all other animals, I could not those of the human kind; and that, not knowing the way, I must perish in the woods.

Henry Louis Gates, Jr., and Nellie Y. McKay, eds., *The Norton Anthology of African American Literature*. New York: Norton, pp. 151–53.

MUTINY AT SEA

Even while aboard the slave boats and ships, the Africans (and, sometimes, junior slave drivers), driven by the basic human need for liberty, fought hard to liberate themselves from their captors. In doing so, some freed themselves and swam out to sea to safety; but those who failed to make it were tortured for causing mutiny at sea. As in the excerpt that follows, it is well-known that some of the crew were sympathetic to the plight of the slaves. However, in order not to offend their captain, they were always vigilant to ensure that no prisoners escaped during their beat. Thus, the slaver was enslaved.

FROM THEODORE CANOT, *ADVENTURES OF AN AFRICAN SLAVER* (1928)

Mutiny at Sea

It was a sweltering July, and the rainy season proved its power by an almost incessant deluge. In the breathless calms that held me on the coast, the rain came down in such torrents that I often thought the solid water would bury our schooner. Now and then a south-western and the current would fan and drift us along; yet the tenth day found us rolling from side to side in the longitude of the Cape Verde Islands.

Day broke with one of its customary squalls and showers. As the cloud lifted, my look-out from the cross-trees announced a sail under our lee. It was invisible from deck, in the folds of the retreating rain, but in the dead calm that followed, the distant whistle of a boatswain was distinctly audible. Before I could deliberate, all my doubts were solved by a shot in our mainsail, and the crack of a cannon. There could be no question that the unwelcome visitor was a man-of-war.

It was fortunate that the breeze sprang up after the lull, and enabled us to carry everything that could be crowded on our spars. We dashed away before the freshening wind, like a deer with the unleashed hounds pursuing. The slaves were shifted from side to side by the owner,—forward or aft—to aid our sailing. Headstays were slackened, wedges knocked off the masts, and every incumbrance cast from the decks into the sea. Now and then, a fruitless shot from his bow-chasers reminded the fugitive that the foe was still on his scent. At last the cruiser got the range of his guns so perfectly that a well-aimed ball ripped away our rail and tore a dangerous splinter from the foremast, three feet from deck.

It was not perilous to carry a press of sail on the same tack with the weakened spar, whereupon I put the schooner about, and, to my delight, found we ranged ahead a knot faster on this course than the former. The enemy went about as quickly as we did, but her balls soon fell short of us, and before noon we had crawled so nimbly to windward that her top-gallants alone were visible above the horizon.

Our voyage was uncheckered by any occurrence worthy of recollection, save the accidental loss of the mate in a dark and stormy night, until we approached the Antilles. Here, where everything on a slaver assumes the guise of pleasure and relief, I remarked not only the sullenness of my crew, but a disposition to disobey or neglect. The second mate—who was shipped in the Rio Nunez and now replaced my lost officer—was noticed occasionally in close intercourse with the watch, while his deportment indicated dissatisfaction, if not mutiny.

The sight of land is commonly the signal for merriment, for a well-behaved cargo is invariably released from shackles, and allowed free intercourse between the sexes during daytime on deck. Water tanks are thrown open for unrestricted use. The "cat" is cast into the sea. Strict discipline is relaxed. The day of danger or revolt is considered over, and the captain enjoys a new and refreshing life till the hour of landing. Sailors share their biscuits and clothing with the blacks. The women, who are generally without garments, appear in costume from the wardrobes of tars, petty officers, mates, and even captains. Sheets, table-cloths, and pare sails are torn to pieces for raiment, while shoes, boots, caps, oil-cloths, and monkey-jackets contribute to the gay masquerade of the "emigrants."

It [was] my sincere hope that the first glimpse of the Antilles would have converted my schooner into a theatre for such a display; but the moodiness of my companions was so manifest, that I thought it best to meet rebellion half way, by breaking the suspected officer, and sending him forward, at the same time that I threw his "dog-house" overboard.

I was now without a reliable officer, and was obliged to call two of the youngest sailors to my assistance in navigating the schooner. I knew the cook and steward—both of whom messed aft—to be trustworthy; so that with four men at my back, and the blacks below, I felt competent to control my vessel. From that moment, I suffered no one to approach the quarter-deck nearer than the mainmast.

It was a sweet afternoon when we were floating along the shores of Porto Rico, tracking our course upon the chart. Suddenly, one of my new assistants approached, and in a quiet tone, asked whether I would take a *cigarillo*. As I never smoked, I rejected the offer with thanks, when the youth immediately dropped the twisted paper on my map. In an instant, I perceived the ruse, and discovered that the *cigarillo* was in fact a *billet* rolled to resemble one. I put it in my mouth, and walked aft until I could throw myself on the deck, with my head over the stern, so as to open the paper unseen. It disclosed the organization of a mutiny under the lead of the broken mate. Our arrival in sight of Santo Domingo was to be the signal of its rupture, and for my immediate landing on the island. Six of the crew were implicated with the villain, and the boatswain, who was ill in the slave-hospital, was to share my fate.

My resolution was promptly made. In a few minutes, I had cast a hasty glance into the arm-chest, and seen that our weapons were in order. Then, mustering ten of the stoutest and cleverest of my negroes on the quarter-deck, I took the liberty to invent a little strategic fib. I told them, in Soosoo dialect, that there were bad men on board, who wanted to run the schooner ashore among rocks and drown the slaves while below. At the same time, I gave each a cutlass from the arm-chest, and supplying my trusty whites with a couple of pistols and a knife apiece, without saying a word, I seized the ringleader and his colleagues.

Irons and double-irons secured the party to the mainmast or deck, while a drum-head court-martial, composed of the officers and presided over by myself, arraigned and tried the scoundrels in much less time than regular boards ordinarily spend in such investigations. During the in-quiry, we ascertained beyond doubt that the death of the mate was due to false play. He had been wilfully murdered, as a preliminary to the assault on me, for his colossal stature and powerful muscles would have made him a dangerous adversary in the seizure of the craft.

There was, perhaps, a touch of the Inquisition in our judicial re-searches. We proceeded very much by way of "confession," and when-ever the culprit manifested reluctance or hesitation, his memory was stimulated by a cat. Accordingly, at the end of the trial, the mutineers were already pretty well punished; so that we sentenced the six accom-plices to receive an additional flagellation, and continue ironed till we reached Cuba.

The fate of the ringleader was not decided so easily. Some were in favour of dropping him overboard, as he had done with the mate; others proposed to set him adrift on a raft, ballasted with chains; but I consid-ered both these punishments too cruel, notwithstanding his treachery, and kept his head beneath the pistol of a sentry till I landed him in shackles on Turtle Island, with three days' food and abundance of water.

New York: Garden City Publishing, pp. 231–35.

CONCLUSION

Black Africa was not always under European rule. It had king-doms, kings, queens, and gentry as well as ordinary people; it had wealth, culture, and civilization; and, above all, it had sovereignty and dignity until the Portuguese opened it up to Europe for the international slave trade. Europeans did not come to Africa pri-marily to save the Africans from hell fire through missionary work. The exploration journeys made by various European powers were, in the main, caused, promoted, and prolonged by sheer greed for the plunder of African human and natural resources. Africans fought hard to stop the trade and to maintain their sovereignty. Unfortunately, however, they were overpowered and overrun by Europeans who possessed superior weapons.

TOPICS FOR WRITTEN OR ORAL EXPLORATION

1. Why was Africa branded a "dark continent," and why are its countries generally referred to as third world countries?

2. Why did European countries make contacts with pre-colonial Africa, and how far did such contacts go?

3. How and why did Achebe localize the European encounter with Africa in *Things Fall Apart*?

4. What specific contributions did ancient Africa make to world civilization?

5. Name the regions of Africa that are known as Black Africa.

6. Why was Black Africa a closed world until the coming of the Portuguese in the fifteenth century?

7. Why did Portuguese mariners first visit Black Africa? What historic events stemmed from that visit?

8. What were the positive and negative effects of that first coming of the Portuguese to the Atlantic coastal shores of Africa?

9. What was "the scramble for Africa," and how and when did it begin?

10. Which European countries took part in the scramble, and why?

11. Which Black African countries were first affected by the scramble?

12. What was the slave trade, and how did it differ from slave raid?

13. How did the scramble for Africa cause, promote, and prolong the slave trade and slave raid?

14. What were the advantages and disadvantages of slave trade and slave raid for the Africans and the Europeans, respectively?

15. What was the "partition of Africa"?

16. Which countries signed the document that legally created the partition?

17. Did the partition bring peace between European powers and their African colonies on the one hand, and between rival European powers on the other?

18. What was the role of European missionaries in promoting the partition?

19. Did missionary activities in Africa help to end slavery or to prolong it?

20. Discuss the missionary activities in *Things Fall Apart*.

21. For the characters in *Things Fall Apart*, what are the advantages and disadvantages of being educated by the missionaries?

22. Who colonized Nigeria, the setting of *Things Fall Apart*, and why?

23. Now that you know what uninvaded Africa looked like, do you think it was a continent without culture and civilization before the coming of the Europeans? Give persuasive reasons for your answer.

SUGGESTED READINGS

Beazley, C. Raymond. *Prince Henry the Navigator*. New York: Barnes and Noble, 1967.

Canot, Theodore. *Adventures of an African Slaver*. New York: Garden City Publishing, 1928.

Collins, Robert C., ed. *The Partition of Africa: Illusion or Necessity?* New York: John Wiley and Sons, 1969.

Gates, Henry Louis, Jr., and Nellie Y. McKay, eds. *The Norton Anthology of African American Literature*. New York: Norton, 1997.

Ogbaa, Kalu. *Igbo*. New York: Rosen, 1995.

Omer-Cooper, J. D., et al., eds. *The Making of Modern Africa: The Nineteenth Century to the Partition*, vol. 1. London: Longman, 1968.

Sesay, Amadu, ed. *Africa and Europe: From Partition to Independence or Dependency?* Dover, N.H.: Croom Helm, 1986.

Shinnie, Margaret. *Ancient African Kingdoms*. London: Edward Arnold, 1965.

3

Historical Context II: The Creation and Colonization of Nigeria

CHRONOLOGY

1808	Great Britain acquires Sierra Leone as its first West African territory
1817	France acquires Senegal as its first West African territory
c. 1880	Great Britain acquires Gambia, Gold Coast, and some territories along the Niger River—the nucleus of what becomes Nigeria in 1914
c. 1880	France acquires Western Sudan, Bamako, Upper Guinea, Ivory Coast, and Dahomey
1880–1887	Great Britain acquires the Northern and Southern protectorates of Nigeria
1897	The British West African Frontier Force (WAFF) patrols the Northern Protectorate, thereby halting French incursions into the Niger territories
1900	The protectorates become Northern Nigeria and Southern Nigeria
1914	Sir Frederick Lugard amalgamates the two protectorates into one colonial country, Nigeria
1929	The Aba [Igbo] Women's Riot is staged

1948	Great Britain establishes the University College, Ibadan, Nigeria
1957	Nigeria becomes a dominion of Great Britain
1960	Nigeria gains political independence from Great Britain
1963	Nigeria becomes a federal republic

HISTORICAL ALLUSION TO THE PARTITION OF WEST AFRICA

In the final paragraph of *Things Fall Apart*, the narrator makes the following remarks:

> The Commissioner went away, taking three or four of the soldiers with him. In the many years in which he had toiled to bring civilization to different parts of Africa he had learnt a number of things. One of them was that a District Commissioner must never attend to such undignified details as cutting down a hanged man from the tree. Such attention would give the natives a poor opinion of him. In the book which he planned to write he would stress that point. As he walked back to the court he thought about the book. Every day brought him some new material. The story of this man who had killed a messenger and hanged himself would make interesting reading. One could almost write a whole chapter on him. Perhaps not a whole chapter but a reasonable paragraph, at any rate. There was so much else to include, and one must be firm in cutting out details. He had already chosen the title of the book, after much thought: *The Pacification of the Primitive Tribes of the Lower Niger*. (147–48)

This passage calls the attention of readers to two important interconnected issues by which the author explains why and how the white men gained a foothold in Igboland and Nigeria, respectively.

The first issue is the bigoted attitude that the whites maintained in their encounter with the Igbo. The whites saw themselves as possessing a superior culture and civilization that must be imposed on a people they, out of ignorance, considered primitive and uncivilized. However, the natives, as well as the narrator (who represents Achebe, the Igbo author), knew that neither were they primitive nor were their culture and civilization inferior to those of the intruding whites; they were simply different. And that is why they fought hard, under the leadership of their strongman Okonkwo, to resist that imposition—a resistance effort that produces much of the tension and conflict in the novel. So, when the Igbo discovered that their leader had taken his own life, they were stunned. They had to regroup under the leadership of Obierika, Okonkwo's best friend and fellow Igbo elder, to keep their clan together. However, the white leader, the District Commissioner, had a sense of accomplishment after the death of Okonkwo, who was a stumbling block to his "civilizing" effort. The Commissioner was already thinking about writing a book in which he would describe his foreign service experiences and accomplishments to his home audience, the English. That way he would become an authority on African affairs.

Achebe points to the bitter irony of the title: *The Pacification of the Primitive Tribes of the Lower Niger*. This echoes Conrad's Kurtz, whose pamphlet, *Suppression & Savage Customs*, ends with "exterminate the brutes!"

The second issue touched on in that final paragraph of *Things Fall Apart* is a historical allusion to the rivalry between the British and the French that developed as they struggled to gain permanent control of that part of West Africa referred to in nineteenth-century colonial history as the Lower Niger. An examination of that British-French struggle and its aftermath, which eventually brought Nigeria under British rule, is the main focus of this chapter.

THE ORIGINS OF BRITISH RULE IN NIGERIA

As discussed in Chapter 2, the scramble for Africa, and specifically for West Africa, was embarked upon by some European nations purely for commercial reasons. However, the missionary activities that followed the commercial interests helped to prick the conscience of European governments and peoples, especially the British and the French, who began the campaign against the slave trade, as they also sought effective ways of protecting the legitimate commerce of their nationals in West Africa. Britain and France built forts and garrisons along the coastal towns of West Africa for that protection. As time went on, however, the humanitarian effort to stop the slave trade and the idea of protecting legitimate European commercial interests gave way to the idea of European conquest of West Africa.

Britain became the first European nation to acquire a West African territory over which it exercised direct political control. That territory, Sierra Leone, acquired in 1808, prompted the French, who would not be outdone, to acquire Senegal in 1817. From these two coastal colonies, the British and the French sought to extend their colonial possessions into the interior of West Africa—a task that necessitated the navigation and exploration of the Niger and the Benue and the territories they drain. By 1880, the French had acquired Senegal, Western Sudan, Bamako, Upper Guinea, Ivory Coast, and Dahomey. By then the British had acquired only Sierra Leone, Gambia, Gold Coast, and some ethnic communities along the Niger River, including Lagos, Abeokuta, Lokoja, and Jebba, that formed the nucleus of the territory that became Nigeria in 1914. Subsequently, the British and the French bought such territories as Togoland and the Cameroons from the Portuguese and the Germans and thus became the only two European powers in West Africa after World War I.

LORD LUGARD AND THE CREATION OF NIGERIA

Nigeria, the most populous country on the African continent, came into being in its present form only in 1914, when the two British protectorates of Northern and Southern Nigeria were amalgamated by Sir Frederick Lugard. Sixteen years earlier, Flora Shaw, who later married Lugard, first suggested in an article for the *Times* of London that the several British protectorates on the Niger be known collectively as Nigeria (Crowder 11).

The protectorates were groups of culturally and linguistically divergent but geographically adjacent ethnic communities which, through the use of powerful gunboats and cunning diplomacy, the British brought together for administrative purposes, and for protection against French and German ambitions in West Africa.

The Southern Protectorate was comprised of the ancient kingdoms of Ife and Benin, the Yoruba Empire of Oyo, and the slave center of Lagos; the city-states of the Niger Delta, where the first European contacts and slave trade began; Old and New Calabar; and the largely politically decentralized but technologically advanced lands of the Igbo-speaking peoples of southeast Nigeria.

Map 2
West African Area of European Contact

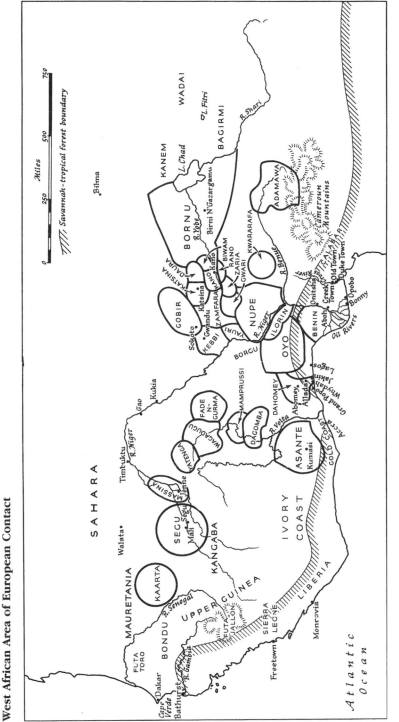

Source: J. D. Omer-Ccoper et al., eds., *The Making of Modern Africa: The Nineteenth Century to the Partition*, vol. 1 (London: Longman, 1968).

The Northern Protectorate included "the great kingdom of Kanem-Borno, with a known history of more than a thousand years, and the Sokoto Caliphate which for nearly a hundred years before its conquest by Britain had ruled most of the savannah of northern Nigeria" (Crowder 11).

The peoples of Nigeria in both protectorates had their own cultures and civilizations, as well as complex political systems, which the intruding British agencies both misunderstood and underrated. In fact, the British, like the French, believed that their culture and social institutions were the best in the world, and made serious efforts to impose them on the Nigerians, whom they perceived as backward. They introduced the idea of "modern" government to the "savage" peoples of Nigeria. But they could not do so effectively without the local assistance of warrant chiefs and court messengers (*kotma* in *Things Fall Apart*).

The method the British used to govern the conquered peoples of Nigeria was called "Indirect Rule." The system originated in 1891 when slave traders along the Niger Delta in the south appointed local chiefs, whose cooperation they needed to run their court of equity, as government agents to assist British officials in bringing law and order to the region. In the north, the Royal Niger Company, which held the Northern Protectorate until British officials came to rule it in 1897, also allowed emirs (Muslim leaders and chiefs) to exercise limited authority over their people. When the British government eventually took over the authority from the trading companies in both protectorates, they "selected some people whom they compelled to become chiefs. They gave these people 'certificates of recognition' which were called "warrants." For this reason these men were popularly known as "warrant chiefs." Apart from trying cases and passing bye-laws, the warrant chiefs also recruited and supervised the men who built the main roads and government stations" (Ayandele et al. 154). The corruption of the warrant chiefs and court messengers is re-created in *Things Fall Apart*, where Okonkwo and other members of *egwugwu* are made to pay more money than the District Commissioner ordered as restitution for the church that the villagers burned down (137–39).

The two protectorates continued to enjoy the protection of the British Parliament and the Royal Niger Company on the Niger territory until 1897, when the Northern Protectorate was threatened by the French. French officers garrisoned permanently in Boussa noticed that Borgu Province on the bank of the Niger was not occupied by the Company or militarily protected by the British garrison, unlike the Southern Protectorate, which was permanently garrisoned by the British West African Frontier Force (WAFF) and patrolled by powerful gunboats. So the French ventured to capture the province. But "in 1897, Mr. J. Chamberlain [a British parliamentarian] sent out Captain Lugard, with the rank of Brigadier-General, to raise a force of 2,000 men, with British officers and N.C.O.'s, stores and guns, with the result that a convention was signed with France in June 1898, and British rights were saved" (Geary 8).

The British government paid the Royal Niger Company for its assets and investments on the Niger, and it ceased to rule the protectorate in 1899. Following his successful military campaign, Brigadier-General Lugard was appointed the first governor of Northern Nigeria that year. In 1914, when Southern Nigeria and Northern Nigeria were joined, he (now Sir Frederick Lugard) became its first governor-general. That way, Nigeria, like the thirteen original American colonies, became both a British colony, and later a member of the British Commonwealth.

As the British established a foothold in the Lower Niger, they divided the territory into administrative districts and appointed district commissioners to govern them. One of these district commissioners is in charge of the Igbo districts that Achebe writes about in *Things Fall Apart*.

EARLY REACTIONS TO THE COLONIZATION OF NIGERIA

The creation and colonization of Nigeria by Britain took the form of a three-pronged frontal attack on the ethnic peoples of the Lower Niger: the commercial front, the socio-religious front, and the paramilitary administration front. The attack was so cunningly coordinated and simultaneously executed on all three fronts by various British forces that before the natives realized what had happened, their land, their culture, their wealth, their gods and goddesses, and their own people had been won over by the alien agencies. Hence it became very difficult for the Nigerians to counterattack their white enemies effectively without harming their fellow clansmen. For not only had some Nigerians become Christians and catechists, teachers and students in mission schools, or court messengers and interpreters, but, above all, the *efulefu* or outcasts (such as the *osu*, the twins and their mothers, and the poor and the sick) had been freed by the new dispensation. In a word, the alien people and their way of life, which offered Nigerians new job opportunities, individual freedoms, and a new and apparently more compassionate religion, understandably now had to be defended by their native converts.

The situation created serious conflicts between the colonized Nigerians and the colonizing Englishmen. And, obviously, the two sides reacted to the situation in different ways. The following pages discuss some of these reactions.

CHINUA ACHEBE AND COLONIALISM

Chinua Achebe, born thirty years after the creation of Nigeria and thirty years before it attained political independence, had direct experience of the British colonization of Nigeria and Igboland. He was raised in the village of Ogidi, one of the first centers of Anglican missionary work in Eastern Nigeria, only a few dozen miles away from the Niger River. As a Christian convert, he was named Albert.

> I was baptized Albert Chinualumogu. I dropped the tribute to Victorian England when I went to the university, although you might find some early acquaintances still calling me by it. The earliest of them all—my mother—certainly stuck to it to the bitter end. So if anyone asks you what her Britannic Majesty Queen Victoria had in common with Chinua Achebe, the answer is, They both lost their Albert! As for the second name, which in the manner of my people is a full-length philosophical statement, I simply cut in two, making it more businesslike without, I hope, losing the general drift of its meaning. (*Morning Yet on Creation Day* 98).

Achebe received his elementary, secondary, and university education, respectively, from a mission school, a (colonial) government secondary school, and a (colonial) university college in Ibadan, staffed and run by London University. All three institutions exerted colonial influences on him, be they religious, administrative, or academic. In his first novel, *Things Fall Apart*, his general reaction to colonialism in Nigeria is unmistakable:

> But apart from the church, the white men had also brought a government. They had built a court where the District Commissioner judged cases in ignorance. He had court messengers who brought men to him for trial. Many of these messengers came from Umuru on the bank of the Great River [Niger River], where the white men first came many years before and where they had built the centre of their *religion*, and *trade* and *government* [emphasis added]. These court messengers were greatly hated in Umuofia because they were foreigners and also arrogant and high-handed. They were called *kotma*, and because of their ash-coloured shorts they earned the additional name of Ashy-Buttocks. They guarded the prison, which was full of men who had offended against the white man's laws. Some of these prisoners had thrown away their twins and some had molested Christians. They were beaten in the prison by the *kotma* and made to work every morning clearing the government compound and fetching wood for the white Commissioners and the court messengers. Some of these prisoners were men of title who should be above such mean occupation. They were grieved by the indignity and mourned for their neglected farms. (123)

WILLIAM NEVILL M. GEARY AND NIGERIA UNDER BRITISH RULE

Coming to West Africa from England as a practicing lawyer, William Geary first landed in Sierra Leone in 1894. From 1895 to 1897 he was appointed attorney-general of Gold Coast (now Ghana). After a leave of absence in England, he returned to West Africa in 1898, this time to Lagos, Nigeria, as a private lawyer. While there Geary worked with British and Nigerian businessmen and British colonial officials, but he also interacted with ordinary Nigerian citizens. His experiences enabled him to write with the kind of authority apparent in the excerpt that follows.

FROM WILLIAM NEVILL M. GEARY, *NIGERIA UNDER BRITISH RULE* (1927)

Progress of Nigeria

How has England benefited, how have the Africans benefited in the result from our self-imposed task of governing Nigeria? How, when, and by whom, has the great task been carried out in the last thirty years? For 1895 is the starting point in this great adventure.

We have benefited by a great and increasing market being raised up for British manufacturers, carried in British bottoms.

In 1925 the Nigerian imports were over £16 million in all, whereof the United Kingdom supplied 71 per cent. In 1895 the imports were under one million.

Our payment has been some £5 million in all granted by the British Treasury mainly for subvention of Northern Nigeria and the West African Frontier Force. It was an emergency grant when without it Northern Nigeria could not have been occupied, and granted when England was rich and income-tax low. Now that Nigeria is prosperous, why should not the over-burdened English tax-payer be refunded?

This sum of £5 million is independent of and different from the ordinary debt of Nigeria. It was given for Northern Nigeria, which had no sufficient revenue to offer as security and so could not come on the market to borrow. On 18 March 1926 the Secretary of State for the Colonies, Mr. Amery, said these grants-in-aid were free grants, not loans, and neither capital nor interest can be claimed.

The benefit to the Natives is that the *Pax Britannica* has been extended over the whole of Nigeria at a minimum of cost mainly met out of import duties on articles which to the African are luxuries.

Natives of Nigeria

There is no unrest in Nigeria—no political assassination—no non-co-operation—no bombs. The Prince of Wales had a universal welcome of enthusiastic loyalty. The Intelligentsia in West Africa is Christian and Protestant mainly; so there is not that division of caste and creed. The Mohammedans are not fanatical. Still there is faithful and shrewd criticism of the Administration. However, these African critics combine a hearty dislike and contempt for official methods with affectionate regard for England, just as many a good Christian has a loathing for the clergy. I have heard the phrase and wish expressed that West Africa will be another India. God forbid. The condition of India is not so satisfactory to either the governors or the governed; and let us avoid methods which might lead to similar results. The sound old system in West Africa was to consider the African as an "Englishman with a black face". In return the African used to talk of going "home to England". A snob might sneer. But this good feeling is the result of the statesmanship of Wilberforce and his friends, including William Pitt; and of Lord Palmerston's ordering the taking of Lagos. Let us take care that no latter-day policy, or lesser men, and least of all any "dam-nigger" prejudice, may undo the work of the great men of the past and estrange the love of our adopted children.

The Indian never laughs. The African, on the contrary, has a loud laugh and is boisterous and noisy, which may irritate the European: in compensation the African has an inherent common sense and an appreciation of a joke whereto one can appeal. The European can never do manual work in West Africa, therefore the execution of all work, whether Government or commercial, depends on Native labour. So the European who would be efficient must be able to handle Native labour so as to secure willing co-operation; for there cannot now be nigger-driving by the lash. The African is utilized as a marine-engineer and also on the railway; and a Krooboy at the donkey-engine can deal quickly and carefully with cargo.

There are in fact twelve Native main line drivers on the railway and twenty-five shunters, who can rise to a maximum salary of £300 a year. Colonel F. D. Hammond, in his report on the railway, recommends that more Native engine-drivers should be employed. The African frequently becomes a skilled mechanic in repair shops and all purely clerical work is done by Africans.

In the professional class the Bar is almost entirely African, though there are one or two European lawyers in Lagos and one in Northern Nigeria. In medicine there are numerous qualified physicians and surgeons, some in the Government service. There has been some tension as to the treatment of African doctors in the Government service, but in contrast thereto stands out a story of African gallantry and patriotism. A young Lagosian returned to Lagos during the War as a qualified doctor, the Nigerian forces were then going on the East African expeditions; this young man sank his rank as a doctor and volunteered to go as a dresser; his services were accepted and he was mentioned for his bravery under fire. Ecclesiastically there are African Bishops of the Church of England and clergy of the Church of England and other denominations. There are but few African Roman Catholic priests—the African has no predilection for celibacy.

Lastly, it is often said, "Black men smell bad." It is difficult to prove a negative, and I can only give in evidence my own experience. For several years when practising, I sat in court on the bar benches side by side with African barristers; and I had numerous African clients, male and female, and I personally never perceived any unpleasant odour. Perhaps carriers coming in after a long march and freely sweating, do smell; but there are similar smells even in Europe.

· · ·

Missionaries

The missionaries have been a wide-reaching influence for good in coastal districts of Nigeria. The Protestants were first in the field, at Badagry and Abeokuta before the taking of Lagos, at Lagos itself after its capture, and in the delta at Bonny, and from these centres they spread churches and schools. The Roman Catholics came later.

In the temporal side of their work the Protestant missionaries educated their converts and thereby provided the Native staff on which the Government and traders depended and without whose help the Government and trade could not have been carried on. It was only later that the Government undertook education, firstly by subventions and secondly by establishing Government schools, as the King's College at Lagos, for secondary education and primary schools, and also training schools for teachers.

The Roman Catholics have undertaken the upbringing of half-castes, "snuff and butters," as is the slang local phrase for their colour, at the convent at Lagos for girls whose parents pay, and at Taupo up the lagoon gratuitously.

On the religious and moral side of missionary effort it is as difficult to judge in Africa as it is in Europe; and many delight in pointing a finger of scorn at any delinquencies of Christian Africans.

A crucial test of the moral effect of Christianity is the conduct of the Christian inhabitants of Nimbe in the Akassa raid. The Royal Niger Company, acting under their charter, had imposed a customs barrier which destroyed the trade and prosperity of Nimbe, and all the inhabitants of Nimbe, Christian and Pagan, determined to raid and destroy Akassa, the head station of the Niger Company. The raid was successful and forty captives were taken, who were divided between the Pagan and Christian inhabitants of Nimbe. The Pagans killed and ate their captives, making a cannibal feast, described by a Roman Catholic missionary, Father Diedenhofer, accidentally present, as a spectator, not a dietary. The Christians refused to kill their captives, treated them fairly and ultimately returned them safely to the Government. A fine instance of fidelity to the faith; but there was one renegade who, though trained for years in a missionary school in the Isle of Man, was one of the cannibals and was observed eating a man's leg.

London: Methuen, pp. 13–17.

C. K. MEEK ON THE EVIL EFFECTS OF INDIRECT RULE IN IGBOLAND

When Lord Lugard assumed office on January 1, 1914, as the first governor-general of Nigeria, he extended the application of the principles of indirect rule, which had worked so well in Northern Nigeria, to Southern Nigeria, which included Igboland. He did so without regard to the peculiar political nature of the individual peoples of Nigeria, especially disregarding the egalitarian nature of the Igbo, who are opposed to any form of imposed government. Furthermore, the native courts and the warrant chiefs that were appointed to run the system of indirect rule became a disastrous failure in both their administrative and judicial functions. As the years passed, the warrant chiefs became oppressive tyrants, imprisoning arbitrarily whoever criticized them openly, receiving bribes from litigants before their cases were tried, and often giving disputed lands to the wrong claimants. In 1929 the women of Aba, an Igbo community, seeing how their husbands, fathers, and brothers were cruelly beaten and falsely imprisoned, engaged in an unprecedented riot that took the government months to put down. The federal government was invited to come and solve the problem.

Lord Lugard sent C. K. Meek, the anthropologist to the government of Nigeria, who had already established a high reputation of conducting invaluable research on Nigerians in the Northern Provinces, to study the problem posed by the 1929 Aba Women's Riot, which became a historic example of feminist movements in Nigeria. In the excerpt that follows, Dr. Meek comments on the riot as well as on indirect rule, which he considers another form of local government, but one without the participation of the people. He makes suggestions on what the federal government must do to improve the system, if the principles of indirect rule are to be applied to Igboland.

FROM C. K. MEEK, *LAW AND AUTHORITY IN A NIGERIAN TRIBE: A STUDY IN INDIRECT RULE* (1937)

Introduction

Towards the close of 1929 riots of an unprecedented kind broke out with startling suddenness in two of the South-Eastern Provinces of Nigeria. The rioters were women—not a few enthusiasts, but women *en masse*—who formed themselves into mobs, armed themselves with cudgels, and marched up and down the country, holding up the roads, howling down the Government, setting fire to the Native Court buildings, assaulting their chiefs, and working themselves generally into such a state of frenzy that on several occasions they did not hesitate to challenge the troops sent to restore order. The rioting continued vigorously for several weeks, and then faded gradually away, as the frenzy subsided and reason began to resume its place. But in the meantime many of the rioters had lost their lives and heavy damage had been done to the property of the Native Administrations and of numerous European trading firms.

Nigeria had always been noted and quoted for the success of its methods of administration and the contentment and friendliness of its twenty million people. This violent and widespread rebellion, therefore, fell upon the Government like a bolt from the blue. A Commission was appointed to inquire into the causes of the disturbances and, after hearing hundreds of witnesses, produced a report which is one of the most interesting commentaries on colonial administration that have been published in recent times. The riots, it appeared, were primarily due to an unfounded fear that direct taxation, which had recently been applied to the male members of the community, was now to be extended to the female. And this fear was intensified by the scarcity of money caused by a heavy fall in the price of palm-produce, the principal source of the people's income, without any corresponding fall in the price of imported goods. But the manner in which the riots had been conducted had made it evident that there were other predisposing causes of discontent, and chief among these was the widespread hatred of the system of Native Administration conducted through the artificial channel of Native Courts, the members of which, under the name of "Warrant Chiefs", had come to be regarded as corrupt henchmen of the Government, rather than as spokesmen and protectors of the people. Had there been a genuine system of Native Administrations based on the institutions of the people and giving full freedom of expression, the riots, if they had occurred at all, could not have attained the dimensions they did, and would not have taken the form of vicious attacks on "Warrant Chiefs" and the wholesale destruction of Native Administration property. Nor were the opinions expressed by the women confined to them. They were shared also by the men. But the women had believed that they could show their resentment with an impunity which would not be accorded to their menfolk.

Elsewhere in Nigeria the form of government known as "Indirect Rule" had been applied with marked success for many years, pre-existing native institutions being fully utilized for the establishment of local self-government on progressive lines. From the large emirates or states such as Sokoto, Bornu, or Kano in the north, and Oyo, Abeokuta, or Benin in the south, to the numerous petty chiefdoms scattered all over the country, there were few areas that could not boast their own Native Administration, including chiefs, counsellors, judges, police, treasuries, hospitals, and schools.

But in South-Eastern Nigeria indirect rule on these lines had not been considered possible, as no framework had been discovered on which Native Administrations could be erected. There were no chiefs with substantial territorial jurisdiction. Indeed, in most areas there were no chiefs at all, and there was no higher unit of government than the commune or small group of contiguous villages. The British system of administration had therefore been direct. For judicial purposes central Native Courts, each with jurisdiction over a large area, had been established to dispose of all but the most serious crimes and torts. No objection had been taken to these courts as such, but the judges of the courts soon became unpopular when they began to assume, as they were often compelled by the British District Officer to assume, executive authority within their own villages. They became, in fact, "chiefs" armed with an authority far in excess of that possessed by the village-councils in former times. This and their venality as judicial officials had made them feared and disliked, though many individuals among them were men of the highest character. With the introduction of direct taxation in 1927 the dislike of the Native Court members became intensified, as they had been used by the Government to persuade the people to accept taxation, and indeed had become the principal agents for collecting the tax. Thus, when in 1929 the price of palm-produce fell to an uneconomic figure, it merely needed the spark of a rumor that women, the preparers and marketers of palm-produce, were to be taxed to set the whole country ablaze.

It might be inferred that the Government of Nigeria had not devoted sufficient attention to the administration of these South-Eastern Provinces, and it must be admitted that there is some ground for this opinion. Yet it had been no mean achievement on the part of the British Administrative Staff that in a single generation the most lawless part of Nigeria had been converted to a state of comparative peace and contentment. Moreover, the administrative difficulties had been largely inherent in the situation, owing to the absence of any form of central authority. The

Government had made numerous attempts to bring to light the indigenous leaders of the people, but little progress had been made prior to the riots, as investigations had not been carried out in the intensive, scientific manner which would alone reveal the framework on which stable Native Administrations could be built. The Secretary of State for the Colonies was not therefore unjustified when he endorsed the opinion of the Lieutenant-Governor and of the Commission of Inquiry that direct taxation should not have been introduced into the South-Eastern Provinces of Nigeria until fuller knowledge had been obtained of the social institutions of the people. The cart had been put before the horse.

• • •

In the Southern Provinces of Nigeria there is almost a mass movement towards Christianity and Western education, and it is true to say that in the most populous tribes the majority of the younger generation are already professing Christians and have some knowledge of reading and writing. The result has been a cultural clash between the old and the young. It would be a fatal mistake, therefore, to concentrate local authority exclusively in the hands of the elders, most of whom are still pagans, and to fail to give to the younger generation, who no longer respect the ancient sanctions, a reasonable share in the administration of local affairs. This would merely alienate or create active hostility among the educated members of the community, and give them just ground for believing that the policy of "Indirect Rule" is indeed an anachronism and a means of keeping them in a state of subjection to institutions which have outlasted their usefulness. "Indirect Rule," after all, is merely another name for the local self-government, and self-government implies a form of government acceptable to the people as a whole. The pursuit of a static policy would defeat the main purpose of "Indirect Rule," which is to enlist the activities of all the social elements in a common loyalty and solidarity. The old and young will have to work out the synthesis by tact and forbearance, but the Government can assist in the adjustment by adhering to a broad dynamic policy. Such a policy has been well and truly laid down in Sir Donald Cameron's recent memorandum on "The Principles of Indirect Administration," and this memorandum should be sufficient to allay, once for all, the fears that have been expressed in recent years regarding the wisdom and purpose of the policy of "Indirect Rule."

London: Oxford University Press, pp. ix–xvi.

ELIZABETH ISICHEI ON THE BRITISH INVASION OF IGBOLAND, 1902–1906

The Aba Women's Riot was not the first instance of Igbo resistance to British rule. On the contrary, the fight the men gave the British between 1902 and 1906 before they were subdued and severely punished gave the women the impetus to fight the British later. The Igbo, who believe in complementary dualism, see the 1929 riot as a complement to the men's armed combat with the British earlier in the century.

In the following excerpt, Elizabeth Isichei, a renowned Igbo historian, gives a partial account of the war of liberation that the Igbo men waged against the British before they were defeated and punished, and their cherished land occupied and colonized.

FROM ELIZABETH ISICHEI, *THE IBO PEOPLE AND THE EUROPEANS: THE GENESIS OF A RELATIONSHIP—TO 1906* (1973)

The Invasion of Iboland, 1902–1906

In the mid 1890s, the rulers of the states of the western Ibo interior gradually came to a resolve to unite in an effort to expel the Royal Niger Company, using the Ekumeku societies as their instruments. Several years of negotiation were necessary to resolve the problems created by the need for united action, and the jealously guarded autonomy of each little state, and even when agreement was reached, each Ekumeku band fought independently, under its own commander, though side by side.[1] In 1898, they rose in an insurrection "for the express purpose of . . . driving out of the country all foreigners and everything foreign."[2] Both missionaries and Company officials fled to the relative safety of Asaba, and soon the Ekumeku controlled the whole Asaba hinterland, except for Asaba itself, the village of Okpanam, some four miles distant, and Issele-Uku, garrisoned by the Company's troops. They used guerilla tactics, attacking, and then disappearing along a maze of forest paths. They sacked the deserted mission stations, and news of their success reached the neighbouring Ishan peoples, who sent reinforcements for the struggle. After suffering several reverses, the forces of the Royal Niger Company succeeded in crushing the rising, with much bloodshed. Strub considered that if it had been united under a single capable leader, the movement could have taken over the whole west bank of the Niger, and threatened the European presence there.[3]

This was not, as was thought at the time, the end of the Ekumeku. Gradually, the societies regrouped, and recouped their strength. In 1900, the Royal Niger Company gave way to the Protectorate of Southern Nigeria. In 1902, in response to the fears of traders and missionaries that another rising was imminent, a patrol was sent against the Ekumeku, capturing many of its leaders and imprisoning them in distant Calabar.[4]

But the Ekumeku survived, and in 1904, despite their memories of the failures of the past, they broke out in another major rising. The immediate occasion was dissatisfaction with the workings of the recently established Native Courts, and the abuses and corruption they manifested.[5] Mission property was unharmed, but "Native Christians and others suspected of foreign sympathies have been made to suffer equally with the foreigners themselves."[6] None lost their lives, but many lost their property and were forced to flee.

In 1904, the Ekumeku changed their tactics. They abandoned the guerilla warfare, which had enjoyed much success in 1898, and concentrated on the separate defence of each town[7]—a decision which reflected the continuing paramountcy of local loyalties. The change of tactics was disastrous, for it was relatively easy to isolate and conquer the little states, one by one, and their defences—clay walls and ditches—offered no protection against machine guns. The turning point of the rising was the siege of Uburuku, a town which, unlike its allies, had excellent natural defences. After several days of gallant resistance, the town fell. It was the end of the rising, for "the others in the league understood that they could not resist an enemy who had conquered the bravest of their number, and returned to their homes."[8]

At least three hundred of those involved in the movement were imprisoned in Calabar, and many died there.[9] A missionary in western Iboland described the consequences of failure in war. "Result: many towns destroyed, four to five hundred killed; four hundred prisoners. On the British side, one European killed, another wounded, a dozen soldiers killed. All the farms are devastated, and yams, banana groves and cassava, all destroyed."[10] But it was still not the end of the Ekumeku, and in 1909, resistance broke out again in the Ogwashi area, which was only suppressed after five months of guerilla warfare.[11] And the western Ibo continue to cherish the memory of the Ekumeku, of those "select men, brave, courageous, with military prowess," such as Dunkwu Isusu of Onicha-Olona, and Nwadiaju, of Issele Mkpitma.[12]

By 1906, the conquest of Iboland was in no sense completed. A missionary wrote in 1910 that "Almost continual expeditions, which the newspapers never mention, take place in the interior of the country."[13]

This resistance continued through the period of the First World War and beyond. The Women's Riots of 1929, with their tragic sequel, were not an isolated protest, but were an affirmation of a continuing tradition of resistance.

Notes

1. Strub, fo. 13.
2. E. Dennis, "The Rising of the Ekwumekwu," *Niger and Yoruba Notes* (1904), p. 83.
3. This paragraph is based on *ibid.* and on Strub, folios 14–15.
4. C.O. 520/18, Fosbery to High Commissioner, Southern Nigeria, 2 January 1903.
5. C.O. 520/24, W.E.B. Copland-Crawford, "Report on the Rising of the Ekumeku Society in Asaba Hinterland, 1904," 25 April 1904; encl. in Egerton to C.O., 22 May 1904. Cf. E. Dennis, *loc. cit.*, p. 84.
6. C.M.S. G3/A3/1904/27, Dennis to Baylis, 19 January 1904. Paul O. Emecete, "Story of My Life," *The African Missionary* (November–December 1919), p. 3.
7. Strub, fo. 21.
8. Strub, fo. 22. C.O. 520/24, "Report on Asaba Hinterland Operations," 14 March 1904, encl. in Egerton to C.O., 7 May 1904.
9. C.O. 520/24, Copland-Crawford, "Report on the Rising of the Ekumeku Society in Asaba Hinterland, 1904," encl. in Egerton to C.O., 22 May 1904. Non-official sources put the number higher. Cf. C.S.Sp. 191/A/II, cutting from Depêche Coloniale, 13 June 1905, annotated "C'est très vrai dit le P. Lejeune."
10. C.S.Sp. 192/B/III, Lejeune to Superior General, 17 March 1904.
11. Ferrieux, letter of 1 October 1910, in *Annals of the Propagation of the Faith* (1911), pp. 72 ff.
12. Asaba oral tradition.
13. C.S.Sp. 192/B/VI, Léna to Superior General, 21 December 1910.

New York: St. Martin's Press, pp. 140–42.

MICHAEL CROWDER ON THE AFTERMATH OF THE UNIFICATION OF NIGERIA

A white professor, Michael Crowder taught history at the University of Lagos during the 1960s and 1970s. While there he researched and wrote an authoritative history of Nigeria so that both Nigerians and Britons could truly understand how Nigeria was created and colonized by Britain. In the following excerpt, Crowder discusses the unification of Nigeria and its impact on the ethnic peoples, especially the Igbo, who, under the leadership of the Aro, refused to be colonized until they were finally subdued around 1918.

FROM MICHAEL CROWDER, *THE STORY OF NIGERIA* (1978)

The Unification of Nigeria

On the withdrawal of the Royal Niger Company's charter [in 1897], the Niger Coast Protectorate and all the company's territories as far north as Idah were, as we have seen, amalgamated into the new Protectorate of Southern Nigeria. The Lagos Protectorate, like the Protectorate of Southern Nigeria, was brought under Colonial Office jurisdiction, and comprised all of Yorubaland except the Emirate of Ilorin, which was included in the Protectorate of Northern Nigeria. By 1900 the major areas of resistance to British authority had been overcome, but in some areas of the eastern provinces British authority was only extended with great difficulty. Yorubaland, with the exception of Ijebu, had been brought under British rule by treaty, Benin had been conquered and the Delta states had all been subdued in the interests of trade. However, it took many punitive expeditions to bring the whole of Igboland effectively under British administration.

The first major operation undertaken by the new Protectorate government was against the Aro, guardians of the famous Aro Chukwu oracle, which still retained its political influence over most of the peoples of the Niger Delta and its hinterland. The Aro bitterly resented the extension of British authority over an area in which for more than two centuries the religious and political supremacy of their oracle had remained unchallenged. They therefore did as much as they could to frustrate the alien administration, particularly by using their religious authority to place embargoes on trade with the Europeans. At first the British had hoped to avoid using force in dealing with the Aro. However, when in June 1901 the latter attacked some Ibibio villages, carrying off a number of their inhabitants for sale as slaves on the domestic market, the British decided to take action. As Anene has put it, "there were no doubts . . . in the minds of the Protectorate administrators that the one remaining obstacle to the consolidation of imperial rule was the Aro." The attack on the Ibibio was considered by the Protectorate government as having been aimed at the frustration of trade in the interior. This, together with the continuing role of the Aro in the internal slave trade, gave them the excuse they needed to mount an expedition against the Aro and their oracle. However, as Anene has pointed out, the Colonial Office, while sanctioning the expedition, was not happy about extending the Protectorate by conquest. The expedition met with comparatively little resistance, and entered Arochukwu itself on 24th December 1901. A number of Aro chiefs were hanged, and the oracle was burnt. Though the destruction of the basis of Aro authority represented a major step forward in the extension of British authority over south-eastern Nigeria, numerous columns, named after the areas they patrolled, were kept on a standing basis. In Ogoja, Owerri, Ibibio, Urhobo and Western Igbo the new government had its most difficult task, often extending control village by village. The local people had the initiative despite their primitive weapons. Great rain forests, meshes of streams and rivers merging into swampland, made rapid communications almost impossible and put the villagers at a great advantage over their well-armed enemies. Thus for the first six years of the Protectorate's life the new administration, particularly in the eastern provinces, was concerned primarily with the assertion of its authority.

Though some parts of Igboland were not finally brought under British control until as late as 1918, the year 1906, when the Lagos Protectorate was merged with the Protectorate of Southern Nigeria and the north was finally pacified, can be taken as marking the beginning of effective British administration in modern Nigeria. Before then cultural contact with the European, with the exception of the coastal ports and certain towns in Yorubaland, had been of marginal significance. During the three centuries that Europeans had been visiting Nigeria they had made remarkably little cultural impact on the bulk of the local population. This is in marked contrast to the trans-Saharan contact in northern Nigeria, which resulted in extensive changes in religion, law, architecture, technology and concepts of social stratification. It was only after 1906 that the way of life of the invaders had any appreciable effect on Nigerian society. From then on can be traced the rapid breakdown of the structure of traditional society, as the various peoples of Nigeria were brought under an administration which if not uniform in its application was at least controlled by a single power. Before then the British had been but a handful and their main interest in Nigeria had been economic. With the exception of the missionaries they had neither deliberately nor unconsciously attempted to alter Nigerian society except in so far as customs hindered trade, or where practices such as human sacrifice were openly repugnant to them.

The period 1906–12, which preceded the amalgamation of the Northern and Southern Protectorates, is one of the most crucial in the history of Nigeria, for it marks both the beginning of effective administration and the beginning of the rejection of standards and customs that had endured almost intact for many centuries. It was the first time that Nigerians were subjected in any large measure to Western influences, which in the next fifty years were to have such a great effect on Nigerian society. A whole new economic world was to be opened to Nigerians. Christianity, as the official doctrine of the colonial masters, began to spread throughout Southern Nigeria and the non-Muslim areas of Northern Nigeria. New forms of administration and justice were introduced. Finally, education in the Western way of life was made available to a wide range of Nigerians as a result of the spread of missions. So although this period appears from the annual reports as a static one, it was in effect the beginning of major changes in Nigeria.

• • •

Neither the economic nor administrative policy of the government set out deliberately to upset the traditional social structure. Indeed the core of the philosophy of indirect rule as it came to be practised in Nigeria from 1906 onwards was the ensurance of minimum interference with "native society." It attempted only to create favourable conditions for trade and to ensure what it considered the basic essentials of human behaviour. By contrast the missionaries, who were excluded from the Muslim areas of the North by Lugard's agreement with the Caliph of Sokoto that he would not interfere with Muslim religion, approached Nigerian societies with a very different attitude. They were convinced that their own society was superior, and also that conversion of the local people would have to be not only from the traditional religion but from the whole way of life which was intertwined with it and supported it. They therefore deliberately set out to change the very structure of traditional society. Until the beginning of the twentieth century they had made only comparatively small inroads into Nigerian society.

London: Faber and Faber, pp. 188–93.

CONCLUSION

The partition of West Africa in 1894–95 gave British trading companies, the Royal Niger Company and the Niger Delta Company, the right and authority to occupy parts of the Lower Niger. However, it took the combined efforts of the trading companies, Parliament, and paramilitary forces to fight and subdue the native armed resistance to the British invasion and occupation of the ethnic communities of the Niger and the Benue. When in 1900 all other ethnic peoples of Nigeria accepted British colonial rule, albeit reluctantly, the Igbo-speaking peoples of southeastern Nigeria continued their war of independence against the British. The British formally invaded Igboland in 1901. The Igbo kept on fighting until 1906, when they were finally defeated and brought into the Nigerian nation after paying a heavy price. Although the Igbo warriors did not win then, their descendants led the struggle for independence against the British again, this time winning in 1960.

TOPICS FOR WRITTEN OR ORAL EXPLORATION

1. Why did the Europeans colonize West Africa?

2. Why were Britain and France the only European powers to colonize West Africa at the end of World War I?

3. When did Nigeria become a country in its present form? How was it created?

4. What was the original form of government that Britain practiced in Nigeria?

5. What kind of government did the District Commissioner establish in Umuofia?

6. How did that government help to promote the establishment of Christianity in Umuofia?

7. Comment on the roles of British government agents such as court messengers and interpreters in Umuofia.

8. Discuss the merits and disadvantages of indirect rule in several parts of Nigeria.

9. When did Igboland come fully under British rule? Why was it the last ethnic community to be subdued by the British?

10. What was the Aba Women's Riot? Why did the Igbo women go to war with the British government forces?

11. What is the historical significance of the Aba Women's Riot?

12. Discuss the roles of the British trading firms, the Niger Delta Company and the Royal Niger Company, in the creation and colonization of Nigeria.

13. What were the Northern, Southern, and Lagos Protectorates? How were they different from Lagos, Northern Nigeria, and Southern Nigeria?

14. Discuss reactions to the British creation and colonization of Nigeria by (1) Achebe the novelist, (2) British colonial functionaries in Nigeria, and (3) British and Nigerian historians.

15. Discuss the overall Igbo leadership in the Nigerian struggle for independence against Britain.

SUGGESTED READINGS

Ayandele, E. A., et al., eds. *The Making of Modern Africa: The Late Nineteenth Century to the Present Day*, vol. 2. London: Longman, 1971.

Crowder, Michael. *The Story of Nigeria*. London: Faber and Faber, 1978.

Geary, William Nevill M. *Nigeria Under British Rule*. London: Methuen, 1927.

Isichei, Elizabeth. *The Ibo People and the Europeans: The Genesis of a Relationship—to 1906*. New York: St. Martin's Press, 1973.

Meek, C. K. *Law and Authority in a Nigerian Tribe: A Study in Indirect Rule*. London: Oxford University Press, 1937.

Ogbaa, Kalu. *Igbo*. New York: Rosen, 1995.

4

Cultural Harmony I: Igboland—the World of Man and the World of Spirits

CHRONOLOGY

c. 3000 B.C.E.	Neolithic men's existence in Igboland
c. A.D. 850	The Igbo people produce iron swords, bronze and copper vases and ornaments, and terra cotta sculptures
1678–89	16,000 Igbo slaves shipped annually to Europe through Bonny
1745	Olaudah Equiano is born in Igboland, but sold later as a slave to Barbados in 1756
1797	Olaudah Equiano dies in England a freed slave
1830	European explorers discover the course of the Lower Niger and meet the Niger Igbo
1835	James Africanus Horton is born to Igbo ex-slaves in Sierra Leone
1850	Europeans penetrate Igboland through the Niger Delta area
1855	William Belfour Baikie, a Scottish naval physician, reaches Niger Igboland
1883	James Africanus Horton dies
1885–1906	Missionary presence in Igboland

1891	King Ja Ja of Opobo (born Jubo Jubogha of Amaigbo) dies in exile, but his corpse is brought back to Nigeria for burial
1896–1906	About 6,000 Igbo children attend mission schools
1906	Igboland becomes part of Southern Nigeria
1910	Southern Nigeria, principally Igboland, exports 172,998 tons of palm kernel and 76,850 tons of oil to Europe annually
1920	A branch of Marcus Garvey's Universal Negro Improvement Association is formed in Lagos to raise people's consciousness of nationalistic movement in Nigeria
1929	The Aba Women's Riot, which marks the first Nigerian feminist movement, is staged
1944	National Council for Nigeria and the Cameroons (NCNC) political organization formed in Lagos
1950	All-Nigeria Constitional Conference meets to recommend the formation of a federal system of government for Nigeria
1957	Eastern Nigeria and Western Nigeria constitutionally become self-ruling
1960	Dr. Nnamdi Azikiwe is installed as the first indigenous governor-general of independent Nigeria
1960	The first indigenous Nigerian university, the University of Nigeria, is built at Nsukka in Igboland
1960–63	Major-General Johnson T. U. Aguiyi-Ironsi serves as the first African Force Commander of the United Nations Peace-keeping Operation during the Congo crisis
1966	General Aguiyi-Ironsi is installed as head of the Nigerian military government following the January 15, 1966 military coup, but is killed on July 29, 1966, following a second military coup
1967	Eastern Nigeria declares itself the Federal Republic of Biafra on May 27; Nigeria declares war on Biafra on May 29
1970	Biafra surrenders to Nigeria, thereby ending the Nigeria-Biafra War (1967–1970), and rejoins the Federal Republic of Nigeria on January 15

1974   The first Nigerian college of education, Alvan Ikoku College of Education, is founded at Owerri, in Igboland

1981   The first Nigerian state university, The Imo State University, is founded at Etiti, in Igboland

INTRODUCTION

In Part Three, Chapter Twenty, of *Things Fall Apart*, Chinua Achebe uses a conversation between Okonkwo and his friend Obierika to suggest that pre-colonial Igboland enjoyed cultural harmony and that the people "acted like one" because of four important elements of Igbo life: their land, language, customs, and religion, which the advent of the white men so seriously disturbed that things began to go badly for the people:

> "Does the white man understand our custom about *land?*"
>
> "How can he when he does not even speak our *tongue?* But he says that our *customs* are bad; and our own brothers who have taken up his *religion* also say that our customs are bad [emphasis added]. How do you think we can fight when our own brothers have turned against us? The white man is very clever. He came quietly and peaceably with his religion. We were amused at his foolishness and allowed him to stay. Now he has won our brothers, and our clan can no longer act like one. He has put a knife on the things that held us together and we have fallen apart." (124–25)

Whether one looks critically at the fictive Igbo community of Umuofia in *Things Fall Apart* or at actual pre-colonial Igbo communities, the importance of the land to the community's way of life is clear:

> Behind [Achebe's] novels, short stories and poems there is this immense presence of a patrimony, a land, a people, a way of life. But while characterizing that land, detailing the history of its many crises, Achebe sees it as the one unchanging feature of the artistic and moral landscape, as the permanent Being to which all efforts of the children of the land must be devoted. If we recognize this, we can then appreciate why Achebe is not the urban African, why his art is not the art of the metropolis. Rather Achebe is the artist in the communal sense of the term, the man of great wisdom, working

within the limits and through the norms of his society as on the universality of his own personal vision. (Echeruo 151)

As a conscious artist, therefore, and with an obsessive commitment to the messages of his art, Achebe not only keeps the history and culture of his cherished Igboland alive, but also plays the role of a keeper of the conscience of his people and defender of their individual liberties and rights. For those reasons, a full appreciation of his classic novel *Things Fall Apart* requires that the serious reader be aware of those elements of Igbo life which created the harmony the people enjoyed before colonialism. This chapter examines Igboland as the world of man and the world of spirits, and how their understanding of the land shapes the worldview of the Igbo and influences their individual and collective behavior.

IGBOLAND

To the Igbo people, Igboland is both a physical place and a metaphysical expression. This dual definition of the land shapes the Igbo worldview and, in turn, affects their spiritual, social, political and, to an extent, economic lives.

Igboland as a Geographical Expression: The World of Man

Geographically, Igboland is located in southeastern Nigeria, spanning Abia, Anambra, Ebonyin, Enugu, and Imo States of Nigeria. However, Igbo people are also found in large numbers in other non-Igbo states, including Akwa Ibom, Delta, Port Harcourt, and Rivers. These are areas that one can point to as Igbo country on any map of Nigeria.

The Igbo, unlike other peoples of Nigeria, are very skeptical about traditions that tell of lengthy migrations of their ancestors from other parts of Nigeria or anywhere else in the world. In fact, the Igbo elders would tell any interviewer that "we did not come from anywhere and anyone who tells you we came from anywhere is a liar." This means that Igboland came into being the very day their creator god, Chukwu, created the universe.

So far as is known from archeological findings and oral and writ-

Map 3
Map of Nigeria Showing Major Ethnic Groups

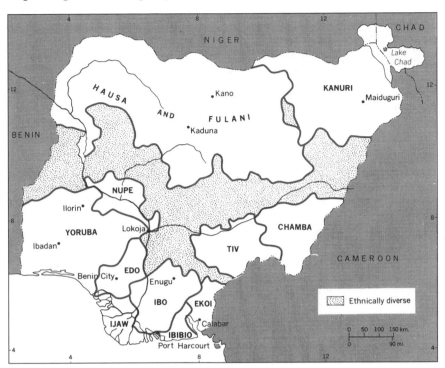

Source: Alan C. G. Best and Harm J. de Blij, *African Survey* (New York: John Wiley and Sons, 1977), 155.

ten history, the Igbo, as a people, have never been carried in captivity to any other place on earth, nor have they colonized other peoples of the world. That is why some say that Igbo people have no history—a claim Igbo historians such as Elizabeth Isichei and A. E. Afigbo have proved erroneous.

Furthermore, given the antiquity of their history and the intra-migrations of their communities, it is easy to understand why Igbo citizens have stood ever ready to resist colonization of any part of their god-given land. That readiness helps to explain why Igboland was the last part of what is now Nigeria to be conquered by Great Britain. British colonial rule had taken root much earlier in Hausaland and Yorubaland, the homes of the other two dominant ethnic groups in Nigeria.

Igboland as a Metaphysical Expression: The World of Spirits

As a metaphysical expression, Igboland comprises two "spirit-lands," *ala mmo* in Igbo. One of them is the abode of the dead-living ancestors, which is a replica underground of the abode of Igbo humans on earth. Achebe describes this spiritland in *Morning Yet on Creation Day*, where he quotes an early anthropological study of the Igbo by Major A. G. Leonard, who reported the following account by one of his Igbo informants:

> We Ibo look forward to the next world as being much the same as this. . . . We picture life there to be exactly as it is in this world. The ground there is just the same as it is here; the earth is similar. There are forests and hills and valleys with rivers flowing and roads leading from one town to another. . . . People in spiritland have their ordinary occupations, the farmer his farm. (133–34)

By way of commentary on the quote, Achebe asserts:

> This "spiritland" where dead ancestors recreate a life comparable to their earthly existence is not only parallel to the human world but is also similar and physically contiguous with it, for there is constant coming and going between them in the endless traffic of life, death, and reincarnation. The masked spirits who often grace human rituals and ceremonies with their presence are representative visitors from this underworld and are said to emerge from their subterranean home through ant holes. At least that is the story as told to the uninitiated. To those who know, however, the masked "spirits" are only *symbolic* ancestors. But this knowledge does not in any way diminish their validity or the awesomeness of their presence. (134)

The second Igbo spiritland is the abode of *chi*, one's personal spirit, guardian angel, soul, or spirit double. Although this second spiritland is also known in Igbo as *ala mmo*, it is not underground, like the abode of the dead-living ancestors; instead, the realm of *chi* is above, and a person's *chi* normally resides with the sun. Achebe writes: "In a general way we may visualize a person's *chi* as his other identity in spiritland—his *spirit being* complementing his terrestrial *human being*; for nothing can stand alone, there must always be another thing standing beside it" (131).

Complementary Dualism: The World of Man and the World of Spirits

The inhabitants of pre-colonial Igbo communities believed that the world in which they lived had its double or counterpart in the realm of spirits, and that all humans on earth had their complementary counterparts, their *chi*, in the spiritland. Hence they developed the notion of complementary dualism, which became central in Igbo thought and philosophy of life. In fact, they developed a spirituality that enabled them to recognize and respect "otherness"—human beings and spirit beings; the Earth and the Sky; the male and the female; the native and the foreigner; the sun and the moon; the living and the dead; the weak and the strong; the young and the old. In the face of things seen and unseen, the Igbo developed religious and ritualistic systems that enabled them to maintain the necessary balance and harmony between opposite beings. The result was that they invoked the attendance of spirit beings during their meetings, rituals, and festivals—a practice that became an essential part of their customs and religious rites. And being conscious of the presence of the spirit beings and their involvement in human activities helped the Igbo to speak and act like one until the advent of the white men into their communities introduced new elements that challenged their traditional way of life. Since that point in their history, the Igbo have never been at ease again.

WRITERS' VIEWS ON COLONIAL IGBOLAND AND ITS PEOPLE

Until the coming of the white men to Igboland, Igbo culture and civilization were transmitted essentially through an oral tradition. All that began to change following the nineteenth-century missionary activities in Igboland (1841–1891), for foreign ethnographers then started to study the people and their land. However, the image of the Igbo that emerged from the pages of European books did not fully and accurately reflect the people's rich culture, customs, land, and religion, primarily because the authors were outsiders to the culture and worked with Igbo interpreters who did not fully understand English and were sometimes reluctant to work with the whites. Another reason for the inaccurate representation of the image of the Igbo in European books was the bigoted attitude of Europeans toward anything African. And yet the faulty image of the Igbo was authoritatively fed to and accepted by European home audiences because their authors were English "gentlemen" and missionaries.

We can now see why Chinua Achebe who formally learned to read and write in the white man's tradition was prompted to write *Things Fall Apart*. He seeks to re-educate both the colonized Africans made to read compulsory European texts by their missionary and colonial teachers and the colonizing Europeans about the rich culture and civilization of his cherished land and people. A similar re-education effort has since been made, however belatedly, by committed Igbo historians.

The following documents, two by European writers and two by their Igbo counterparts, give contrasting perspectives on Igboland and its people.

ELIZABETH ISICHEI ON IGBO HISTORY

Elizabeth Isichei lives in and writes from Igboland. Her field work, professional training, and experience, as well as her commitment to her adopted homeland (through marriage), all combine to enable her to publish authoritative books on Igbo history. The excerpt that follows comes from one of the few history books that give authentic images of the Igbo and their land, delineating the geography of Igboland and the intra-migrations of its people.

FROM ELIZABETH ISICHEI, *A HISTORY OF THE IGBO PEOPLE*
(1976)

The Dawn of Igbo History: Origins of Settlement

. . . The first human inhabitants of Igboland must have come from areas further north—possibly from the Niger confluence. But men have been living in Igboland for at least five thousand years, since the dawn of human history. One of the most notable facts of Igbo history is its length and continuity. Igbo began to diverge from other related languages, such as Edo and Yoruba, perhaps four thousand years ago;[1] 4500 years ago people in Nsukka were making pottery which was similar in style to that still made in the area today.[2] The words of the elder of Mbaise, ["We did not come from anywhere and anyone who tells you we came from anywhere is a liar. Write it down."] quoted as epigraph to this chapter, embody an essential historical truth.

The first cradles of human habitation in the Igbo area were probably the Cross River and the Anambra Valley-Nsukka escarpment. In each of these areas, later Stone Age sites have been excavated. A rock shelter at Afikpo was first inhabited about five thousand years ago, by people who made rough red pottery and a variety of stone tools—hoes, knives, pounders and so on. Excavations at the University of Nsukka uncovered the pottery, 4500 years old, mentioned above, and Ibagwa, a town in the Nsukka area, has a rock shelter which yielded both ancient pottery and tools of stone.[3]

This picture of an early nucleus of settlement in northern Igboland is confirmed by Igbo traditions. The traditions of the Umueri clan—which includes the ancient state of Nri—state that both they and the Igala are descended from a still more ancient community in the Anambra Valley. "We are all descended from Eri, but Igala went one way, Aguku another,

Bronze Roped Pot, c. 1000 B.C.E. (Height 32.3 cm.). From Thurstan Shaw, *Igbo-Ukwu: An Account of Archaeological Discoveries in Eastern Nigeria*, vol. 1 (Evanston: Northwestern University Press, 1970).

Bronze Pottery: An Example of Igbo Artwork, c. 1000 B.C.E. (Height 40.6 cm.).
From Thurstan Shaw, *Igbo-Ukwu: An Account of Archaeological Discoveries in
Eastern Nigeria*, vol. 2 (Evanston: Northwestern University Press, 1970).

Amanuke another, Nteje another and Igbariam another. This separating
of the Igala from us happened so long ago that now we do not hear Igala,
nor can they hear our language."[4]

As time went on, these proto-Igbo populations dispersed more widely
in the forests of Igboland. They came to Owerri, Okigwi, Orlu and Awka
divisions. Most scholars follow G. I. Jones in regarding this as an Igbo
heartland, basing their views on linguistic and cultural evidence.[5] It is
also strikingly confirmed by demography, for a glance at a modern population map shows that it is also the area of densest population. As one

moves further from the heartland, the population density falls, in a series of steadily diminishing rings.

The traditions of Nri, in the northern part of the high-density belt, preserve a memory of the original migration to the south. "At the time of Ndri's arrival in this part of the world, there were no other towns in the immediate vicinity, nothing but open country, and so the settlement was called Aguku, meaning, the great field."[6]

This theory of the Igbo heartland, however, suggests a number of problems. In particular, why did the population concentrate on sandy uplands of limited fertility, with frequent water shortages, rather than on the well-watered alluvial soils of the river valleys? There are a number of possible answers to this question. Floyd points out that the uplands offered a number of positive advantages to agriculturalists with limited technical resources: the land was more easily cleared, and well-drained soil favoured yam cultivation, the staple crop.[7] Why did they avoid the more fertile river valleys? Tsetse fly is one stock answer, but trypanosomiasis (sleeping sickness) seems almost unknown among the present-day inhabitants of Igboland's river valleys, and I can see no convincing reason why it should have been more common in the past. There are, of course, other water-linked diseases, such as malaria, borne by mosquitoes, and schistosomiasis (bilharzia) which are both very common in Igboland. The tendency of the rivers to overflow their banks in the rainy season may have been a factor. Defence certainly was, because riverain settlements were very susceptible to canoe-borne attack. Onitsha was placed on an inland site for this reason, and Illah moved to an inland site, to avoid piracy.[8] There was a remarkable demonstration of this factor in the 1890s, after the extension of British rule to the Cross River, when a major shift of population occurred, with whole villages moving to a riverain site.[9] Whatever the reason, Igbo communities regarded settlement near water with definite apprehension. "The ancestors believed that these streams were meant to quench the thirst but not to serve them as 'homes.' The streams and rivers are the homes of gods and other spirits. It is true that the present generation is too wise . . . but that is the reason why man no longer lives long."[10]

The suggestion has been made that the Igbo heartland, isolated from external influences, shows us the original character of Igbo culture, and that the study of, for instance, the Owerri-Orlu-Okigwi area gives us a baseline with which we can assess the nature of change in other Igbo areas.[11] This is a technique which has been used very fruitfully elsewhere, and in the Igbo context it is suggestive (the heartland, for instance, lacks witchcraft beliefs, secret societies, and title societies). But it involves us in a number of difficulties. The heartland, too, was subject to change. Thus the institution of *osu* (ritual slavery) is very typical of the area, but the evidence suggests that it is of relatively recent origin, and adopted its present form in the era of the trans-Atlantic slave trade.[12]

What is most ancient is not necessarily most typical, as witness the institutions of Nri, with its priest-king, which are most untypical of Igboland as a whole. What is important may not be ancient, as witness the great importance of the Aro oracle and trading network in nineteenth-century Igboland—which dated, as we shall see, only from the seventeenth century.

What is clear, is that the Igbo heartland repeatedly built up levels of population pressure which the ecological environment was unable to sustain, and which from time to time gave rise to migrations to other parts of Igboland.

One can assume an early dispersion from this center to the Nsukka-Udi highlands in the east and an early drift southward towards the coast. . . . One can more positively distinguish a later and more massive dispersal . . . which was mainly south-eastwards . . . into what is now Eastern Isuama area. From this subsidiary dispersion area there was one movement south-south-east into the Aba Division to form the Ngwa group of tribes, and another movement east into Umuahia area and thence to the Ohaffia-Arochuku ridge, with an offshoot that struck north . . . to develop into North-Eastern Ibo.[13]

The antiquity of these migrations is reflected in the high population densities obtaining throughout Igboland, and the remarkable extent to which the original vegetation has been modified by the human presence. Igboland is in the rain-forest belt, but it is difficult to find any rain forest; the whole countryside is covered with farms, or secondary vegetation where farms lie fallow. Nor is this a recent phenomenon—a British forestry official described it over sixty years ago, and so did a number of nineteenth-century observers, though with less technical expertise.[14]

Notes

1. R. E. Bradbury, "The Historical Uses of Comparative Ethnography with Special Reference to Benin and the Youruba," in Jan Vansina, Raymond Mauny and L. V. Thomas (eds.), *The Historian in Tropical Africa* (London, 1964) p. 150.

2. Donald D. Hartle, "Archaeology in Eastern Nigeria," *Nigeria Magazine*, 93 (June 1967) 136–7.

3. Ibid., pp. 136–7, 139; Donald D. Hartle, "The Prehistory of Nigeria," mimeo (Nsukka, 1973) pp. 64–6.

4. L. Frobenius, *The Voice of Africa*, I (1913) pp. 274–5, quoted in M. D. W. Jeffries, "The Divine Umundri Kings of Igboland," Ph.D. thesis (London, 1934) ch. 2, n.p.

5. G. I. Jones, *The Trading States of the Oil Rivers*, repr. (London, 1964) p. 30.

6. M. D. W. Jeffries, "The Umundri Tradition of Origin," *African Studies*, XV (1956) 121.

7. Barry Floyd, *Eastern Nigeria, A Geographical Review* (London, 1969) pp. 52–3.

8. Information re Illah collected in the author's fieldwork.

9. Donald M. McFarlan, *Calabar, The Church of Scotland Mission Founded 1846*, rev. ed. (London, 1957) pp. 100–1.

10. James Aniekwe of Adazi-enu, Aginyi, aged c. 87, transcribed in J. I. Ejiofor, "A Precolonial History of the Aguinyi Clan," B.A. history special project (Nsukka, 1973) p. 131.

11. A. E. Afigbo, "Igbo Historians and Igbo History," mimeo (Nsukka, 1972) pp. 9–10.

12. G. T. Basden, *Niger Ibos*, repr. (London, 1966) p. 249.

13. Jones, p. 30.

14. *Journal of the African Society*, X (1910–11) 130.

London: Macmillan, pp. 3–6, 257–58.

G. T. BASDEN ON THE IGBO VILLAGE

A missionary who came to Nigeria from Liverpool, England, in September 1890, G. T. Basden lived among the Igbo of Nigeria for many years. In 1921 he published *Among the Ibos of Nigeria*, an account of his missionary experiences in Igboland. Although he tried very hard to be accurate, his biases toward Igbo culture are reflected in the words he chose to express his ideas. Consider, for instance, the following passage: "Let not this be thought strange, for the black man himself does not know his own mind. He does the most extraordinary things, and cannot explain why he does them. He is not controlled by logic: he is the victim of circumstance, and his policy is very largely one of drift. The will of the tribe or family, expressed or implied, permeates his whole being, and is the deciding factor in every detail of his life" (9–10). Since the publication of Basden's book, Igbo writers have written books and essays that attempt to explain the Igbo world to people like Basden who write about it from foreign perspectives.

FROM G. T. BASDEN, *AMONG THE IBOS OF NIGERIA* (1966)

The Ibo Village

Life in an Ibo village is at once simple and picturesque. The houses, the general environment, the dependence upon local natural resources, and the contentment with the barest modicum of those articles which are usually regarded as indispensable in a household, all these, together with the easy-going spirit amongst the village folk, foster and maintain a life of extreme simplicity. Discontent with primitive conditions comes only with the introduction of novelties from the outside world, and then, like a child, the Ibo covets what he sees. Left to himself he neither needs nor desires foreign luxuries, but once the possibility of securing them presents itself, be they ever so incongruous, he will not relax his efforts until they become his cherished possessions.

A missionary has unique opportunities of becoming acquainted with village life, for from the very nature of things the soundest policy is for him to live in the closest communion with the people whom he seeks to influence. So it comes about that he enters freely into the life of the natives; their huts are always open to him and he goes in and out more or less as one of themselves. In like manner they expect the missionary's house to be free to them, and to come and go as they please.

• • •

Every village has its own market-place, fetish-houses and public meeting ground. The markets are designated by the names of the day on which they are held, viz. "Ekke," "Afaw," "Oye" (Olie) and "Nkwaw," these corresponding to the four days of the Ibo week. The life of the womenfolk largely consists in a continual round of marketing and the preparation of food, varied by farm work in the season.

The fetish-houses are usually small and very crude; indeed they are neglected and allowed to fall into great disrepair, until some wave of religious zeal leads to their temporary restoration. The people do not appear to worry concerning the ju-ju. Wind and weather may play havoc upon it during the period that their fervour is at a low ebb, and, as a considerable number of these gods are composed of clay, the result is somewhat disastrous, especially during the rainy season. However, a little patching, at the admonition of the Chief, or at the time of some special crisis, satisfies the people, and they conclude that the god ought to be satisfied also. This is a mere statement of fact, not a point of sentiment. A charge is sometimes levelled at missionaries that they entertain neither respect nor regard for the native religion; but they probably understand the situation, and know the underlying currents of thought better than their critics, who too often trumpet forth their opinions, though some of ' them have never visited the country at all, and others have made but a "so-many-miles-in-a-fortnight" sort of tour. I remember a case in which a colleague was interrogated by one such visitor. An opinion was asked concerning a certain custom. My colleague answered that he could not commit himself to anything definite, as he had not been able to probe to the bottom of the matter. The visitor thought this strange, and went on to remark that he had *quite* a clear conception of the custom, underlying principle and all, as he had been asking questions for *the last two days!*[1] My colleague replied that he had been working at the idea over a space of two whole years, and he was still far from being in a position to dogmatise on the subject under discussion.

The public meeting ground (Ilo), is a charming spot; a large open space shaded by one or more Awbu trees. Beginning a few feet from the ground, these trees throw out, at right angles to the stem, huge wide spreading branches. As these extend they are supported by props. The leaves are large and abundant and the tree when fully grown gives an almost perfect circle of shade sometimes as much as one hundred yards in circumference.

These natural arbours eclipse all enclosed meeting halls. The crowd sits or lies upon the sandy floor, completely sheltered from the sun, each man assuming any attitude he pleases. Of course, fair weather is necessary to appreciate the advantages of the open-air conditions. The chief drawback is that the attention of the audience is apt to be diverted by every casual passer-by, and often some trivial incident will throw the meeting into hopeless disorder, and bring all business abruptly to an end. The people go off at a tangent on the slightest provocation—they are much like children and find it difficult to concentrate their minds for long together. Very similar conditions prevail in Hyde Park and other resorts of like character in England. It takes very little to attract the attention of the crowd, and the numbers fall off immediately anything transpires which shows the least promise of being more entertaining.

Meetings for many purposes are held in these open spaces: for the adjustment of differences between individuals or households: for the celebration of fixed feasts; the offerings of common town sacrifices and on specially appointed occasions. Hundreds of people will assemble when an important question is under discussion, or a great function is in progress. Frequently the ilo serves also as the market-place, in which case it is the rendezvous of great crowds of haggling buyers and sellers who create a din only to be compared to that of an English fair—minus the steam organs.

London: Frank Cass, pp. 45, 48–50.

M. M. GREEN ON IGBO VILLAGE AFFAIRS

M. M. Green, an English social anthropologist, lived in Igboland from 1934 to 1937, during which time she did field work in and wrote about an Igbo village, Umueke Agbaja. In the excerpt that follows, Green describes her chosen village and its affairs as being typical of Igbo villages of the time. However, her emphasis on the significance of "bush and forest" to the people, as well as the apparent lack of unity among the villages that make up Agbaja clan, would be questioned by the Igbo who have actually lived in such villages. That is to say, Green described the appearance rather than the reality of Igbo village affairs. Her perspective limited what she saw.

FROM M. M. GREEN, *IBO VILLAGE AFFAIRS* (1964)

The Village Group

The village of Umueke is one of eleven villages that together make up what may be called the village-group of Agbaja. The name "town" is sometimes given, particularly in official reports, to social units of this kind, but the designation "village-group" is preferred here for two reasons. In the first place, conditions of life are rural, not urban. In the second place, in this part of Ibo country a village is not a compact circle of houses as in and near Owerri, nor are the villages huddled together to form a town-like agglomeration of the Owerri "town" kind. They are usually scattered over a considerable area of forest, though two of them may sometimes be contiguous.

Agbaja lies about a hundred miles inland from the sea and four hundred feet above sea-level, where the great coastal belt of forested plain is beginning to rise and break up into tree-covered hills and sudden, steep-sided valleys, with frequent outcrops of rock. It is within sight—where one can get a glimpse from high ground through the forest—of the fine rolling uplands of Okigwi. The annual rainfall here is about 90 inches. This is considerably less than that of the coast, but enough to make a damp sticky heat which does not encourage energy either of mind or of body and makes more remarkable the amount of activity the Ibo people, and particularly the women, achieve. Most of the rain falls between April and November, but there is intermittent rain even in the dry season. In

December and January there may be a certain amount of Harmattan, the dry, cool, desert wind. But it is unreliable and always short, and it is the only time that one's spare shoes do not grow green mould.

The forest is less lush and rank than the real tropical rain forest near the coast. There are magnificent trees which dwarf the serried ranks of palms in this, the thick of the oil palm belt. Between the trees there is dense bush which is cut down every few years for purposes of cultivation but which quickly grows up again.

Bush and forest—it is difficult to convey a sense of their pervading influence. Even living in it one does not realise it till one has got away into open country and one's eyes go out to the horizon as from a prison. From the European's point of view, the forest, beautiful as it sometimes is, can none the less become stifling. For the people who live in it there is also a double-edged quality. It may hide them from the enemy, but it also enables the enemy to ambush them in his turn. Nowadays it is perhaps against the white man—or white woman—that it is most useful. The first time I walked through Agbaja on a prospecting trip, to see if it looked a likely spot to settle in, I would have thought from appearances that it was devoid of inhabitants instead of being in the "problem" population belt, so thickly is it peopled. At the sight of an unknown white woman the people had vanished into the bush—a feat they could perform with disconcerting rapidity. Not long after my settling in the village of Umueke Agbaja, and while I was still definitely on probation, I was talking to a crowd of villagers near my house when a white man suddenly arrived to call on me. It was the first car that had navigated the bush path into the village and in my surprise at hearing it I looked round to see what was happening. When I turned again to continue my conversation with the villagers, there was no one in sight. There was just trees and bush.

One gradually becomes accustomed to the way in which even the details of existence are conditioned by the forest. The village, for instance, had the local equivalent of a telephone system. If a mother wanted her child, it was no use going to the door of her house to look for it. Ten yards away it would be invisible either in the bush or, at the right season, among yam vines or maize stems. So the village rang with the cries of parents seeking their children or friends calling to each other. Often when I was talking to one of the villagers in my house he would unexpectedly let out a shrill whoop and I would realise that he, with his trained and sensitive hearing, was answering a call that I had failed to hear.

It was largely forest and tsetse fly that kept out of Ibo country the horse and cattle-owning Fulani who overran so much of Nigeria in their Islamic Holy War in the nineteenth century. How far the protection of the forest can be correlated with the social fragmentation of the Ibo people cannot be assessed. But that there is some connection between the two can hardly be doubted. There is also the isolating effect of the bush upon the people who live in it, which can hardly have failed to contribute to the separatist tendency that is so marked among these people. The mere fact that every village is as invisible from the next as though it were twenty miles away cannot but affect one's mental outlook. To a considerable extent the hidden neighbours seem like strangers. And the bush breeds a constant fear of ambush that is at times only too well founded. Again and again does the ambush motif make itself heard.

Before considering the nature of the village-group of Agbaja we must notice that it counts itself as descended from the same mother as the next door village-group of Umukabia, and reckons that it has kinship links with the neighbouring village-groups known collectively as Umu Ehime. Reference is sometimes made to even wider connections. But these mythical kinship links have at the present day only a limited practical significance so far as one could judge. In past times, before the British cut the country up into Native Court areas under Warrant Chiefs, the significance may have been greater. It may conceivably grow again now that the Native Courts have been reorganized with a view to bringing them more closely into line with indigenous institutions.

As to Agbaja itself, a number of different principles of social grouping enter into the make-up of this village-group, as of most other Ibo social units of this kind. In the first place it is a local unit in the sense that its inhabitants[1] occupy a common territory, the villagers being scattered through the bush over an area that is roughly speaking about three miles square. It is also a mythical kinship unit with relationship becoming genealogical traceable within, and often between, the kindreds that make up the villages. All the people born in Agbaja, with a few exceptions which do not invalidate the principle, claim descent from a mythical pair of ancestors, a man called Ngalaba and a woman called Okpu Ite, who originated in the centre of Agbaja having been created by Chi, and Eke, and who lived in the spot which is now the central Agbaja market place.[2]

• • •

It was evident that Agbaja was an ideological unit in the sense that its members were conscious of their membership and called themselves by the name of Agbaja. But it also appeared that the prestige of each village was an important factor in the eyes of its own inhabitants. From the accounts, I looked forward with interest to seeing the joint action of all Agbaja on the appointed day. When the time came the difference between description and experience was perhaps even more marked than usual. As our village of Umuaka approached the market on its path clearing expedition, shouts and cries could be heard dying away on the other side. I learned somewhat to my surprise that it was another village on its way home having finished its clearing. When our villagers got to the market place they took possession of it alone, dancing and waving their knives in great excitement. As another village came stamping up, also with knives, ours withdrew. I waited, still hoping to see the great assembly. But the elders of my village were clearly uneasy at my lingering and finally insisted on my going home with them and the rest of the villagers. In some surprise I asked why the villages did not all gather in the market place and was told that there would be much too great a risk of their fighting. Evidently it would not do to put an undue strain on the ideal of Agbaja unity, a fact that emerged only too clearly later in my stay when our village and another of the group had a bitter and prolonged dispute.

Notes

1. A Government Intelligence Report gives the population of Agbaja as between four and five thousand. This is probably an underestimate.

2. Ngalaba means forked, and can therefore be used to denote a human being with two legs. Okpu Ite means potter. Agbaja has women potters and also clay. Chi and Eke are the two creating spirits.

London: Frank Cass & Co. Ltd.

VICTOR C. UCHENDU ON THE IGBO OF SOUTHEAST NIGERIA

The sociologist Victor C. Uchendu was one of the first Igbo scholars to do serious ethnographic studies of Igboland and its people.
Not surprisingly, in his book on the Igbo, written from an insider's
point of view, he disagrees with his European counterparts on
many points.

FROM VICTOR C. UCHENDU, *THE IGBO OF SOUTHEAST NIGERIA*
(1965)

The Igbo World

To know how a people view the world around them is to understand
how they evaluate life; and a people's evaluation of life, both temporal
and nontemporal, provides them with a "charter" of action, a guide to
behavior. The Igbo world, in all its aspects—material, spiritual, and so-
ciocultural—is made intelligible to Igbo by their cosmology, which explains how everything came into being. Through it, the Igbo know what
functions the heavenly and earthly bodies have and how to behave with
reference to the gods, the spirits, and the ancestors. In their conception,
not only is cosmology an explanatory device and a guide to conduct; it
is also an action system. As an explanatory device, Igbo cosmology the-
orizes about the origin and character of the universe. I am not concerned
with this aspect of the Igbo world view here. Rather, I am concerned with
two other aspects: cosmology as a system of prescriptive ethics, which
defines what the Igbo ought to do and what they ought to avoid; and
cosmology as an action system, which reveals what the Igbo actually do
as manifested in their overt and covert behavior. The latter is very important if we are to understand the dynamic factors in Igbo culture. But
the three aspects of Igbo cosmology must not be regarded as isolated
phenomena. They are interrelated. I have isolated them for analytical
purposes, as a way of organizing the data and illustrating this well-
accepted fact: that cosmological ideas express the basic notions underlying cultural activities and define cultural goals and social relations.

The World of Man and the World of Spirits

The Igbo world is a "real" one in every respect. There is the world of
man peopled by all created beings and things, both animate and inani-

mate. The spirit world is the abode of the creator, the deities, the disembodied and malignant spirits, and the ancestral spirits. It is the future abode of the living after their death. There is constant interaction between the world of man and the world of the dead; the visible and invisible forces. Existence for the Igbo, therefore, is a dual but interrelated phenomenon involving the interaction between the material and the spiritual, the visible and the invisible, the good and the bad, the living and the dead. The latter are a part of the Igbo social world.

In the Igbo conception, the world of the "dead" is a world full of activities; its inhabitants manifest in their behavior and thought processes that they are "living." The dead continue their lineage system; they are organized in lineages with patrilineal emphasis just as are those on earth. The principle of seniority makes the ancestors the head of the lineage; it gives the lineage its stability and continuity. An Igbo without umunna—a patrilineage—is an Igbo without citizenship both in the world of man and in the world of the ancestors. In the Igbo view, there is a constant interaction between the dead and the living: the dead are reincarnated, death making the transition from the corporeal to the incorporeal life of the ancestors possible. An illustration of the reality of the Igbo dual but interrelated world is provided by this dialogue. Father Shanahan, a great Roman Catholic missionary among the Igbo (who later became a bishop), wanted to baptize a condemned murderer before his death.

> *Murderer*: "If I accept baptism, Father, will it prevent me from getting my enemy in the next life?"
>
> *Father*: "Well, no, you will probably meet him one way or the other."
>
> *Murderer*: "Then baptize me by all means, and as soon as I do meet him, I'll knock his head off a second time." . . .

Apparent in this dialogue is the Igbo conviction that there is a carryover of social status and other personal qualities from the world of man to the world of the dead. The murderer accepted baptism, not because he believed that it would cleanse his sins, but rather because of the reassurance that the baptism was not meant to prevent a face-to-face meeting with his enemy, whose head he wanted to "knock off a second time," thus demonstrating his physical superiority over his enemy in the world of man and the world of the dead.

For the Igbo, death is a necessary precondition for joining the ancestors, just as reincarnation is necessary for the peopling of the temporal segment of the lineage. Therefore death which occurs at a ripe age is a cause for joy, being an index of high status among the ancestors. But since the young as well as the old die, death is received with mixed feelings. Death is personified and dealt with as a powerful spirit which gains mastery over *Ndu*, the life-giving principle. It is the severance of this life-giving principle from the human, corporeal body. Without death, there will be no population increase in the ancestral households and correspondingly, no change in social status for the living Igbo.

Maintaining Cosmological Balance

The world as a natural order which inexorably goes on its ordained way according to a "master plan" is foreign to Igbo conceptions. Rather, their world is a dynamic one—a world of moving equilibrium. It is an equilibrium that is constantly threatened, and sometimes actually disturbed by natural and social calamities. The events which upset it include natural disasters like long, continuous droughts, long periods of famine, epidemic diseases, as well as sorcery and other antisocial forces; litigation, homicide, violation of taboo, and other incidents which the Igbo define as *Nso* or *Alu*—taboo.

But the Igbo believe that these social calamities and cosmic forces which disturb their world are controllable and should be "manipulated" by them for their own purpose. The maintenance of social and cosmological balance in the world becomes, therefore, a dominant and pervasive theme in Igbo life. They achieve this balance, for instance, through divination, sacrifice, appeal to the countervailing powers of their ancestors (who are their invisible father-figures) against the powers of the malignant, and nonancestral spirits, and socially, through constant realignment in their social groupings.

Death, for example, disturbs the existing social and ritual relationships and demands a new mode of adjustment for the bereaved family. The status goal of the one who dies young seems frustrated, and in his family creates a vacuum in its role structure through the loss of a member. The uncertainty about the cause of such an untimely death is a source of concern for all. Divination settles this uncertainty by specifying the cause of death and recommending ritual remedies. The diviner's verdicts follow a culturally expected pattern: the deaths of young people are usually blamed on the sins committed during their previous life on earth; deaths of adults may be attributed to "ripe" age, or senility, a breach of taboo or other antisocial behavior, such as sorcery, false oath, or theft committed in his previous or present life. Whatever the verdict, the loss of ritual balance is implicit and ritual remedies are recommended. If sorcery is involved, the deceased adult is denied "ground" burial (a privilege accorded only to those who die without blemish), and the corpse is cast into *ohia ojoo*—a "bad bush" fit only for the outcast. The ritual purifications are primarily designed to dissociate the living from the deceased's blemish and thus reestablish the ritual balance his breach of taboo has destroyed.

Indeed, whatever threatens the life of the individual or his security as well as society is interpreted by the Igbo as a sign of warning that things must be set right before they get out of hand. Losses in trade indicate to the trader that his *Mbataku*—the wealth-bringing deity—is threatening action for being neglected, while drought or too long a rainy season is a warning that society has lost its balance with nature.

Not only deities and spiritual forces are manipulated. Human beings and social relations are also subject to manipulation. . . . the Igbo individual balances his conflicts in one agnatic group with his privileges in another. His *umune* (mother's agnates[1] among whom he enjoys *okene* privileges) stand with him against the perennial conflicts he faces among his *umunna* (his own agnates). Although he is exposed to physical danger among his *umunna*, his person is sacred in his *umune*. It is the place of his exile should he be convicted of sorcery by his *umunna*. Assured of the support of a strong *umune*, the Igbo can challenge his *umunna* successfully; with the support of both his *umunna* and his *umune*, he can move his world.

When we come to the domain of Igbo legal process, the same principle of balance of forces is seen at work. Legal procedures aim essentially at readjusting social relations. Social justice is more than law, and the spirit of the law is more important than the letter of the law; this seems to be the Igbo juridical principle. The resolution of a case does not have to include a definite victory for one of the parties involved. Judgment among the Igbo ideally involves a compromise. They insist that good judgment "cuts into the flesh as well as the bone" of the matter under dispute. This implies a "hostile" compromise in which there is neither victor nor vanquished; a reconciliation to the benefit of—or a loss to—both parties.

• • •

The world of man and the world of spirits are also interdependent. Between them there is always some form of interdependence, a beneficial reciprocity. The principle of reciprocity demands that the ancestors be honored and offered regular sacrifice, and be "fed" with some crumbs each time the living take their meal; it also imposes on the ancestors the obligation of "prospering" the lineage, protecting its members, and standing with them as a unit against the machinations of wicked men and malignant spirits. The same principle requires that all spirits and deities whose help is invoked during a period of crisis and who stand firm throughout it be rewarded with appropriate sacrifice.

Because reciprocity is the organizing principle of Igbo social relationships, near equality is their ideal. Domination by a few powerful men or spirits is deeply resented. A relationship that is one-sided, either in its obligation or in its reward system, does not last long among them. Imbalance, either in the social or in the spiritual world, is considered a trouble indicator. Through mutual interdependence and his ability to manipulate his world, the Igbo individual tries to achieve equality or near equality in both the world of man and the world of the spirits.

Note

1. Agnates are patrilateral kinsfolk. They are men and women to whom one is related through males only. In other words, a descent link from a man to a child is called an *agnatic* link while a descent link from a woman to a child is called an *uterine* link. A social group tracing descent through males only is an *agnatic group*.

New York: Holt, Rinehart and Winston, pp. 11–15.

CONCLUSION

Basden and Green make the point that the "village-group" forms the hub around which Igbo life and civilization revolve. *Things Fall Apart* makes the same point, although from a different perspective, suggesting that Achebe may have read Basden's and Green's books.

However, in interpreting Igbo village affairs, Green and Achebe saw totally different values: in Green's book the Igbo bush and forest are ominous, sinister, and divisive, and the villagers are uncivilized, pagan, and barbaric. In Achebe's novel, however, the bush and forest are protective, nurturing, and life-supporting, for they are the sources of the villagers' spirituality and livelihood (since the people are essentially farmers and marketers of their farm products); also, the people are cultured, pious, humane, and altruistic (for they play the role of their brothers' keepers).

Things Fall Apart romanticizes the lives of the Igbo, which we come to appreciate through their dances, festivals, rituals, and religious practices, all of which are celebrated in honor of their ancestors, gods, and goddesses, especially the earth goddess, Ani, who is in charge of morality and the fertility of the soil and womb. In fact, bush and forest, *ofia* in Igbo, are so central in Igbo village affairs that Achebe named the Igbo people of his novel Umuofia *obodo dike*. They are "bush" people, in the eyes of the British who see them as uncivilized, but they are also *obodo dike* (land of the brave)—an epithet that suggests that the clan's bravery lies in the coming together of the nine villages that make up the clan, and their bravery and unity are sustained by the provisions of the land, *ofia*. As soon as the British colonized their land and urbanized parts of it (bush and forest), the people became "no longer at ease," the title of Achebe's second novel.

TOPICS FOR WRITTEN OR ORAL EXPLORATION

1. What is the geographical location of Igboland in Nigeria?
2. Discuss how its people define Igboland, and explain how that definition has shaped their worldview.
3. Discuss Igboland as both a physical and a metaphysical expression in *Things Fall Apart*.
4. Identify and discuss the two kinds of "spiritland" known to the Igbo people.
5. Discuss the importance and role of Ala, the earth goddess, in the socio-spiritual lives of the Igbo.
6. Discuss the extent to which the advent of Europeans in Umuofia disturbed the socio-spiritual lives of the Igbo in *Things Fall Apart*.
7. Name the Igbo states of Nigeria and the non-Igbo states in which the Igbo are found in large numbers.
8. Why are Igbo citizens always ready to resist colonization in any part of their God-given land?
9. Did the missionaries treat land with the same respect the Igbo did in *Things Fall Apart*?
10. Why was it almost inevitable that Igboland would be colonized by the British despite the fierce war of resistance fought by the Igbo?
11. Discuss the centrality of village and clan to Igbo life, culture, and civilization in *Things Fall Apart*.
12. Discuss the perspectives of M. M. Green and Chinua Achebe on the importance of land, bush, and forest to the Igbo people.

SUGGESTED READINGS

Basden, G. T. *Among the Ibos of Nigeria*. London: Frank Cass, 1966.

Echeruo, M.J.C. "Chinua Achebe." In *A Celebration of Black African Writing*. Ed. Bruce King and Kolawole Ogungbesan. Zaira, Nigeria: Ahmadu Bello University Press, 1975. 150–63.

Green, M. M. *Ibo Village Affairs*. London: Frank Cass & Co., 1964.

Isichei, Elizabeth. *A History of the Igbo People*. London: Macmillan, 1976.

Uchendu, Victor C. *The Igbo of Southeast Nigeria*. New York: Holt, Rinehart and Winston, 1965.

5

Cultural Harmony II: Igbo Language and Narrative Customs

INTRODUCTION

Language, customs, and religion were important factors in creating the cultural harmony that existed among the Igbo people before colonialism. This chapter discusses the Igbo language and Igbo narrative customs, which in practice are so interrelated, so dovetailed, that it makes sense to explore them together. Chapter 6 deals with religion and material customs, which are also interrelated.

THE IGBO LANGUAGE

The language of the Igbo people is also called Igbo. A member of the Kwa language sub-family of West Africa, it developed as a separate language about 4,500 years ago. However, the language remained unwritten until the late 1800s, when white missionaries established churches and mission schools in Igboland. The missionaries developed the Igbo alphabet and orthography that enabled them to translate the Bible into Igbo for their new converts, and the teachers translated English primers and children's literature for their young pupils, who later became catechists and interpreters for the church and the British administration, respectively.

The Igbo Alphabet

A	B	GB	D	E	F		a	b	gb	d	e	f
G	GH	H	I	Ị	J		g	gh	h	i	ị	j
K	L	M	N	Ñ	O		k	l	m	n	ñ	o
Ọ	P	KP	R	S	SH		ọ	p	kp	r	s	sh
T	U	Ụ	V	W	Y		t	u	ụ	v	w	y
Z	CH	GW	KW	NW	NY		z	ch	gw	kw	nw	ny

The Igbo alphabet has thirty-six letters instead of the twenty-six in the English alphabet. The extra ten Igbo letters, known as twin letters, for example, "gb," are used to represent sounds found in Igbo that are non-existent in English. The absence of such sounds in English made it difficult for the early missionaries and British administrators in Igboland to spell many Igbo words correctly, including names of towns, the language, and the people, whom they called the Ibo. For example, Okonano, a town, was spelled Awkawnanaw, which the Igbo could neither spell nor pronounce; in Igbo orthography, clusters of consonants are not found without the interpolation of vowels, except in the cases of sounds produced with twin letters (gh, kp, sh, ch, gw, kw, nw, and ny). Also, when the Igbo were taught such English words as "three" and "blessing," they would improvise by saying "tiri" and "beleziñ," respectively. However, since the turn of the twentieth century, courses in English linguistics have helped educated Igbo to pronounce English words correctly.

The misspellings of some Igbo words in books written by white authors were forced on colonial Igbo students and writers, including Achebe, who, following the British way, spelled "Igbo" as "Ibo" in *Things Fall Apart*. However, since Nigeria's independence in 1960, Igbo writers and teachers have started to write Igbo words, including names of people and places, in the Igbo way.

Even though Igbo was an oral language before the coming of Europeans, its basic nature and function were the same as those of other written and unwritten languages. As William G. Moulton puts it in "The Nature of Language":

> Language is a wonderful rich vehicle for communication. We can use it to convey wishes and commands, to tell truths and to tell

lies, to influence our hearers and to vent our emotions, and to formulate ideas which could probably never arise if we had no language in which to embody them. We can even use language to communicate with ourselves; in fact, such self-communication seems to constitute much of what we call "thinking." In our own particular culture, such "talking to ourself" is permissible as long as we do it silently; it becomes a problem if we are caught doing it out loud. (3)

While sharing the general nature and function of language that Moulton outlines above, the Igbo language is characterized by such linguistic elements as proverbs, folk stories and chants, metaphor, and imagery that reflect the people's peculiar thought patterns, grammar, ontology, philosophy, worldview, and humor, which are not easily expressed in any other language. In essence, the language is the clearest, most potent means of expressing the Igbo culture and civilization. And because all the members of the Igbo communities used Igbo as their *only* language of communication (albeit in different dialects) before the coming of the Europeans, they could think, relate, and formulate ideas without interpreters, which made their human and interpersonal relationships easier and more harmonious. Unfortunately, however, the advent of the white culture necessitated the use of *kotma* as both interpreters for and intermediaries between the whites and natives—a role that created a lot of havoc in Igboland (which will be fully examined later in this book).

The Igbo language, more than any other element of Igbo life, kept the pre-colonial Igbo societies united:

> Since Igbo people did not construct a rigid and closely argued system of thought to explain the universe and the place of man in it, preferring the metaphor of myth and poetry, anyone seeking an insight into their world must seek it along their own way. Some of these ways are folktales, proverbs, proper names, rituals, and festivals. (*Morning Yet on Creation Day* 132)

The myth, poetry, folktales, proverbs, proper names, rituals, and festivals mentioned in the passage constitute the folklore that has kept the Igbo culture and civilization alive all through the ages, despite challenges by Western education and culture.

Unlike some primordial cultures that depended on written records for survival, traditional Igbo culture, essentially oral, did not die at any point in history because it was actively handed down from one generation to another by living people. Hence, Igbo has continued to be a living language in spite of the antiquity of its development. And the Igbo people are lucky that even when their land was colonized by the British, their language was never taken away from them. Under the British colonial system in Nigeria, the educated Igbo became bilingual: they spoke perfect English on school premises, and perfect Igbo at home. In order to communicate fully with their non-Igbo speaking neighbors, some Igbo people learned a third language, pidgin English, which is now another viable means of communication in modern Nigeria. In that sense some Western-educated Igbo people are trilingual. All three languages are used by various characters in Achebe's novels depending on whether the novels are urban or rural.

Achebe appears to be obsessed with preserving the folkways that constitute Igbo culture and civilization and has managed to re-create them in all his novels, especially *Things Fall Apart*. For, according to him, first and foremost, "the African novel has to be about Africa. A pretty severe restriction, I am told. But Africa is not only a geographical expression, it is also a metaphysical land-scape—it is, in fact, a view of the world and of the whole cosmos perceived from a particular position" (*Morning Yet on Creation Day* 66). As an educated African, indeed, an educated Igbo, Achebe realized early enough that the colonial educational system delib-erately did not teach African students things African. Consequently, when he began his writing career after college, Achebe decided to play the self-imposed role of "the novelist as teacher." He told his critics: "Perhaps what I write is applied art as distinct from pure. But who cares? Art is important but so is education of the kind I have in mind. And I don't see that the two need be mutually ex-clusive" (58). How well he has played that role, and how clearly he has enunciated some of the Igbo folkways in his novels, form the topic of many critical works. In addition, other African writers and critics have followed Achebe's example by expressing in Eng-lish their individual ethnic folkways originally expressed only in their indigenous African languages.

IGBO NARRATIVE CUSTOMS AND VERBAL FOLKLORE

Igbo folklore has been handed down from generation to gen-eration through a tradition of narrative customs.

Narrative customs are conventional means of expressing and transmitting a culture orally and through body movement and sign language. Igbo verbal folklore takes various forms, including ritual incantations, proverbs, myths, legends, folktales, folk chants and dances, folk drama, folk instrumental music, folk speech, folk similes and metaphors, and traditional names and naming. These types of Igbo verbal folklore are discussed here under four headings: ritual incantations, proverbs, folk stories, and folk festivals.

Ritual Incantations

A traditional Igbo man's day or a traditional public ceremony begins with ritual incantations (folk prayer) in which the male head of the family invites and acknowledges the presence of the dead-living ancestors with three ritual items, *oji* (kola nut), *nzu* (white chalk), and *mmanya ngwuo* (palm wine). With the wine he pours a libation on the floor or ground, which symbolically opens the earth through which the ancestors enter the physical world from the spiritland underground. With the chalk he draws lines on the floor to pray for and symbolize the safe cyclic passage of the ancestors to and from the spiritland. The kola nut is broken and shared among the visible men (human beings) and the invisible men (spirit beings), after which the wine is served. The kola is eaten and the wine drunk as a sign of the spiritual communion and unity that is intended to bring life and prosperity to the people. The ritual must also precede all traditional Igbo public events, including weddings, naming ceremonies, meetings, and political gatherings.

The entire ritual is called *Iwa Oji* (Breaking of Kola). It must be done in the Igbo language, even when the ceremony takes place in English-speaking countries such as the United Kingdom and the United States of America, which have large Igbo communities. The reasoning behind the "use of Igbo only" rule is that the dead-living ancestors, whose presence and attendance are being invoked, do not understand or speak English, which, at any rate, the ancestors ridicule as a language spoken through the nose. That is why quite often a man who attempts to perform the *Iwa Oji* ritual in English is chided with the phrase, "*Oji anaghi asu Bekee*" (Kola does not speak English).

Women are excluded from the performance of this ritual, because Igboland, both at home and abroad, is patriarchal. The kola nut is never shown to women before it is broken; and when it is shared, all males (however young) must be given their shares before the women (however old) receive theirs. Also, women are not taught the esoteric or proverbial language in which the ritual is conducted.

Achebe re-creates a version of the *Iwa Oji* ritual in *Things Fall Apart*:

> One day a neighbor called Okoye came in to see him [Unoka]. He was reclining on a mud bed in his hut playing on the flute. He immediately rose and shook hands with Okoye, who then unrolled the goatskin which he carried under his arm, and sat down. Unoka went into an inner room and soon returned with a small wooden disc containing a kola nut, some alligator pepper and a lump of white chalk.
>
> "I have kola," he announced when he sat down, and passed the disc over to his guest.
>
> "Thank you. He who brings kola brings life. But I think you ought to break it," replied Okoye passing back the disc.
>
> "No, it is for you, I think," and they argued like this for a few moments before Unoka accepted the honor of breaking the kola. Okoye, meanwhile, took the lump of chalk, drew some lines on the floor, and then painted his big toe. As he broke the kola, Unoka prayed to their ancestors for life and health, and for protection against their enemies. When they had eaten they talked about many things: about the heavy rains which were drowning the yams, about the next ancestral feast and about the impending war with the village of Mbaino. (4–5)

Apart from its sacred import, the Breaking of Kola ritual evidences Igbo traditional hospitality. The alligator pepper spices up the nut, and the white chalk painted on the big toe is a sign of the safe arrival of the guest and a wish for his safe departure, lest he should dash his feet against the stones on the unpaved roads. What is missing in this passage is the palm wine to wash down the kola and alligator pepper, as it were. Unoka is too poor to provide that essential item of entertainment, and that does not please the ancestors, whom he has displeased in other ways as well.

Proverbs

The most important form of Igbo narrative custom is the proverb. As a rhetorical aid and stylized verbal form, the Igbo proverb is described by Achebe as "the palm-oil with which words are eaten." The metaphor is apt because few Igbo menus or recipes fail to include palm oil, just as there is hardly any good Igbo speech that is not interlaced with proverbs. Proverbs are very important in Igbo language and literature, for they express the life and civilization of the people. That is why they are found in folktales, folk songs, drum language, and dirges as well as in common prayers and incantations. Some are esoteric in the sense that they are used by groups of elders and titled men and are hard to interpret because sometimes they are oracular. Their images are drawn from all areas of human and animal life, including farming, eating, sex, hunting, wrestling, angling, ritual sacrifice, and story-telling.

Furthermore, the proverbs are both old and current in the linguistic habits of the people: old in the sense that they are usually the prerogative of the elders, who use them to teach the younger generations the wisdom and lore of the people; current in that a man can create his own proverbs as long as he observes the conventions, presenting them in a way that is acceptable to the people, since proverbs are a highly stylized form of verbal art. The easiest way to present new proverbs is to introduce them with either "As our elders said" or "As the saying goes." Some people even identify their fathers as the source of their proverbs. This is a way of making proverbs "the wit of one, and the wisdom of many."

Achebe recognizes these formal requirements for creating proverbs and incorporates them in his novels. Proverbs are one of the most important rhetorical devices available to the traditional Igbo, especially if introduced at the right times, for the right occasions and purposes, and for the right audiences.

Here are some examples of Igbo proverbs (*Ilu Igbo*) and their English equivalents:

Igwe bu ike. [Crowds engender strength.]

"Unity is strength."

Egbe bere ugo bere; nke si ibe ya ebela nku kwaa ya. [Let the kite perch and let the eagle perch; whoever says the other should not perch, may his own wings break.]

"Live and let live."

Oburu na agwo dum ebikota onu n'otu ebe, onye ga abia ha nso? [If all the snakes lived together in one place, who would approach them?]

"United we stand, divided we fall."

Nwata kwoo aka ya, ya na ogaranya erikoo ihe. [If a child washed his hands he could eat with kings and elders.]

"Good conduct and achievement elevate a person."

Onye choo iri awo, ya rie nke gbara agba. [If you want to eat a toad you should look for a fat and juicy one.]

"Whatever you want to be, be the best of it."

Ma onwu egbuchu utu, o rie anu gbara afoonu. [If the penis does not die young it eats the bearded meat.]

"A patient dog eats the fattest bone."

Iji na enweghi onye ndumodu na eso ozu alakpu n'ili. [The fly that has no one to advise him follows the corpse into the ground.]

"To be forewarned is to be forearmed."

Oburu na oke enweghi ike igba oso, ya chaara mbe n'uzo. [If the rat cannot flee fast enough let him make way for the tortoise.]

"Don't be a dog in the manger."

Onye kwe chi ya ekwe. [If a man says yes his *chi* says yes also.]

"A man is the architect of his own destiny."

Otu mkpisi aka ruta mmanu o zue oha. [If one finger gets the oil it smears the rest.]

"One bad apple spoils the barrel."

Anaghi eji ngborogwu ochie agwo oria obiara ohuu. [A disease that has never been seen before cannot be cured with an everyday herb.]

"New problems require new, innovative solutions."

Onye kpara nku ahuhu siri ka nkwere bia oriri n'ebe ya. [The man who brings ant-ridden faggots into his hut should not grumble when lizards begin to pay him a visit.]

"Whatever evil one sows that will he reap."

Onye na elo mkpuru udala, ya chetakwa ka ike nsi ya ha. [He who will swallow *udala* seeds must consider the size of his anus.]

"Bite as much as you can chew." Or "Cut your coat according to your size."

Ahu anyuru n'elu nkwu na agba iji no n'elu gharii. [When the air is fouled by a man on top of a palm tree the fly below is confused.]

"The corruption of leaders in high places disorganizes the rank and file below."

Onwu na egbu nwa nkita anaghi ekwe ya nuu isi nsi. [When death wants to take a little dog it prevents it from smelling even excrement.]

"An ill-fated person disregards all warnings against danger."

Agwo adighi amu nwa mkpukpu. [The snake does not give birth to a short child.]

"Like father, like son."

Jiri ehihie choo ewu ojii. [Look for a black goat in daylight.]

"Make hay while the sun shines."

Ibu uzo na anu mmiri oma. [The early comer to the spring drinks the clearest water.]

"The early bird catches the worm."

Ebe onye oso ruru bu ebe onye ije ga eru. [The destination of the runner is also the destination of the walker.]

"The race is not always to the swift."

Agwa bu mma. [Good behavior is beauty.]

"Handsome is as handsome does."

Folk Stories

The generic name for folk narrative in Igbo is *akuko nde ichie*, "told by the fireside." Instead of the common term *folktales*, Achebe prefers the term *folk stories*, which he uses in Chapter Five of his second novel, *No Longer at Ease*, to embrace all the major tales in Igbo folklore.

In general, folktales, *akuko ifo*, are told to explain natural phenomena and the Igbo worldview. However, particular narrative types serve particular functions. Mythological tales *(akuko mmalite/odinala)*, for example, narrate the founding and origins of Igbo communities and tell of wars, folk heroes, and legends, as well as metaphysical events. As such they serve as the basis of Igbo oral history, which is taught to children from one generation to another. To such children, folk stories are mainly evening entertainment, while adults regard them essentially as a useful forum for handing traditions down to the younger generations.

Also, as a stylized verbal art of the folk, folk stories serve as noncreative Igbo oral literature (orature). Those who tell them, including story-tellers, chanteurs, chorus leaders, and (in modern times) researchers, are not the original creators, performers, or writers. Rather, they are regarded merely as instruments through which the collective folk mind, mentality, worldview, morality, and ethos are kept alive and handed down from generation to generation. Hence, the authorship or origin of folk stories cannot be attributed to any one individual artist or performer. However, individual artists and performers can add to or subtract from every enactment of the stylized performance, as long as the original essence of the act is not destroyed.

A type of folk story Achebe frequently appropriates in his novels, especially *Things Fall Apart*, is the didactic animal tale. He either alludes briefly to Igbo didactic animal tales (or fables) or reconstructs in full familiar ones as a way of commenting on a particular character. For instance, after Okonkwo beats up one of his wives during the Week of Peace, he is made to offer a purification sacrifice. In addition to observing that Okonkwo is repentant, the narrator remarks, "They called him the little bird *nza*." In the tale of *nza*, *nza* so overfeeds himself that he forgets how little he once was and challenges hunters to shoot at him. By alluding to the tale in this episode, the narrator is succinctly saying that Okonkwo has a false sense of his momentary affluence; after all, Okonkwo has not yet escaped his poor parentage completely. However, the narrator makes this remark warily. Having said earlier that Okonkwo was repentant, it would be a contradiction if he simply said that Okonkwo is the little bird *nza*, implying that Okonkwo is not repentant. So he allows the clansmen to discern the difference between the observation of the omniscient reporter, which is internal and objective, and that of Okonkwo's fellow clansmen, which is external and limited. Thus the omniscient narrator represents Achebe, who reports what he sees and hears as accurately as he possibly can, thereby making his narrative objective and trustworthy (22).

Achebe draws from a list of animals found in classic Igbo folktales in developing the folk stories in his novels. The list includes:

Agụ—Tiger	Eneke-ntị-ọba—Swallow	Nkwọ—Hawk
Ebulu—Ram	Iji—Fly	Nwa Ologbo—Cat
Egbe—Kite	Igurube—Locust	Nza—Sparrow
Ejula—Snail	Mbe—Tortoise	Obu—Wren
Eke—Python	Ngwere—Lizard	Udele—Vulture
Enwe—Monkey	Nkịta—Dog	Ugo—Eagle

TWO IGBO FABLES

The two folk stories that follow exemplify the kinds of didactic
animal tales told to Nwoye and Ikemefuna in *Things Fall Apart*.

FROM E. NOLUE EMENANJO, ED., *OMALINZE: A BOOK OF IGBO FOLK-TALES* (1977)

Mbe na Ejula

Otu mgbe otu eze na nwunye ya nwere so otu nwa nwanyi. Mgbe nwa
ahu ruru ilu di, eze wee si na etu nwa ya ahu ga-esi luo di bu na ndi
mmadu nile choro ilu ya ga-abia ya enye ha olu o ga-abu onye buru uzo
luchaa o wee nye ya nwa ya ka o luba.

O ruo n'uchichi odibo eze wee maa ekwe, zie ndi mmadu ihe eze
kwuru. N'isi ututu, Mbe na Ejula wee yiri bia be eze maka na ha bu enyi.
Eze si odibo ya gaa gosi ha olu ahu. Ha wee na-alu olu wee ruo ka ike o
ga-agwu ha, nwunye eze wee jee n'ebe Mbe no alu olu si yatichapu ya
mgburu akwu di ya n'azu. Mbe si, 'Mba ana m alu olu. Atufuzila m oge'.
O nojuo wee jezie na nke Ejula. Ejula wee tichapu ya mkpuru akwu ahu.
Umu okorobia asaa wee maputa nyere ejula aka o luchaa olu ya.

Ejula wee jee gwa Mbe na ya aluchaala olu ya. Mbe juo ya etu o si mee
o gwa Mbe na ya tichapuru mkpuru akwu di n'azu nwunye eze, umu
okorobia asaa maputa nyere ya aka.

Mbe jee juo nwunye eze si, 'I siri m tichapu gi mkpuru akwu di gi
n'azu?' Nwunye eze agbachi ya nkiti, o tie ya ihe n'azu, nwunye eze dapu
nwuo. Mbe wee jee n'afa juo ya ihe o ga-eme. Afa si ya ka o buru nwunye
eze je zoo n'ohia, echi ka o gwa Ejula ya duje ya nta. Mgbe ha ruru ka o
tuoro Ejula aka ebe ozu ahu di si ya gbaa egbe.

Mbe wee mee etu afa siri gwa ya. O wee kpoo ejula si, 'I mara na I bu
ezi enyi m, ihe m siri gi mee, I mee ya. Mgbe ha ruru n'ohia, Mbe si Ejula
ya gba egbe ebe a. Ejula wee gba egbe. Ha jeru hu na o bu ozu nwunye
eze.

Mbe wee si Ejula na o gbuola nwunye eze, na ya ga-eje koro eze. Ejula
si ya, 'Ookwa gi siri m gbaa.' Mbe si ya, 'Mgbc m si gi gbaa, I kpuru isi?
O bu m si gi tinye isi n'ite, I ga-etinye?'

Ejula wee kwe jebekwa n'afa. Afa wee si ya je gota efe na akpukpo
ukwu. O kechaa ekike, ka o je si Mbe na o bu ihe eze nyere ya maka na
ya gburu nwunye ya. Na eze siri na o teela nwanyi ahu mebere ihe ojoo.
Ejula mee etu afa si kwu wee gosi Mbe ekike ya.

Anya wee gha mbe. O si Ejula ka ha jee be eze, ka ya gwa ya na o bu ya gburu nwunye eze. Mbe wee je gwa eze. Eze wee tichaa, tie mkpu, si umu odibo ya kpuru Mbe je gbuo, wee kporo ada ya nye Ejula o wee lubazie.

Ihe akuko a na-akuziri anyi bu na anya ukwu adighi mma. (132–33)

The Tortoise and the Snail

Once upon a time, a king and his queen had only one daughter. When the daughter was ready for marriage, the king announced that he would give her suitors a task to perform, and that whoever was the first to finish the task would be given the princess to marry.

In the evening, the king's page made the announcement to the people. Early the next morning, Tortoise and Snail went to the king together because they were friends. The king asked the page to show them the task. As they worked and began to get tired, the queen came to Tortoise and asked him to kindly remove palm fruits from her back. But Tortoise said to her, "No, I can't, for I am working. Don't waste my time." The queen then went to Snail and made the same appeal; and Snail kindly removed the palm fruits from the queen's back. At that time, seven young men appeared and helped Snail to finish his task very quickly.

Snail went and told Tortoise that he had finished his task. Tortoise asked him how he managed to finish so quickly. Snail told him that after he removed palm fruits from the queen's back, seven young men came out and helped him.

After hearing that, Tortoise went and asked the queen angrily, "Did you ever ask me to remove palm fruits from your back?" The queen kept quiet. Tortoise then hit the queen on the back, and she fell and died. On seeing what had happened, Tortoise went to consult the oracle for help. The oracle told him to go hide the queen's corpse in the forest, and to ask Snail to go hunting with him in that forest the next day. Then, when they arrive in the forest, Tortoise should ask Snail to shoot his gun towards the spot where the corpse lay.

Tortoise did as he was told. He then said to Snail, "You know you are my best friend. So whatever I ask you to do, do it." When they came to the forest, Tortoise asked Snail to shoot his gun towards the direction of the corpse. Snail did so. They then went and found out that what Snail shot was the queen's corpse.

Tortoise accused Snail of killing the queen, and threatened to tell the king about it. Snail said to him, "Aren't you the one who asked me to shoot my gun there?" To which Tortoise said, "When I asked you to shoot, were you blind? If I asked you to put your head into a pot would you do so?"

Like Tortoise, Snail went to consult the oracle on how to solve his problem. The oracle advised Snail to buy new clothes and shoes; after dressing up in them, he should go show himself to Tortoise, telling him that what he wore was an award presented to him by the king for killing the queen, who had been misbehaving towards the king for too long. Snail did exactly as he was told by the oracle.

Tortoise became jealous. He then told Snail that they should both go to see the king so he can tell the king that he killed the queen. Tortoise informed the king that he truly killed the queen. The king grew angry and ordered his pages to arrest and kill Tortoise. Thereafter, he gave his princess to Snail for marriage.

The moral of this story is that covetousness is bad.

(Translated by Kalu Ogbaa)

Etu onwu si bia n'uwa

Otu mgbe Chukwu kporo umu anumanu nile si ha hoputa otu onye n'ime ha mara agba oso ka o jeere ya ozi n'uwa. Ha wee laa, gaa hoputa Nkita. Mbe wèe wee iwe si na o bu ya kachasi mara ihe na ya ga-akakwa mara zie ozi.

Chukwu asi na ya ahorola Nkita ndi umu anu ndi ozo nile hoputara. Chukwu wee si Nkita ya jee n'uwa ka ogwa umu mmadu na onwu agaghi adi n'uwa. Na onye o bula ga-anogide e bighi ebi n'uwa.

Mgbe Mbe nuruchara ozi ahu o wee gaa dochiere Nkita nsi n'uzo wee buru uzo gaba n'uwa. Nkita aputa, hu nsi ahu wee ribe ya. Mgbe o norii na-eri ya, Mbe agbarala garuo n'uwa, jee si ndi mmadu nile gbakoro na-eche ozi Chukwu, 'Na e mee elu mee ala na onwu ga-adiriri n'uwa'.

Ndi mmadu ahu nile wee dapu bebe akwa. Mgbe Nkita jiri rute o juo ha ihe na-eme ha, ha wee kooro ya ihe Mbe kwuru. Nkita si ha gbaa ya nkiti, na o bu ya ka Chukwu ziri ozi. Na Chukwu siri na onwu agaghi adi n'uwa.

Umu mmadu wee zukoo ziga ozi be Chukwu je juo ya nke ha gaewe, o bu ihe Mbe kwuru ka o bu ihe Nkita kwuru. Chukwu aza ha si na okwu bu uzo eruola be mmuo, na nke ha buru uzo nu ka ha ga-ewe.

Ya mere onwu jiri dizi n'uwa taa. (200)

How Death Came into the World

Once upon a time, God summoned all the animals to his presence, and asked them to choose from among them the fastest runner, who would carry an important message from God to human beings on earth. When they went back home, they deliberated and chose Dog. However, Tortoise grew angry, saying that he should have been chosen to run the errand because he was the wisest animal, and one who also knew how best to deliver messages.

When the animals informed God of their choice, he said he was happy with it. He then asked Dog to go to the world and tell all human beings that there will be no deaths in the world; that everyone will live forever.

After overhearing the mesasge, Tortoise went and put a heap of dung in Dog's way to the human world to divert him. When Dog came to the spot where the dung was, he stopped to eat it. As he did so, Tortoise ran to the human beings, who had gathered to await anxiously the message from God. Tortoise then told them that the message is "Come what may, there will always be deaths in the world of Man."

The people began to weep. When Dog arrived and asked why they wept, they told him what Tortoise had told them. He asked them to ignore what they heard from Tortoise because he, Dog, was the true messenger of God; and that God's message was that there would be no deaths on earth.

Human beings met again and sent word to God, to find out from him if they should accept the mesage that Tortoise brought or the one that Dog brought as the true version. God replied, saying that the first version has already reached death's kingdom, and whichever version they heard first, they should take.

That is why death is everywhere in the human world.

(Translated by Kalu Ogbaa)

Ibadan, Nigeria: University Press plc, p. 200.

Nwoye would prefer the first story, which is about a trickster who is beaten at his own game (as he beat his father), rather than the second, which is an etiological animal story that saddens him because the humans are helpless, like his adoptive brother Ikemefuna.

All Igbo folk stories contain lessons for the young on humility, gratitude, candor, and community. They are presented as simple proverbs, parables, or evening entertainment stories. However, the elders and the story-tellers would normally drive home the lessons by saying, "*Ibe ozizi ya bu nke a . . .*," which means "The moral of the story is this . . ."

Folk Festivals

Of all the narrative customs of the Igbo, folk festivals are the ones that most often bring people together, fostering cultural harmony and peace regardless of social and economic class. Among these festivals are wrestling matches, wedding feasts, naming ceremonies for individual babies and for age-grades, new yam festivals, and ritual dances. Some of the festivals are seasonal, while others are yearly. All of them, though, include folk instrumental music and professional singers and dancers, although everyone is drawn to clap, sing, and dance, depending on the nature and occasion of the festival. The ritual nature of traditional Igbo festivals, even those that seem very secular, such as wrestling and weddings, brings men and gods together in one crowd. During the merriment of the festivals "a man might look to his right and find his neighbor and look to his left and see a god standing there."

Above all, because the festivals involve drumming, clapping of hands, and dancing, as well as folk chants and songs, they embody folk drama and entertainment. However, it is important to observe that folk drama and entertainment, in their many manifestations, including their ritual manifestation, are very specifically communal in character. More than any of the other arts, they require a group audience at all stages of enactment; quite often, in fact, they demand the participation of the audience in the action or song. For this reason, some theorists, for example, Michael Echeruo, have argued quite convincingly that drama flourishes most in a society that has developed a strong consciousness of itself as a *community*. We should, however, add that drama flourishes best in a community that has satisfactorily transformed ritual into celebration and converted the mythic structure of action from the religious and priestly to the secular plane (see Ogbaa, *Gods, Oracles and Divination* 89–90).

Igbo folk festivals are as diverse as the Igbo-speaking peoples of Nigeria. However, there are pan-Igbo festivals commonly celebrated throughout Igboland. They include the new yam festival, second yam harvest festival, age-grade naming festival, traditional wedding ceremony, as well as esoteric festivals such as the title-taking festival, war dance pageant, Dibia cult outing, and Okonko cult outing.

The new yam festival is a public celebration of the first harvest of the king of Igbo crops, the yam. The public merriment, which involves a "fashion" parade, dances, wrestling, and feasting, is preceded by a series of sacrifices offered by the heads of each family to the Igbo yam god, Ifejioku, Nfijoku, or Njoku; to Ala, the earth goddess, who is in charge of the fertility of the soil and of the womb; and to the ancestors for their blessings of bumper crops, especially the yam.

Yam, being a "male" crop and a major staple food for the people, symbolizes the Igbo source of strength, sustenance, and endurance. Because the traditional Igbo society is agrarian, all the ceremonies involved in taking titles include eating plenty of food prepared with yams. Also, when sold, yams fetch more money for the farmer than any other Igbo crop.

The new yam festival takes place during the months of July, August, and September of each year.

The second yam harvest festival is celebrated in the same way as the new yam festival. The new yam is harvested mainly for eating and marketing. The second harvest also produces yams for eating and marketing, and, in addition, yields seed-yams for sowing during the next planting season.

The second yam harvest festival takes place during the months of November, December, and January of each year. As such, it marks the end of the old year and the beginning of the new. The celebrations are more flamboyant than during the first harvest festival because the majority of other festivals take place at this time, when yams are available for preparing the festal meals, and the weather is dry. In modern times, the festival coincides with Christmas and New Year celebrations, when Igbo people from all parts of Nigeria and the world return to renew their lives with their kith and kin, including the dead-living ancestors.

Since the Nigeria-Biafra War (1967–70), the second yam harvest festival has expanded to the intellectual realm: In November 1979, the renowned Igbo scholar, poet, and critic Michael J. C. Echeruo began the Ahiajoku Lecture Series, otherwise known as the Igbo intellectual harvest. Like the yam harvest, the lecture series celebrates the source of Igbo intellectual strength and sustenance while defining aspects of Igbo culture and civilization as essential elements of Nigerian and African culture and civilization. Since its inception, Ahiajoku has afforded Igbo scholars the opportunity to conduct fundamental research on chosen aspects of the Igbo culture and worldview, and to share their findings with *oba na eze*,

New Yam Festival of Nde Igbo. From Umuahia, Abia, State of Nigeria, Ministry of Information.

all and sundry. It is a celebration that yearly reminds the Igbo of who they are, as well as calling on them to dedicate their lives to serving the people and maintaining their noble heritage.

The age-grade naming festival is a ceremony in which those born within a period of three years (ages 18 through 21) are officially recognized as a group and named as an age-grade. The naming is usually conducted by village elders during public ceremonies, which may involve sacrifices and dances to the gods and ancestors, as well as feasting and wrestling among the people.

The naming ceremony is conducted separately for girls in some communities, and collectively with boys in others. Be that as it may, boys and girls who are born within the same age bracket belong to the same age-grade. As a group, they are expected to contribute money and services to help carry out their chosen community projects, and to maintain social control over their members.

Naming ceremonies, which are rites of passage, take place during the new yam festival in some Igbo communities and during the second yam harvest festival in others. The ceremonies involve the preparation of feasts with plenty of yams.

The traditional wedding ceremony is a public celebration of a marriage pact between the families of the bride and bridegroom. It is usually preceded by a long period of courtship between the couple, completion of farmwork by the bridegroom for his prospective in-laws, payment of a bride-price by the bridegroom, and a private ritual sacrifice to the ancestors for the blessing of the marriage.

The public ceremony takes place in the village *ilo* (village green) with music, the dance of the maidens, and presentation of the dowry to the bride by her parents and relations. After that, the pageant moves to the bridegroom's compound, where, after a few more dances and ululations, the wedding feast, which includes yam foofoo and egusi soup made with smoked fish and goat meat, is convivially served to the villagers and their visitors.

Like the age-grade naming festival, the traditional wedding ceremony is an important and joyous rite of passage. Parents and elderly villagers are always vigilant in ensuring that the wedding ceremony is not prevented or marred by news of pregnancy or premarital sex by the prospective bride, which can result in the cancellation of the marriage pact and the ostracism of the young woman by her age-grade and other village organizations.

Esoteric festivals include the title-taking festival, war dance pageant, Dibia cult outing, and Okonko cult outing. Since each of these esoteric organizations functions in secrecy, only the initiated know what they do privately, and they normally take oaths not to divulge their secrets. However, in public ceremonies, the title holders wear certain dresses, exchange greetings, and use body language and signs that mark them out from the rest of the villagers.

The war dancers wear war garb and carry human skulls in a basket as they dance in celebration of their prowess and war victories. Many of the dancers serve as a traditional local army who guard their inter-ethnic borders. In fact, the war dancers were members of recognized armed forces in the Old Bende and Afikpo areas of Igboland (now Abia and Ebonyin states of Nigeria) charged

The Award-Winning Nkwa Umuagbọghọ Dancing Troupe from Afikpo Performing "Dance of the Maidens." From Umuahia, Abia State of Nigeria, Ministry of Information.

The War Dancers Carrying the Oyaya (Basket of Human Skulls). Author's photo.

with the duty of fighting head hunters and slave raiders from Akwa Ibom, Cross River, and Rivers states of Nigeria before colonialism.

The members of the Dibia cult are traditional medicine men or healers, and the Okonko cult is a mystical or magical group. However, whereas the Dibia cult appears in all areas of Igboland, only the Cross River Igbo, principally the Igbo of Abia and Ebonyin states, have the Okonko cult, which developed through their interaction with their riverine neighbors. Since colonialism opened up all parts of Igboland, the Okonko cult has become almost a pan-Igbo organization.

In every case, the festivals touched upon here began as traditional Igbo religious or esoteric rites but later turned into secular rituals and ceremonies. When the white missionaries came, they condemned the festivals as pagan practices. As a result, divisions quickly developed in the Igbo community between Christians and "heathens" to the point of threatening the communal lives and unity of the people. Since independence, however, the Igbo, like the Greeks, have been attempting to force myth out of their religious and cultic rituals, creating secular festivals out of the once religious and esoteric ones.

Some of the Igbo festivals Achebe romanticizes in *Things Fall Apart* and in his other novels embody dramatic elements that qualify them as folk drama, folk opera, or simply folk entertainment. Despite their religious origins and import, they provide much-needed entertainment to the people year round, since they may be enacted as weekly, monthly, or yearly rituals and ceremonies.

CONCLUSION

The Igbo language, like any other human language, functions as a wonderful and effective vehicle for communicating the culture and civilization of the people, including the enactment and expression of their rituals and festivals. Until the British colonization of Nigeria, Igbo culture was transmitted orally. However, since the introduction of Christianity and mission schools in Igboland during the 1800s, the language has developed into a viable written language, a development that has made it possible for the Igbo to share their literature and culture with non-Igbo people throughout the world.

TOPICS FOR WRITTEN OR ORAL EXPLORATION

1. What is the language of the Igbo people, and what are its general nature and functions?

2. Why has the Igbo language survived both the British colonization of Nigeria and the introduction of English as the official language of colonial and post-colonial Nigeria?

3. What cultural roles do proverbs play in Igbo society?

4. Identify five proverbs found in *Things Fall Apart* and discuss how they promote the narrative action of the novel.

5. Why are Igbo proverbs described as "the palm-oil with which words are eaten"?

6. What are Igbo narrative customs, and how have they promoted or hindered Igbo culture and civilization?

7. Discuss narrative customs in relation to the Igbo people's rituals, ceremonies, literature, and informal education.

8. Identify and discuss four Igbo rituals and ceremonies found in *Things Fall Apart*.

9. Name and discuss three Igbo esoteric organizations or festivals.

10. Name and discuss four pan-Igbo festivals.

11. Discuss the importance of folk stories in traditional Igbo informal education.

12. Discuss the types of folk stories Nwoye liked in *Things Fall Apart*.

13. Discuss the nature and importance of the second yam harvest festival.

14. Compare and contrast the Igbo wedding ceremony in *Things Fall Apart* with the traditional American wedding ceremony.

15. Discuss the difference between bride-price and dowry and the reasons both are involved in the Igbo institution of marriage.

16. Why did white missionaries prevent their converts from participating in Igbo festivals?

17. Do you think Igbo Christians should or should not participate in Igbo festivals?

18. What is an age-grade, and what are its functions?

19. Why do the Igbo in *Things Fall Apart* consider premarital sex an offense?

SUGGESTED READINGS

Dundes, Alan. *The Study of Folklore*. Englewood Cliffs, N.J.: Prentice-Hall, 1965.

Emenanjo, E. Nolue, ed. *Omalinze: A Book of Igbo Folk-tales*. Ibadan, Nigeria: Oxford University Press plc, 1977.

Isichei, Elizabeth. *A History of the Igbo People*. London: Macmillan, 1976.

Moulton, William G. "The Nature of Language." In *Language as a Human Problem*. Ed. Einar Haugen and Morton Bloomfield. New York: Norton, 1974. 3–21.

6 _____

Cultural Harmony III:
Traditional Igbo Religion and
Material Customs

INTRODUCTION

In Chapter Twenty-Two of *Things Fall Apart*, Achebe discusses the alien religion, Christianity, as the most divisive element of Igbo life, because its tenets are at odds with those of traditional Igbo religion. Out of ignorance of Igbo culture and civilization, Christian missionaries branded most Igbo customs as heathenish. In order to enlighten his readers about Igbo religion, Achebe makes it a focal aspect of the lives of the characters and their society.

TRADITIONAL IGBO RELIGION

The Igbo, whether in ancient or modern times, arc a very religious people, so much so that they do not separate their religious life from the secular. In fact, their pious nature made it all too easy for Christian missionaries to make eager converts, who then aided British government agents in their efforts to conquer and colonize Igboland at the turn of the twentieth century. At any rate, the pre-Christian traditional religion that the Igbo still practice is organized around four theological concepts, namely, *Chukwu*, non-human spirits (deities or oracles), ancestors, and *chi*.

Chukwu

All Igbo people believe in Chukwu, who is almost the equivalent of the Supreme Being in some other world religions. He is the creator of the universe. However, unlike the Christian God, or Chineke in Igbo, Chukwu was far removed from human beings soon after he created them. Also, the creation of humans as part of the universe is the handiwork of Chukwu (literally, Chi ukwu or high god) and his creative double, Eke. In other words, Chukwu is supreme in the sense of being higher or greater than the lesser gods and goddesses (who derive their being and powers from him); but as creator god, he is Chi-na-Eke (Chi and Eke). Unfortunately, the Igbo creator god, Chi-na-Eke, has been misrepresented by both foreign and native Christian clergy as Chineke. Also, while the Christian concept of God emphasizes the Trinity (God the Father, God the Son, and God the Holy Spirit), the Igbo concept of Chukwu emphasizes duality (Chi-na-Eke, implying creation and destiny of man).

Furthermore, Chukwu is omnipotent and omniscient; yet he is not considered omnipresent by the Igbo, who believe he dwells above and beyond the heavenly dome, *Igwe*, which is very distant from the abode of humans. In various parts of Igboland he is described by such names as *Obasi bi n'elu* (Spirit that dwells above), *Olisa bi n'elu* (Lord who lives above), or *Igwe ka ala* (Heaven that is greater/higher than earth).

In addition, as a result of Chukwu's distance from human beings, the Igbo give him the descriptive name *Ama-ama-amasi-amasi* (One who is known but never fully known). Through faith and by seeing his creations (some of which are worshipped as gods and goddesses), the Igbo know that Chukwu exists (*Chi di*), but he is not fully known because his dwelling place is beyond human reach and comprehension. That is why Chukwu is not represented with statues (*nkwá*) and other religious icons used in representing the lesser gods and goddesses, who are closer, hence better known, to humans.

Non-human Spirits, Deities, and Oracles

The non-human spirits, deities, and oracles that the Igbo believe in are man-made gods, goddesses, and oracles as well as nature

Mbari Shrine—Igbo Pantheon of Gods and Goddesses. Photo by Herbert M. Cole, 1967.

gods and goddesses. Both are essentially the manifestations of the divine forces of Chukwu, and they exist as intermediary agencies between Chukwu and humans. No one can accurately trace the origins of the deities, especially the older man-made ones, who may be deified heroes and mythological figures. The origins of the latter gods and goddesses are known, but quite often different narrators give what impartial readers may consider conflicting mythological accounts of the deities. To their Igbo worshippers, however, what cannot be scientifically proved is accepted unquestionably through faith and tradition—the basic and necessary ingredients of all religions.

The man-made deities and oracles include Ibini Ukpabi of Arochukwu, Opia of Umuchiakuma Ihechiowa, Agbala of Awka, and Iyi Oji of Nkwere. In fact, there are myths that confirm that such deities were created by men possessed and inspired by the spirit of Chukwu. For instance, Chief Kalu Ogoro of Ihechiowa, himself a creator of latter-day gods, told the author he was often visited in dreams by spirits who instructed him on how to create some gods for troubled societies. The Igbo believe that their gods, goddesses, and oracles are sons and daughters of Chukwu who are powerful and intelligent beings that roam the world but have their permanent homes in the rivers, mountains, caves, forests, and trees, which worshippers regard as the shrines of individual divinities.

Superior to the man-made gods are nature gods and goddesses such as Ala (Ani), Anyanwu, Amadioha, and Nfijoku (Ifejioku, Njoku), whom the Igbo regard and revere as the spirits of nature or personifications of natural forces. Unlike man-made deities, these gods cannot be treated with disrespect when they fail to fulfill human expectations; rather, human beings are always prepared to accept blame for the apparent failure of such deities. For instance, should there be a drought like the one in *Things Fall Apart*, the general belief is that someone must have committed an abominable offense against the god or goddess in charge of rain. Therefore, the people will have to consult an oracle to divine the will of that god or goddess, a means by which the right items of sacrifice are determined. In other words, natural disasters are generally attributed to offenses that people commit against the gods. The traditional Igbo also believe that however great an offense may be, it can be atoned for with a matching sacrifice, which may include the sacrifice of human beings.

Whether natural or man-made, the divinities are believed to have been delegated by the absentee high god, Chukwu, as his strong representatives in the world of humans, and they must take charge of all walks of human life. That way Chukwu is able to establish a strong presence and influence in the human world. Among the gods and goddesses the Igbo universally worship are Ala (Ani), Amadioha, Nfijoku (Ifejioku, Njoku), Anyanwu, and Ikenga.

Ala, the earth goddess, is the most important divinity after Chukwu in traditional Igbo religion. She is in charge of the fertility of the womb (including the wombs of animals) and of the soil; she bears in her womb the dead-living ancestors, hence she is Mother Earth. She is also in charge of Igbo laws and customs, known as *Omenala* Igbo, as well as their group morality. Any offenses against her, such as adultery, killing of one's clansman, giving birth to twins, or thievery, are all *nso ala* (offenses against Ala). While Chukwu is beyond the reach and comprehension of the Igbo, the presence of Ala is felt every minute of their existence: when they plant their crops, bury their dead kinsmen, wrestle in the village *ilo*, dig up the earth and turn it into mud for building homes, take oaths or make pacts between clans and villages, or even walk on the earth in their everyday activities. Above all, the earth is sacred for harboring the dead-living ancestors, to whom libations are poured and incantatory prayers offered many times a day.

Amadioha, the god of lightning and war, is the very opposite of Ala in the sense that while Ala is seen as a mother figure, nurturing and caring, Amadioha is a destructive god. His worshippers use him as the "angel of death," for his main role is to wreak deadly vengeance on those who have hurt or offended his worshippers. In times of war, Amadioha is invoked to strike dead the enemies of the people, and his victims are never mourned, but are buried only when very expensive cleansing rituals have been performed by Amadioha's priest. In various parts of Igboland, Amadioha is known as Igwe, Kalu, Kamalu, Kanu, or Akanu.

Nfijoku, the yam god, is offered sacrifices by the Igbo before and after their planting seasons so he may bless them with a bumper harvest of crops, especially yam, the king of Igbo crops. Because of the subsistence, economic, social, and sacred values of yam, Nfijoku is regarded as one of the most important gods, and the new yam festival in which he is honored is the highest celebration in Igboland.

Anyanwu, the sun god, is regarded as the eyes by which Chukwu sees through human beings, knowing their inner thoughts, their joys, and their sorrows. That is why when a person is wrongfully accused of an offense, he or she throws up their open palms toward the sun, saying, *"Chukwu lekwa, aka m di ocha"* (Look, Chukwu, my hands are clean), to proclaim their innocence, which no one but Chukwu can establish. In addition, Anyanwu is honored as the male counterpart of Ala in the cyclic process of reproduction, growth, and maturation of Igbo crops. His two roles, as the eyes of Chukwu on earth and as a reproductive agent in the agricultural life of the people, make Anyanwu an important Igbo god.

Ikenga (literally, "right hand"), one of the Igbo man-made gods, is the personification of the strength of a man's arm and fortitude in the face of adversity, which create good fortune for him. The statuette Ikenga holds a sword that symbolizes the weapon with which a man fights those who stand between him and his fortune. In their agragrian society, the traditional Igbo believe in hard work as the key to prosperity, which depends on the strength of a man's "right arm." This work ethic characterizes the Igbo as the most ambitious and hard-working ethnic group in Nigeria. Each man draws inspiration and strength from his Ikenga as he prepares to go to work every day. Ikenga is a personal god; his image is split and buried with the owner at death.

Other man-made but non-universal Igbo gods appear in primarily local **oracles**, including Ibini Ukpabi, Opia, Agbala, and Iyi Oji, mentioned before. They are deities whose roles are purely prognostic: as agencies of divination, they serve both humans and other gods and goddesses. Their creation is always necessitated by adversity and misfortune, which can be averted or removed if the proper sacrifices are offered to the gods and goddesses. The only way to determine the proper and matching sacrifices is by consulting the oracles that divine the will of the gods and goddesses. Unfortunately, however, the Igbo belief in the role of sacrifice in their relationship with the divinities has degenerated into a strong belief in manipulation and bribery. In other words, just as they believe that adversities and misfortunes can be averted or changed by offering sacrifices that can change their gods' wills, they believe that persons in authority who control their progress in all areas of human activity can be manipulated to take actions favorable to those who offer the proper "sacrifices"—namely, persuasive appeals, rendering good services, and, in some cases, offering outright bribes. In all parts of Nigeria, these various forms of manipulation and bribery are expressed by the phrase "offering of kola," which derives from the ritual habit of offering kola and pouring libations to appease the gods and ancestors.

Ancestors

Ancestors are the dead-living forebears from whom all Igbo people are reincarnated (from the spirit world) and descended (from people in the human world). They are at the center of the cyclic existence of human beings in the Igbo world, earlier described as the world of humans and the world of spirits. The ancestors are described as dead-living because they may be dead in the world of humans but alive in the world of spirits.

The birth of a child into the Igbo world begins with the reincarnation of part of an ancestor's spirit from the spirit world into the womb of a woman, where it takes human form and is later born into the world of humans. He grows and lives as a man until he dies physically, but his soul lives on. However, before his body is buried in the earth, propitiation sacrifices are offered to cleanse him of all earthly offenses, thereby making him worthy of reentering the womb of Mother Earth, the portal of the spirit world. If this ritual is not performed, the body may be interred but the spirit cannot enter. So it roams the earth as *ajo mmuo*, an evil spirit.

A second burial rite enables him to rejoin the other half of his spirit in the spirit world, thus making him a whole ancestor again, and ready to be reincarnated in the future. This state of being of the human soul is known as descent or ancestry in Igbo theology, which is the equivalent of ascension in Christian doctrine.

Because of the Igbo belief in ancestors and reincarnation, humans in the physical world honor and court the deceased ancestors with sacrifices during rituals and ceremonies, so that the ancestors may reincarnate into the families from which they descended into the spirit world. In fact, young married couples have been observed competing to take very good care of an elder on his death-bed in the hope of having him reciprocate the favor by reincarnating into their family as a first child. All told, the three levels of human existence—in the spirit world of the ancestors, in the womb as the world of the unborn, and on earth as the world of humans—define the Igbo trinity.

Chi

Of all the Igbo divinities, *chi* is the most difficult to explain, because of the dynamic, often conflicting roles that *chi* is believed to play in the lives of human beings. A brief discussion is presented here to enable readers of *Things Fall Apart* to understand the roles *chi* plays in the lives of the Igbo characters, especially Okonkwo. (Those who wish to know more about the concept may consult the sources listed at the end of the chapter.)

Chi is a person's spirit double, a concept that derives from the Igbo belief in duality: that all things have their complementary opposites even in the realm of spirits. In that sense, *chi* is a person's *spirit being* in the spirit world, complementing his *human being* in the human world. Unlike Chukwu, who is far removed from human beings, *chi* is always in close proximity to people and functions as a transcendent force, guardian angel, personal god or spirit, or soul of *chi*'s individual human double.

Defined strictly in terms of its principal roles, *chi* is creator, fate, or destiny: the Igbo believe that as a dead-living ancestor in the spirit world prepares for reincarnation into the human world, he is presented a number of gifts and talents by Chi-na-Eke from which he alone with his *chi* (as creator spirit) makes choices that become his portion or fortune in the human world. Though guided by *chi*, the reincarnating ancestor exercises free will in making choices. Whatever choices he makes are ratified by *chi*. That is why the Igbo say, "*Onye kwe chi ya ekwe*" (When a man says yes his *chi* will also agree).

After his birth into the human world, the ancestor, now a person, makes use of his chosen gifts and talents under the strict supervision of his *chi* (as guiding spirit). If his use of talents results in misfortune despite every cautionary measure, people would normally rationalize the situation by saying, "*O bu otu ya na chi ya si kwuo*" (It is how he and his *chi* bargained), a philosophical way of attributing responsibility for misfortune to the man and his *chi*.

Whether a man's portion in life is good or bad, he must live with it to the end of his human existence. *Chi* (as guardian angel) will not allow him to be deprived of the opportunity to experience his total destiny. That is why when a man escapes an accident, the Igbo would say *"Chi ya mu anya"* (His *chi* is awake); but when he suffers a series of misfortunes, they call him *"Onye ajo chi"* (a man of bad *chi*), which implies that his fortune rather than his character is bad.

Chi is fate. Two brothers, for instance, may be brought up by good parents, but one may turn out good and the other bad. To the Igbo, the situation may not be surprising. They have a popular saying, *"Otu nne na-amu, ma otu chi anaghi eke"* (One mother gives birth, but different *chi* create). The implication of the statement underscores the role *chi* plays in the creation and endowment of humans with fortune or misfortune that becomes their fate on earth, which is what makes each human being a unique creation.

Finally, although *chi* is a spirit, it does not dwell in the same spiritworld underground with the dead-living ancestors. Instead, it dwells above, somewhere near the sun. Nevertheless, *chi* is close to human beings, who invoke his presence from an earthly shrine, especially at sunrise. *Chi*, together with Chi-na-Eke, created humanity, but *chi* alone, as a person's spirit double, guardian angel, guiding spirit, or personal god, controls the fortune, fate, or destiny of humans on earth.

Ofo

Ofo is not a spirit or god like any of the divinities discussed so far. Yet its centrality in the religious, political, and socio-cultural lives of the Igbo elevates its position almost to that of a god. *Ofo* is the consecrated symbol of Igbo ancestral authority handed down from one generation to another through the first-born sons of each family, village, or clan. So there are *ofo* for the family, village, and clan in ascending order of authority.

As a religious emblem, *ofo* symbolizes the chain links between humanity and Chukwu, humanity and the ancestors, and humanity and the unborn children in the womb. The linkage centers around people in the human world (the center of the Igbo worlds), where the virtues of justice, truth, and equilibrium (all embodied in the *ofo*) are required for ordered, harmonious coexistence of humans and the spirit beings.

During political and socio-cultural events, the holder of the *ofo* becomes speaker, chairman, or president. As he presides over the conduct of the people's affairs, his authority is never impugned by anyone, for the *ofo* he holds assures the people that he does his job with justice and in truth, without fear or favor. Should the *ofo* holder fall short of that expectation, the people believe that he will be severely punished by the gods and ancestors whose sacred trust and authority he has betrayed and abused.

Oracles, Divination, and Sacrifice

In traditional Igbo societies, one of the problems in having several gods and goddesses is that any allegiance one pays to one god may turn out to be an offense against another god, because the man-made gods are as envious as their makers. Achebe emphasizes this conflict when he asserts in *Morning Yet on Creation Day*: "Nothing is absolute. *I am the truth, the way and the life* would be called blasphemous or simply absurd, for is it not well known that a man may worship Ogwugwu to perfection and yet be killed by Udo?" (133). To avoid offending the gods, the people always watch out for signs. Therefore omens and premonitions play a large part in the fortunes of the Igbo. Ordinary people can interpret ordinary omens, but those with psychic tendencies can recognize some omens and have premonitions of some disasters before they happen. To prevent envisaged disasters from happening, the people constantly consult priests and priestesses who divine the will of the gods.

Oracles are the places where, or the mediums through which, the Igbo deities are consulted. Divination is the practice of trying to foretell the future, especially using the priest and his oracle to know the will of the gods. According to Ruth A. Firor:

> Divination is the active counterpart of omens and premonitions. It is the *sortilegium* and *augurium* of the ancients, practiced lawfully only by the priest or the head of a family. Among the Germanic tribes, divination, like the priestly office, was hereditary. It was held

unlawful when practiced by any not recognized as a priest of a cult. Such a practitioner was believed to use his knowledge chiefly for the selfish benefit or active hurt of individuals rather than for the social weal. (11)

Many of the characteristics that Firor outlines apply to Igbo divination: divination as the active counterpart to omens and premonitions is practiced lawfully only by the priests of cults or by the head of a family, village, or clan; in some cases the priestly office is hereditary; and the practitioners of Igbo divination use their knowledge for the benefit of society.

Once the wills of the gods are known through divination, the next thing to do is offer appropriate sacrifices to the gods. Igbo sacrifice is a sacred offering, as of a life or object, to a deity. It takes four forms, namely, sacrifice as atonement, sacrifice as defense against unknown evil forces, sacrifice as petition, and sacrifice as thanksgiving.

Sacrifice as atonement: The Igbo offer this type of sacrifice to make amends for any abominable offenses committed against Ala, the ancestors, and fellow clansmen. Such offenses include giving birth to twins, murder, adultery, suicide, incest, and rape. Whenever any of these offenses is committed, Ala, the earth goddess in charge of morality, is offended, and her abode, also known as Ala, is desecrated. She must be appeased with animal blood, including that of fowls, sheep, goats, cows, and humans, depending on the gravity of the particular abomination, known in Igbo as *nso-ala*.

Sacrifice as defense against unknown evil forces: This type of sacrifice is offered to ward off evil forces that attack people, or series of misfortunes that come one's way without rational causes or explanations. The oracle is consulted to guide healers (*nde dibia*) not only to exorcise the evil spirits but also to build "charms" to prevent future occurrences.

Sacrifice as petition: This refers to the sacrifice that Igbo people offer as petition to the ancestors, Chukwu, and specific deities in charge of specific human activities and departments. For instance, if there is a drought, rain-makers are consulted to offer sacrifices to Ala, who has been unfairly denied water, so she can sustain farm crops with left-over water in her bowel until the next rainfall. Also, the rain-makers are asked to offer another sacrifice to some oracles so that they can reveal the hidden cause of the drought. Once the cause is known, the necessary propitiation sacrifice is offered so that rain will begin to fall again.

Sacrifice as thanksgiving: This is the most common type of sacrifice the Igbo offer to their ancestors, Chukwu, and other gods and goddesses for the blessings of childbirth, bumper harvest, new marriages, good health, long life, and so on. Such sacrifices precede the public rituals and ceremonies that the people perform weekly, monthly, or yearly. As a grateful people, the Igbo offer sacrifices in the belief that the more often they show gratitude for the blessings they receive, the happier the divinities will be in giving them more blessings.

All four types of sacrifice may involve the slaughter of animals, feasting, and merriment in the form of rituals and ceremonies. But they require also the use of material customs, which are both sacred and secular.

MATERIAL CUSTOMS

Material customs are comprised of the equipment, implements, and structures that the Igbo traditionally produce to aid and promote their culture and civilization. They include traditional buildings and their decorations, farm implements and tools, folk costumes and ornaments, war gear and weapons, talking drums, gongs and fiddles, masks and raffia skirts, as well as body decorations and scarifications.

Religious Icons and Symbols

Igbo religious icons and symbols include shrines and the pantheon that harbor the myriad of gods and goddesses to whom the people offer their sacrifices, or divine the wills of the deities. In the shrines are found such sacred objects as masks, raffia skirts (the costumes of the *egwugwu*), wooden and earthen statues, long drums and cannons, as well as gongs and fiddles. In addition to siting the shrines and pantheon in appropriate geographical locations to reflect the natural habitats of the deities, great care is taken by those who create the masks to give them male or female faces and other physical features that depict them as gods or goddesses. The professionals who create, carve, sculpt, or weave the icons

A Masked Spirit, Mgbadike Masker Near Awka in Igboland. Photo by Herbert M. Cole, 1966.

receive divine inspiration and guidance and occupy important social and spiritual positions in their communities.

Sacred Buildings and Ornamentation

Before the shrine of any god or goddess (especially a man-made one) is erected, the oracle is consulted about the site, shape, and decoration of the shrine. Also, before the builders themselves embark on their sacred duty to their people and their gods, they must be purified with a cleansing sacrifice offered to the gods. Some of them go through mystical "eye-opening" rituals known as *iwa anya* or *itu ogwu*. Once they have gone through the cleansing and eye-opening processes, it is believed that they are then possessed by the gods and goddesses, who guide them to construct the sacred structures, each of which looks different because the appearance, functions, and temperaments of the gods who occupy them are also diverse.

Body Decorations and Scarifications

Body decorations range from simple hairstyles and traditional cosmetic makeup, using such items as *nzu* (white chalk), *uri* (black dye), *odo* (yellow dye), and *ufie* (carmine) for women and priests during rituals and ceremonies, to complex scarifications (*igbu ichi*) on the faces of titled men and on the faces and bellies of titled women. Facial scarifications are also made to distinguish the various clans and communities of the individuals that bear them.

Igbo material customs, like the narrative customs discussed in Chapter 5, function as a subtle means of expressing and transmitting the folklore and traditions of the people. The difference between narrative customs and material customs is that whereas the former are verbal and explicit, the latter are more symbolic and implicit. Taken together, they reflect the quality of Igbo-ness in whatever the people do, which Achebe has expertly appropriated in *Things Fall Apart*.

Facial Scarification of a Titled Woman, *Iwo Ilo*. Photo by Herbert M. Cole, 1983.

FOREIGN AND NATIVE WRITERS' VIEWS ON IGBO RELIGION

European missionaries and anthropologists who lived in Igboland during the colonial period published the first works on the traditional religion of the Igbo people. As a result, works on the subject later published by Igbo writers sounded either revisionist, because they attempted to correct what they perceived as inaccurate representations of their native religion, or imitative, because the Igbo authors, themselves Christian converts, made use of biblical terms and Christian concepts to describe Igbo religious ideas.

The following excerpts, two by European clergy and two by Igbo scholars, describe aspects of traditional Igbo religion.

FROM M. M. GREEN, *IBO VILLAGE AFFAIRS* (1964)

The Supernatural Sphere

Village Cults

As for the beliefs and sentiments associated with the tutelary deities of village-group and village, we have seen how they contribute in a number of ways to the sense of identity of the village and village-group community, and to its stability. They also reflect the kinship and local pattern of Ibo organisation. Moreover, the lack of well-defined tribal consciousness is accompanied by the absence of a tribal deity. But just as the people of Agbaja marry and trade with the people of the village-groups near to them, so they recognise the guardian spirits of these groups though they are not directly concerned with their cults. When their annual ceremonies are performed, there is much exchange of hospitality between relations by marriage. Moreover, an Agbaja man may call on the priest of the guardian spirit of a neighbouring village-group to bring the *ofo* of the spirit so that he may swear his innocence on it in a case. In some instances there is a recognised order in which the ceremonies of different spirits must be performed. The new yam ceremonies which are initiated, in Agbaja, by the village of Abosi, must be done before those of the village-group of Umu Ezeala can start. In this case certain distant kinship bonds are recognised between Agbaja and Umu Ezeala. The right to start any ceremony is a matter of prestige. When, in 1937, there was conflict between Abosi and Umueke, and the sacred spear of the yam spirit, Ajioku Ji, was planted as a threat in Umueke, the time for the new yam ceremonies drew on and they could not be done in the absence of the spear. Among other causes for anxiety in the situation was the fact that if Abosi did not keep up to time, Umu Ezeala would go ahead without waiting for them, and thus the prestige of Abosi would be impaired.

Whether or not there is any conception of deities that are either universal or at any rate more than local, it is not easy to know. We have seen that Ala, the ground, seems to be a village or village-group conception rather than anything wider.

As for *Chi*, the spirit who creates people and whose name, as in *Chineke*, has been taken by the Christians to denote the Creator, it is difficult to know what the real Ibo significance of the word is. *Chi* and Eke together create an individual but each person is thought of as having his own *Chi* and whether, over and above this, there is any conception of a universal *Chi* seems doubtful.

Ancestor cult is an important factor in the life of the people. Apart from the performance of certain burial and second-burial ceremonies which are the concern of the whole village, its sphere is that of the individual or extended families rather than of the village as a whole, and does not therefore fall directly within our province, which is the organisation of the village. But the supernatural sanctions which stress the virtues of filial piety and mutual responsibility among kinsmen so far as the dead are concerned cannot fail also to promote them among the living. This will provide a cohesive element in village life so long as it does not overstress the particular kinship bonds of small units within the village in opposition to others. There is always, as we have seen, this tension between the separatist kinship interests of the extended families and the unity of the village as a whole.

Nde Dibia

The two sets of people who pre-eminently deal with the supernatural side of life are the priests and the *nde dibia*, and it is important to be clear as to the marked difference between them. A priest, though he observes taboos and performs ceremonies, is yet what one might call an ordinary member of society. A *dibia*, on the other hand, though he still joins in many of the generalised activities of farming, trading, housebuilding and the like, is none the less a specialist, a member of a profession which entails hard and costly training and initiation, and complicated and often arduous technical activities.

The word "*dibia*" can perhaps best be translated either as "diviner" or as "doctor-magician." A *dibia* will normally specialise in one or the other of these two branches of his profession, though some combine the two activities, and all seem to have a smattering of both.

Entry into the profession is characteristically Ibo in being open to anyone. There is no question here, or anywhere else so far as I saw in Ibo society, of a closed hereditary guild system. There is probably a tendency for sons or other young relations to follow in the footsteps of a *dibia* father or senior relative, but the principle on which an individual starts on the career of diviner is that he shows signs of mental derangement. His parents then, as in all cases of sickness or misfortune, consult a diviner to know the cause and cure of the trouble, and in these mental cases they may be told that Agwu Nshi, the spirit of divining and of magic, is troubling the youth and that he must become a *dibia* and therefore a servitor of Agwu Nshi. People distinguish clearly between a man they consider mad and a man "troubled" by Agwu Nshi. The latter is probably, at this stage of his life anyway, psychologically unstable: whether or not, as seems likely, his training as a *dibia* helps to stabilise him is a matter that would repay investigation. In any case, he is made socially useful and respectable instead of being regarded as an outcast and a liability.

Becoming a *dibia* involves much expense and a long process of teaching and, in the case of a diviner, of initiation by other *nde dibia*, a description of which cannot be given here.

What must be stressed, however, is the part played by the *dibia* in the daily life of the Ibo. When anyone is ill or overtaken by disaster, either he or his relations will hurry to a diviner to know why, since most if not all misfortune has a supernatural cause, and it is the diviner who by the vision he has acquired during his training can see these causes. He will then prescribe the sacrifices to be made or the ceremonies to be performed. Except for the few annual occasions of more or less public sacrifice, offerings and ceremonies for the ancestors and the spirits are performed at the behest of the diviner. The diviner can also be consulted in cases of theft. In addition to all voluntary cases of consultation, if anything habitual can be so described, custom decrees that a diviner shall be consulted in the two fundamental crises of birth and of death. He must be visited on the fourth day after a child's birth by the child's kinsmen in order to ascertain what ancestor or spirit is incarnated in the baby, and therefore what name it should be given. When anyone dies, kinsmen again must go to ask a diviner, and if need be, several, the cause of death. The cause is always, so far as I have seen, held to be supernatural—an offended ancestor or spirit, or the magic or sacrifice made by an enemy.

Clearly the diviner needs a considerable local knowledge to deal with his clients, and this must extend over a wide area since a man will usually go some distance, several miles at least, to consult a *dibia*. There is, I think, little doubt that the diviners, whatever their supernatural or supernormal powers, have methods by no means supernatural of learning a great deal of what goes on, and from the very nature of their clients' cases they must gain a considerable insight into the private lives of many people. They must also, particularly in giving reasons why people have died, be a considerable factor in expressing and upholding the moral code of the community, since death often comes as a result of an offense against this code.

London: Frank Cass & Co. Ltd.

FROM G. T. BASDEN, *AMONG THE IBOS OF NIGERIA* (1966)

Some Aspects of Religion

Amongst the Ibo people there is a distinct recognition of a Supreme Being—beneficent in character—who is above every other spirit, good or evil. He is believed to control all things in heaven and earth, and dispenses rewards and punishments according to merit. Anything that occurs, for which no visible explanation is forthcoming, is attributed either to Him or His eternal enemy Ekwensu, i.e. the Devil. But Chukwu (as He is called) is supreme, and at His service are many ministering spirits whose sole business it is to fulfill His commands. It is interesting to note that Death is spoken of as one of the servants of God.

This Supreme Being is designated by different rites, the chief of which are Chukwu (=Chi-ukwu) i.e. the Great God; Olisa bulu uwa, usually shortened to Osebulu uwa; or Olisa simply. The underlying idea of the name is, "God who fashions the world." In the southern districts Chineke (God the Creator) is the prevailing name.

The knowledge of the Supreme Being is practically confined to the name and the interpretation thereof. Besides the recognition of a Beneficent Being, there is a profound belief in an Evil Spirit. The two are eternally opposed to each other, each striving to influence mankind for good or evil, but Chukwu is always classed as superior to Ekwensu.

Certain actions such as murder, theft, and adultery, are esteemed offences against God, as well as against man. The natives hold that in committing such offences, a man is acting contrary to the will of God and the appropriate punishment will assuredly follow. Should the actual sinner escape, his descendants must bear the burden. The fear of retribution, however, is not profound; it certainly does not act as a deterrent to evil. Though such deeds are reckoned as ajaw-awlu (bad works) there is no actual "sting" in the committal of them. The greatest of all sins is "to be found out," and any man who works so clumsily that his misdeeds are discovered deserves all the punishment that comes to him. . . .

Over the greater part, if not over the whole, of the Ibo country the python is sacred, more especially the smaller species called ekke-ntu. These likewise are referred to as "our mother," and to injure one is a very serious offence. If a man has the misfortune to kill one accidentally he will mourn for a year and abstain from shaving his head. Monkeys, birds and various animals are treated similarly in the different districts where they are held sacred.

If a person be injured by any sacred animal or reptile, or by the fall of a sacred tree or stone, it is inferred that some grievous offence has been committed, and that nneayi is meting out an appropriate punishment to the transgressor. Favour can be regained only by resort to the medicine-man, who will advise as to the sacrifice to be offered in the circumstances. If the injury should be fatal, as it may be when a tree falls upon a person, then the assumption is that the offence was such as could only be atoned for by the god thus exercising his powers of vengeance. The unfortunate person is left to his or her fate, a crowd of spectators probably looking on with callous indifference, in the belief that the sufferer is but getting his just deserts, and that to attempt a rescue, or to interfere in any way would be but to bring retribution upon themselves.

We turn now to the private and family gods—those which are kept within the house and compound and which have a much closer connection with the individual than those which are public and general. It must be again emphasised that no object in itself is worshipped by the Ibos; it is sacred only as the habitation of a spirit. It has only that relative sanctity to which it is entitled as the shrine or home of a certain spirit. Very seldom are the objects themselves called upon by name; the petitions are invariably addressed to the igaw-maw, i.e. the spirits. Occasionally the god Ikenga is invoked under the title of Ikenga Oweawfa, i.e. "he who splits the shield (of the enemy), hence the strongest one: the bravest one." Under certain conditions this spirit-worship exercises a tremendous influence over the lives of the natives.

Each house contains many sacred objects, but they have not all equal significance, for among the "gods many and lords many" there are higher and lower degrees of importance. The most universal of these household gods, and that which is given first rank, is the Ikenga and no house may be without one. It is the first god sought by a young man at the beginning of his career, and it is the one to which he looks for good luck in all his enterprises.

The Ikenga is always carved from a solid block of uroko-wood. The height varies from one foot upwards. It represents a man seated upon a stool; two long horns, curling backwards, are the symbol of strength and power. Many examples have a long-stemmed pipe in the mouth, the bowl of the pipe resting on the knees. The right hand of the larger Ikengas grasps a sword, point upwards, whilst the left holds the head of the conquered enemy—this again denoting strength. Occasionally the horns project from a headless trunk and no limbs are provided. Such are simply of cheaper design. For religious purposes all figures of Ikenga stand equal. As a rule only the head of the household may offer sacrifice to them; should he be prevented for any reason the awkpala (next of kin, male) officiates in his stead.

London: Frank Cass, pp. 215–16, 218–19.

FROM VICTOR C. UCHENDU, *THE IGBO OF SOUTHEAST NIGERIA* (1965)

Igbo Gods and Oracles

Igbo Ideas of the High God

The idea of a creator of all things is focal to Igbo theology. They believe in a supreme god, a high god, who is all good. The logical implication of the concept of a god who is all good is the existence of a devil (*agbara*) to whom all evil must be attributed. This is not peculiar to Igbo thought. It is a characteristic of all known religions which accept the doctrine of a high god who does no evil.

The Igbo high god is a withdrawn god. He is a god who has finished all active works of creation and keeps watch over his creatures from a distance. The Igbo high god is not worshipped directly. There is neither shrine nor priest dedicated to his service. He gets no direct sacrifice from the living but is conceived as the ultimate receiver of all sacrifice made to the minor deities. (In fact, Igbo sacrifice to any unknown and uninvited deities who might be present.) He seldom interferes in the affairs of men, a characteristic which sets him apart from all other deities, spirits, and ancestors. He is a satisfied god who is not jealous of the prosperity of man on earth.

Although the Igbo feel psychologically separated from their high god, he is not too far away, he can be reached, but not as quickly as can other deities who must render their services to man to justify their demand for sacrifices. The Igbo recognize that the high god can do all things. It is their experience, too, that he lets the minor, malignant deities torture them, rob them of their property, kill their children, and make trade unprofitable and women and land barren and unproductive. Their appeals to him at the height of their distress and despondency do not always meet with immediate response. Is it any wonder that they sometimes feel that the distance between them and the high god is too great? Although the high god may be distant and withdrawn, he is not completely separated from the affairs of men. He is still the great father, the source of all good. He interacts with each Igbo during each reincarnation cycle. He sometimes intervenes in favor of the living but not as quickly as suppliants would like.

The high god is conceived of in different roles. In his creative role, he is called Chineke, Chi-Okike (Chi—God; Okike—that creates). To distinguish him from other minor gods he is called Chukwu—the great or the high god. As the creator of everything, he is called Chukwu Abiama, while as the pillar that supports the heavens, he is called Agalaba ji igwe. The sky is regarded as his place of residence and people invoke his name as Chi-di-n'elu—"God who lives above."

Besides the high god, there are other minor gods called nature gods, sometimes described as kind, hospitable and industrious; at other times, they are conceived of as fraudulent, treacherous, unmerciful, and envious. They are, in general, and, in fact, used to further human interests.

The organization and power structure of these nature gods mirror Igbo social structure. Like the latter, the nature gods are not conceived of as forming a hierarchical pantheon. There is no seniority or authority implied in the conception of these minor deities. It is the Igbo practice to appeal to one god or to a number of gods simultaneously without any consideration of their rank or status. The Igbo demand from their gods effective service and effective protection. If they fail in this duty, they are always threatened with starvation and desertion. Given effective protection, the Igbo are very faithful to their gods.

Ala, the Earth-Goddess

The minor gods are not normally ranked in importance. The Igbo regard *Ala*, the earth-goddess, nearest to them, with the possible exception of their ancestors. *Ala* is an earth-goddess, a great mother. She is the spirit of fertility. She increases the fertility of man and the productivity of the land. Without her, life would be impossible for the Igbo, who attach much sentiment to the land. It is out of respect to the earth-goddess that the Igbo are ideologically opposed to the sale of land. As was noted earlier, where there is a "sale" of land the earth-goddess must be ritually pacified if the transaction is to be consummated. The Igbo feel guilty and ashamed to have to sell their land.

Every Igbo community has a myth about its settlement—a myth which validates its claim to the piece of land it inhabits. Some villagers claim that their founding parents were created on the spot; others lay claim to priority of settlement. Whatever the basis of the charter, the first settlers are always said to have founded *ihu ala*—the face of the earth—which thus becomes sacred for the people. *Ihu Ala* is the place where all major decisions, like going to war, summarily dispatching a sorcerer, or giving a democratically reached decision a ritual binder, are made. The Igbo are fond of changing their mind, but decisions taken at *ihu ala* are not lightly treated and are often respected.

Ala is a merciful mother. She intercedes for her children with other spirits. Minor deities may not take action against Igbo without asking *ala* to "warn" her children, but no spirit may intercede or intervene when *ala* has decided to punish. But she does not punish in haste; she gives many signals of her displeasure. Quite reluctantly, after many unheeded warnings, *ala* may kill by bouncing the wicked on the ground until they are dead. She does not kill for minor offenses. Only such offenses classed as *nso—ali* (taboo)—warrant her anger. Incest is a good example. As the custodian of Igbo morality, *ala* must take action to save the community. Death is not considered enough punishment for an Igbo who has offended against *ala*. He is denied ground burial, the worst social humiliation for any Igbo.

Ala helps the Igbo with many things. They ask her for children, for prosperity in trade, and for increase in livestock. As the source of strength, she must be notified before her children go to war. It is a great privilege to be a priest of *ala*. This requires a *diala*-status, which is ascribed to all children born of a freeman and a freewoman. Every *diala* is therefore a potential priest of *ala*.

• • •

The Ancestors

Ancestors occupy a special place in Igbo religious practice. The Igbo conceive of their ancestors as the invisible segment of the lineage. The ancestors are "honored" and not "worshipped" in the strict sense. The ancestral honor is a religion based on reciprocity. There is a loving reverence for the deceased ancestors, who are expected to come back to reincarnate and "do to the living members what they did for them."

Ancestors are scolded as if they were still living. This can be noticed in any sacrifice. They are reprimanded for failing in their duty to their children, by closing their eyes to the depredations of evil spirits which cause death to the family, cause crop failure, and make trade unprofitable. No elaborate sacrifices are made to ancestors. They are given the ordinary foods eaten in the home: water, raphia wine, and a piece of kola may be all.

The Igbo idea that the ancestors and other deceased members come back to "temporal life" is rooted in their theory of reincarnation. Belief in reincarnation gives the Igbo hope of realizing their frustrated status goals in the next cycle of life. Transmigration, on the other hand, is regarded as the greatest possible punishment for the incestuous, the murderer, the witch, and the sorcerer. *"Ilodigh uwa na mmadu"*—"May you not reincarnate in the human form"—is a great curse for the Igbo. The reincarnation of those who violated taboos is usually said to be inauspicious. They are born either feet first or with teeth or as members of a twin set—all of which are in themselves taboo.

Although death of old age is accepted as a blessing by general consent, and death in childhood or youth and death through accident is regarded as a tragedy, some Igbo reincarnate as *ogbanje*—repeater. The *ogbanje* die prematurely without any sign of ill-health. They can, however, be "stabilized" by specialist doctors, provided they can be detected in time.

Sacrifice is an integral part of Igbo religious practice. Igbo seek the divine will through oracles and divination. Revelation must be followed by some form of sacrifice, which may involve the whole political community, a lineage, a compound, or a family. Some sacrifices are obligatory (those recommended by the diviner) and others may be routine. Whatever their form, sacrifices show gratitude to the gods for past blessings, express hope for future favors, and request protection against all evils from wicked men and malignant spirits.

Igbo religious beliefs and practices are complex. They are based on the conception of a high god who has subordinate but "free" spirits, on the reincarnation doctrine which rationalizes people's status, and on the ancestors who protect the living from the wicked spirits. The revelation of divine will, which is ascertained through divination and oracular opinion, must be followed by sacrifice.

New York: Holt, Rinehart and Winston, pp. 94–95, 102.

FROM MAZI ELECHUKWU NNADIBUAGHA NJAKA, *IGBO POLITICAL CULTURE* (1974)

Igbo Religion and Politics

Ofoism

The Igbo belief in Chukwu depends essentially on man's belief in himself. For example, the Igbo cannot conceive of his own existence without Chukwu. However, to exist, live, die, and be reincarnated, the Igbo believes that he possesses some godhood—as do other created things, although to lesser degrees. Hence he assigns himself a chi and assigns lesser chi to other created things. This is primarily based on the Igbo belief that without Chukwu nothing can exist, even inanimate objects. Ukuru ("breath" or "essence of") Chineke sustains all things animate and inanimate; hence he is called Olisa or Orisa ("the sustaining penetrating being").

The Igbo are essentially religious. They live in a world of Chukwu, man, and spirits. The Ofo links these three entities. Thus the concept of Ofo tends to envelop all the spirits, man, and Chukwu and at the same time is a way of life and of religion. As the Ofo is the central symbol of Igbo religion, so man is the central and ultimate beneficiary of the religion. To the Igbo, Chukwu created the world for man, who is sustained by Chukwu. Man, like Olisa, will never die, man's sole purpose being to cultivate and enjoy the world, as Chukwu has ordained.

The Igbo society is a place where men live in a convenant with spirits as well as a convenant with Chukwu and man. Men and spirit commingle and communicate with each other on an everyday basis. The spirits play a vital part in a whole series of human relationships, resulting in a humanism where the society finds ethical imperatives of social and political welfare in the mythic and cultic aspects of its religion.

The above can be said to be a partial description of Ofoism, the religion of man, which conceptualizes Chukwu, ndiishii [ancestors], chi, Ala, and other spirits mingling with men in all aspects of life. It is a religion which influences the political system of the Igbo without making it essentially theocratic. Instead, the political processes of the Igbo are, in the main, secular but protected with the aura of religion (which is of man) only as a measure to maintain law and order in the extremely individualistic populace.

Ofosim, therefore, is highly social and political; it has been successfully used to sanctify laws and thus prevent their violation. The Igbo has utilized his religion in the regulation of the social order, in the adjudication of cases, and in the maintenance of effective administration. Ofoism is thus a religion of man artfully oriented to enable him to carry out the human activities necessary for the full exploitation of the world which is his abode.

Therefore, as we have said about Igbo society, Igbo traditional culture successfully united, from its very inception, the mythic and cultic aspects of religion with the ethical imperatives of social law and political organization. Law and order are maintained because the ancestors so desire and oha [the people] so commands. And the ancestors desire law and order because Chukwu must have approved them. For example, murder is supposed to be an action against Chukwu, the ndiishii, and oha because there is no dichotomy between Ofoism and the state. The will of the oha is necessarily the will of the ndiishii, which is assumed to be the will of Chukwu because the ndiishii can never go against Chukwu. Therefore ethical justice and political responsibility are not separable. To extend this concept further, kinship (umunna, mkpuru, ogbe, ebe, etc., in the concept of ikwu and ibe [kith and kin]) includes responsibility to the laws of both Chukwu and man. Therefore, it is the oha and not the rulers who possess the sovereign rights of the state.

Ofoism, for all practical purposes, permeates every aspect of Igbo society and is consequently the major catalyst in Igbo culture. From the family ikenga to the town-state arusi [shrine or oracle], religious symbolism constantly restrains and shapes the conduct of those for whom it was devised. A new law legislated by a state assembly undergoes consecrational ceremonies in order to be clothed with inviolability. The head of a city-state places his two feet on the ancestral Ofo or piously holds it in his hand, makes the pronouncement (purported to come from the ancestors with Chukwu's attention, direction, and sanction) to Ala, and all the elders with their Ofo, each representing the ancestors of the segmentary units, reply in unison: "Iha, Iha, Iha, E-o-oh, Iha" ("Let it be, let it be, let it be, we all agree, so let it be!"). From that time onward, any violation is considered a violation of the constitution and will be followed by a penalty and cleansing rites. Otherwise the Igbo is free to behave as he pleases until restricted by nso ala. These nso ala, however, can be changed, modified, or interpreted to yield to the forces of change under the pretext of carrying out the wishes of the ancestors.

Evanston: Northwestern University Press, pp. 45–47.

CONCLUSION

The traditional religion of the Igbo, organized around four the-ological concepts—Chukwu, non-human spirits, ancestors, and *chi*—influences every aspect of Igbo life. In Igbo cosmology, the world is peopled at three levels of existence—human beings, dead-living ancestors, and unborn children in the womb—as well as by invisible and visible forces. It is a world in which the forces inter-act, affecting and modifying behavior, including the behavior of human beings and divinities. The religious and socio-cultural phi-losophy known as complementary dualism encourages coopera-tion among the inhabitants of and forces in the Igbo cosmos to maintain a state of balance. Oracles, divination, and sacrifice form the essential elements of traditional Igbo religion.

The fictive society in *Things Fall Apart* is peopled with characters who engage in ritual practices that reflect the religious and pious nature of the Igbo. In public events and ceremonies, ordinary peo-ple and *egwugwu* (who represent the ancestors and deities), men and women, boys and girls, the rich and the poor are brought together. Through his depiction of traditional village life Achebe shows that the Igbo possessed a viable religion that governed their lives long before the introduction of Christianity into Igboland.

TOPICS FOR WRITTEN OR ORAL EXPLORATION

1. How does your definition of religion help you to understand traditional Igbo religion?

2. Name the four theological concepts around which traditional Igbo religion is organized.

3. Discuss the concept and nature of the Igbo high god, Chukwu.

4. Discuss the concept and roles of *chi* in the Igbo's traditional religion and worldview.

5. Discuss the role of Ala, the earth goddess, in the religious and moral life of the Igbo.

6. Who are the Igbo ancestors? Why is their presence so important in rituals, ceremonies, and religious practices?

7. Discuss the roles of the *egwugwu* as important factors in Igbo socio-religious life in *Things Fall Apart*.

8. What are Igbo oracles, and how do they promote religious practices and social control in Igboland?

9. What is ofo? How does it keep the roles of Chukwu, Ala, the ancestors, and the gods and goddesses in balance?

10. What is ofoism, and what are its social and political functions?

11. Why is it difficult, if not impossible, to separate the spiritual life of the Igbo from the secular?

12. Name the two religions discussed in *Things Fall Apart* and comment on one of them.

13. Identify and discuss the most serious social and religious weaknesses in pre-colonial Igboland.

14. Discuss the importance of the *Iwa Oji* ritual to Igbo religious life in *Things Fall Apart*.

15. Compare and contrast the concepts of the Christian godhead and the Igbo high god, Chukwu, in *Things Fall Apart*.

16. What do you admire in pre-colonial Igbo customs, traditions, and religion, and why?

17. What Igbo religious beliefs and practices helped white missionaries to make easy converts in Igboland?

18. What are material customs? How are they different from narrative customs?

19. Name three kinds of material customs. Discuss those that are purely religious.

SUGGESTED READINGS

Achebe, Chinua. "Chi in Igbo Cosmology." In *Morning Yet on Creation Day*. New York: Anchor/Doubleday, 1976. 131–45.

Arinze, Francis A. *Sacrifice in Ibo Religion*. Ibadan, Nigeria: Ibadan University Press, 1970.

Firor, Ruth A. *Folkways in Thomas Hardy*. Philadelphia: University of Pennsylvania Press, 1931.

Mbiti, John S. *African Religions and Philosophy*. New York: Frederick A. Praeger, 1969.

Nwoga, Donatus I. *The Supreme God as Stranger in Igbo Religious Thought*. Ekwereazu, Nigeria: Hawk, 1984.

7

Things Fall Apart: The African Novelists' Novel

> At the university I read some appalling novels about Africa (including Joyce Cary's much praised *Mister Johnson*) and decided that the story we had to tell could not be told for us by anyone else, no matter how gifted or well-intentioned.
> —Chinua Achebe, "Named for Victoria, Queen of England"

CHRONOLOGY

1930	Chinua Achebe is born in Ogidi in Igboland, Nigeria
1948–53	Achebe attends the University College, Ibadan; B.A. (London) 1953
1958	*Things Fall Apart* is published
1960	*No Longer at Ease* is published
1964	*Arrow of God* is published
1966	*A Man of the People* and *Chike and the River* are published
1971	*Beware, Soul Brothers* is published
1972	*Girls at War and Other Stories* and *How the Leopard Got His Claws* are published
1975	*Morning Yet on Creation Day: Essays* is published
1977	*The Drum: A Children's Story* is published

1978	Achebe edits (with Dubem Okafor) *Don't Let Him Die: An Anthology of Memorial Poems for Christopher Okigbo* (1932–1967)
1982	Achebe edits (with Obiora Udechukwu) *Aka Weta: Egwu aguluagu na Egwu edeluede*
1983	*The Trouble with Nigeria* is published
1987	*Anthills of the Savannah* is published
1988	*Hopes and Impediments* and *The University and the Leadership Factor in Nigerian Politics* are published
1992	Achebe edits (with C. L. Innes) *The Heinemann Book of Contemporary African Short Stories*

INTRODUCTION

Things Fall Apart is the result of its author's urgent and dynamic response to a negative situation. While studying at a British colonial university, the University College at Ibadan, Achebe and his fellow African students read "some appalling novels about Africa." So some of them decided to write their own novels that told true stories about their native Africa. They, of course, knew that what they were being taught was not true of the Africa they lived in, which disturbed them. So to challenge and correct the situation, well-informed African writers, critics, and researchers developed an indigenous literature out of oral traditions comprised of folktales, proverbs, folk songs, rituals, and folk dances—a literature that attempted to obliterate the negative image of Africa conveyed in novels by foreign writers. Novels by African writers bore protest messages that paralleled those of African political leaders who were struggling to win independence from European colonial powers.

Ironically, the very expatriate university professors who adopted "offensive" European novels as compulsory texts provided the stimulus for their students to experiment with creative writing as well as a conducive environment in which to work. Those who mastered the craft, Achebe for example, later published books that laid the foundation for what became known as "African literature today." Achebe asserts in an interview with Robert Wren: "They weren't teaching us African literature. If we had relied on them to teach us how to become Africans we would never have got started. They taught us English literature; they taught us what they knew"

(Wren 51). One of Achebe's professors, Molly Mahood, confirms Achebe's assertion: "We were very keen to have Anglo-Irish literature, Irish literature because it seemed relevant to me in the learning situation. If you've read Soyinka's early plays you'll realize a play such as *The Strong Breed* is pure Synge" (Wren 22–23). But if the professors did not teach African literature, they surely created a nationalistic feeling among their Nigerian students that helped them to produce works that later became Nigerian national literature. Commenting on the quality of their students at Ibadan, Mahood says:

> We were extraordinarily lucky in Ibadan really in the late '50's or even before that. There was an extremely good secondary school tradition. We got the cream. Of course that meant that we were called elitists. Perhaps we were. But it did mean that we could keep up a very high standard. We got the backing of London, holding the standard firm. The infrastructure of the school is, I think, all important. Now there were very good schools who worked on building up their courses to the University. . . . They were nearly all boarding schools which had of course the disadvantage that, in theory, they took people away from their own environment—detribalized them. But then they had the advantage that it de-tribalized them. They thought of themselves as Nigerians. . . . But they lived very happily together, Igbo, Yoruba, and the others too, as far as I could see. I mean, they were asking questions, of course, but I think they were enthusiastic churchgoers, too. Both chapels were always packed. We had, in those days, very few northerners, rather few Muslims. But they all kept up their traditions and ceremonies when they went home. (23)

Keeping up their traditions and ceremonies when they went home—traditions and ceremonies they internalized—became thematic maternal that Achebe used to write *Things Fall Apart*, an African novel in English, intended to re-educate both the Africans and their colonizers on true African cultures and civilizations.

THE NEED FOR NOVELS ABOUT AFRICA BY AFRICAN WRITERS

One passage in a European novel about Africa that Achebe found appalling is from Joyce Cary's *Mister Johnson* in which a northern Nigerian town and its inhabitants are described:

Fada is the ordinary native town of the Western Sudan. It has no beauty, convenience or health. It is a dwelling place at one stage from the rabbit warren or the badger burrow; and not so cleanly kept as the latter. It is a pioneer settlement five or six hundred years old, built on its own rubbish heaps, without charm even of antiquity. Its squalor and its stinks are all new. Its oldest compound, except the Emir's mud box, is not twenty years old. The sun and the rain destroy all its antiquity, even of smell. But neither has it the freshness of the new. All its mud walls are eaten as if by smallpox; half of the mats in any compound are always rotten. Poverty and ignorance, the absolute government of jealous savages, conservative as only the savage can be, have kept it at the first frontier of civilization. Its people would not know the change if time jumped back fifty thousand years. They live like mice or rats in a palace floor; all the magnificence and variety of the arts, the ideas, the learning and the battles of civilization go over their heads and they do not even imagine them. (105)

Many literate Africans who have read this lurid description of an African town and its people—albeit fictional—have wondered the temerity of its author. It is the same temerity that one finds in the white District Commissioner who, in the closing paragraph of *Things Fall Apart*, plans to write a book about Umuofia culture and civilization despite his total ignorance of them. Like Joyce Cary, "the District Commissioner is an archetype of those numerous Europeans, particularly missionaries and administrators, whose instant expertise on Africa has contributed to the Westerner's profound ignorance of the continent. And the ethnocentric bias of the Commissioner's imperial handbook underlines the historical inability of the Western scholar to emancipate himself from the usual perspectives on African 'primitives' " (L. W. Brown 138).

The Westerner's profound ignorance of the African continent and his ethnocentric bias also appear in Joseph Conrad's *Heart of Darkness*, where he describes the African natives as "savages," "primitives," and "black shadows," a people without any culture and human language, and their continent as "the heart of darkness." The lush pre-colonial African forest that was able to provide sustenance for the people has been turned into a "greenish" grove with "gloom," and the inhabitants into "diseased" and "starving" people as a result of the nineteenth-century invasion and partition that gave the Congo to the Belgians and the French:

They were dying slowly—it was very clear. They were not enemies, they were not criminals, they were nothing earthly now—nothing but black shadows of disease and starvation, lying confusedly in the greenish gloom. Brought from all the recesses of the coast in all the legality of time contracts, lost in uncongenial surroundings, fed on unfamiliar food, they sickened, became inefficient, and were then allowed to crawl away and rest. These moribund shapes were free as air—and nearly as thin. I began to distinguish the gleam of the eyes under the trees. Then, glancing down, I saw a face near my hand. The black bones reclined at full length with one shoulder against the tree, and slowly the eyelids rose and the sunken eyes looked up at me, enormous and vacant, a kind of blind, white flicker in the depths of the orbs, which died out slowly. The man seemed young—almost a boy—but you know with them it's hard to tell. I found nothing else to do but to offer him one of my good Swede's ship's biscuits I had in my pocket. The fingers closed slowly on it and held—there was no other movement. He had tied a bit of white worsted round his neck—Why? Where did he get it? Was it a badge—an ornament—a charm—a propitiatory act? Was there any idea at all connected with it? It looked startling around his black neck, this bit of white thread from beyond the seas. (Conrad 31–32)

The stereotypical depiction of the African in this passage (and others like it in *Mister Johnson*) that Achebe and other African readers resent does not seem offensive to Western readers who assert that Conrad's depiction of African characters in the novel is art for art's sake. Nevertheless, some African critics take a middle course. For example, Ben Obumselu, one of Achebe's contemporaries at the University College, who was taught *Mister Johnson* by the same white professors, reads the novel differently from the way Achebe does:

Mister Johnson was included in Robinson's course when I got to Ibadan. I think I was there just one year after Achebe, so we are contemporaries. I must say that my reaction to Johnson is the diametrical opposite of Achebe's. Johnson is a very amusing character, and nobody likes to be told that he is like a clown. That is the real point of Achebe's reaction. But I'm afraid that I read literature in an entirely different way from Achebe. Because I think I've given a lot of time and thought to the study of Joyce Cary, and to the study of his French background and his background in the arts, I know that Johnson is a representation of what Cary at one other point calls the spirit of life, which in its—how does it go?—"in its struggle to realize itself in newness and innocence always creates eternal delight." Well, Johnson dominates the novel and he dominates the world in which he is. And if there is any reflection in that novel, on the African, I think that what Cary is saying is that the African ought to have charge of his own affairs because his instinctive desire for novelty will create a new world for him out of the old. You know, Johnson gets in there, and he builds a new road—and the district officer can't even understand how this road came about. That is the point of the novel. I might add that Eric Robinson's treatment of Johnson, on reflection, was wrong. He was trying to recall old Africa except what he read. Not before he came to Africa, but ten years after he went back to England. You know, what he read in the Bodleian Library often was not even Africa, but just generalized anthropology about the primitive. That was the way that Robinson taught it, and that was wrong. (Wren 91)

Although Obumselu does not read *Mister Johnson* the same way Achebe does, his answers to Robert Wren's interview questions confirm Achebe's fears that the message of Cary's novel can easily be misunderstood even by the most enlightened readers. For example, Obumselu was able to comprehend the point of the novel only after he had "given a lot of time and thought to the study of Joyce Cary, and to the study of his French background," which many readers, including Obumselu's own professor, Eric Robinson, whose "treatment of *Johnson*, on reflection, was wrong," are not able to do. Also, like Robinson "trying to recall old Africa except what he read," many readers of European novels about Africa were not given accurate representations of Africa, "but just generalized anthropology about the primitive . . . and that was wrong." In making this assertion, Obumselu agrees with Achebe.

To those Europeans—and even Africans—who believe in the concept of "art for art's sake," Achebe once said in a very testy mood, "Art for art's sake is just another piece of deodorized dog shit." In other words, he insisted that "art is, and was always, in the service of man. Our ancestors created their myths and legends and told their stories for a human purpose (including, no doubt, the excitation of wonder and pure delight); they made their sculptures in wood and terra cotta, stone and bronze to serve the needs of their times" (*Morning Yet on Creation Day* 25). Contextually, what Joyce Cary did in *Mister Johnson* was to portray Africans as persons without any respectable culture, human language, and intelligence. With such a rationalization they were bought and kept in perpetual bondage in foreign countries, and colonized in their own countries by European powers, who arrogated to themselves the sole ownership of culture, language, and intelligence that must be taught to the Africans.

That distorted image of Africa as being "primitive" and "savage" persisted until African writers challenged it. Here lies the impetus for the writing of not only novels about Africa by Africans themselves, but also the kind of novels that Achebe wrote, which served as a model for modern African writers.

THE ACHEBE TRADITION IN AFRICAN FICTION

Chinua Achebe was not the first Igbo or Nigerian to publish a novel in English. That honor went to Cyprian Ekwensi, an Igbo, who published his major novel, *People of the City*, in 1954, and to Amos Tutuola, a Yoruba, who published *The Palm Wine Drinkard* in 1952. However, their novels remained relatively unknown until the publication of *Things Fall Apart* in 1958. Achebe's novel persuaded readers that, contrary to the impression created by European novels about Africa, African folkways, cultures and civilizations were worthy of romanticizing, like those of other peoples of the world. With *Things Fall Apart* and three other novels published in succession—*No Longer at Ease* in 1960, *Arrow of God* in 1964, and *A Man of the People* in 1966—Achebe established a modern African literary tradition that came under what his publishers, Heinemann Educational Books Limited, London, fondly titled African Writers Series, appointing Achebe its first editor.

As noted in Chapter 1, *Things Fall Apart* makes use of elements common in European fiction—plot structure, point of view, figurative language, tone and voice, setting, characters, and symbols and imagery—to convey its theme. However, the local color—the unique quality of Africanness Achebe gives those elements—makes the novel a hybrid genre: African writers and readers have since validated its story and verbal art, setting, cultural context, characters, and overall theme as authentically African. In effect, the style and content of *Things Fall Apart* triggered and helped to establish what can be called the Achebe school of writers and the Achebe tradition in African fiction, the great literature with the power to dispel European-manufactured myths about African cultures, providing readers, native and foreign, with insiders' perspectives on African cultures and civilizations.

So, what is the Achebe tradition, and how has it helped to humanize Africans in the very eyes of readers? And how has it established modern African literature? Answers to these fundamental questions must be sought through careful examination of the uniquely African aspects of *Things Fall Apart*.

The Story and Igbo Verbal Art

To general readers, the fundamental function of the novel is to tell a story. First and foremost, they are eager to know what happens. Whether or not the story is well told depends on the novelist's art and technique.

As Achebe began his professional writing career, he reflected on the distorted images of Africa found in European novels about Africa. He realized that merely condemning such images and their creators was pointless. So he decided to go beyond condemnation and to experiment on the import of an Igbo wrestling proverb, "*I kpopu nwatakiri n'ogbo mgba, i nochie ya*" (If you take a young and inexperienced wrestler off the wrestling arena, you stay on to wrestle in his place). Achebe not only condemned the distorted images of Africa and its peoples presented by European writers, but also wrote a novel in which the images of an African people, the Igbo, and their folkways are realistically delineated.

The Western narrative technique Achebe adopts to tell his story is laced with an Igbo narrative technique full of Igbo cultural assumptions. For, while his narrator realizes that the story must have a beginning, a middle, and an end, with exposition, climax, and denouement, as in Western novels, his language of narration contains the vigor, poetry, and integrity of Igbo vernacular, especially proverbs and other sententious sayings. In other words, although written in English, the novel deals with vernacular characters who are essentially untouched by modern influences, so their ideas are best expressed in a form of language with indigenous sensibility. That is why some sentences in *Things Fall Apart* sound like transliterated Igbo expressions, and why others contain pure Igbo proverbial expressions. Achebe's technical expertise makes it easy for

Igbo and non-Igbo readers alike to appreciate the complex narrative action of the novel in its totality, despite the peculiar nature of its language of expression.

The story is basically about the cultural conflict between the Igbo clan of Umuofia and the intruding white missionaries and British colonial agents. And yet Achebe's focus is on Igbo folkways: namely, Igbo language, traditional religion, rituals, ceremonies, beliefs, values, customs, and festivals. As an insider to Igbo culture, Achebe uses the novel as a means of giving his readers—especially non-Igbo readers—meaningful insights that enable them to overcome negative stereotypes created by Europeans.

Setting

Things Fall Apart is set in Umuofia, in what became the southeastern part of modern Nigeria. Umuofia was a closed society whose village-based culture was intact until the coming of the white missionaries in the 1860s. The society's values were enforced by the masked spirits (*egwugwu*) who represented the founding fathers of the nine villages that made up the clan, by the age-grades, and by other social groups within the village setting. The society itself was patriarchal, highly stratified, and very traditionally religious. It observed numerous rituals and ceremonies, including rites of passage and title-taking festivals.

Status symbols and gender roles were clearly defined as a set process through which the young were taught. Games, story-telling sessions, and instructions preceding age-grade naming ceremonies served as formal and informal traditional education. Achebe realistically appropriates the settings of these Igbo social institutions in *Things Fall Apart* as thematic material. Sentences such as "Fortunately, among these people a man was judged according to his worth and not according to the worth of his father" and "Age is respected but achievement is revered" underscore the importance of personal achievement. Igbo men were in constant quest of titles and status, and a man who lacked them was looked upon as *agbala* (woman). However, that is not to say that traditional Igbo women felt as dominated as their counterparts in the Western world. Women may have been portrayed as less visible than men in Umuofia, but their roles were as important as those of men. Male and female roles complemented each other, resulting in the social philosophy of "complementary dualism," defined in Chapter 4. The importance of mothers was emphasized in the role that Okonkwo's maternal uncle, Uchendu, played in his exile in Mbanta, and in the name Nneka, "Mother is supreme."

By setting the novel in pre-colonial Igboland, in a patriarchal society at war with the white missionaries and British colonial agents, Achebe enables readers to understand not only the traditional Igbo social matrix, but also the sterner stuff that the Igbo men, represented by Okonkwo and his friend Obierika, were made of. The war situation that produces the rhythm of violence and the antagonistic atmosphere is delineated to explain why, in spite of his bravery and military prowess, the strongman Okonkwo commits suicide rather than be taken alive by the District Commissioner and imprisoned like other lesser men. Also, the social weaknesses of Umuofia are described in an ambience of socio-economic class warfare, making it clear why the *efulefu*, the dregs of society, side with the white people.

Cultural Elements

The Igbo culture is given expression in their folktales, proverbs, proper names, rituals, and festivals. Achebe, writing from an insider's point of view, appropriates all of them fully in *Things Fall Apart* and in his second rural novel, *Arrow of God*. Proverbs, for example, serve as necessary linguistic and rhetorical devices in Igbo oratory and are one element that differentiates African and European novels. Whereas proverbs are seldom used in European works, they are put to active, everyday use in Igbo oral and written discourse.

Furthermore, Igbo society is communitarian rather than individualistic, and its rituals and festivals are a means of fostering that community life, even with their dead-living ancestors, Chukwu, gods and goddesses, and unborn children. Also, their folktales, folk songs, and dances have enabled them to develop happy and child-like attitudes toward one another, their neighbors, and even their colonizers—attitudes the whites misunderstood as childish, leading them to address African men as boys and to treat them without respect or dignity.

Achebe uses *Things Fall Apart* as a window through which to reveal both the serious and the lighter aspects of Igbo men, whether engaged in individual activities at home or during folk festivals. He shows layers of interaction in the public, private, and personal lives of the characters, especially that of the hero, Okonkwo, succinctly delineating them to give readers an overview of traditional Igbo life and folkways. These various layers of interaction are seldom differentiated in European novels about Africa.

Characterization

People in a novel are called characters. Perhaps the fact that characters are invented non-human beings may have led those who advocate art for art's sake to overlook the irreparable damage that Cary and Conrad did to African peoples by the way they portrayed Africans in *Mister Johnson* and *Heart of Darkness*, respectively. Achebe, who, like his ancestors, believes that art is in the service of man, set out to show Africa as it is (good and bad) in his writing. Characters like Okonkwo and Obierika are found not only in Igbo villages but everywhere. The realistic characterization in *Things Fall Apart* dispels the exotic aura and mystique found in European novels about Africa, allowing readers to easily appreciate Okonkwo's problems as human problems, an appreciation that creates catharsis in the reader. In a word, Achebe's characters are fully realized human beings.

Theme

Since Achebe the novelist is an Igbo like the characters he creates in *Things Fall Apart*, he has an affinity with and a deep understanding of his subject matter that is absent in European novels about Africa. In a lecture titled "The Role of the Writer in a New Nation" he states the overall theme of his work:

> This theme—put quite simply—is that African peoples did not hear of culture for the first time from Europeans; that their societies were not mindless but frequently had a philosophy of great depth and beauty, that they had poetry and, above all, they had dignity. It is this dignity that many African people all but lost during the colonial period and it is this that they must now regain. (*Nigeria Magazine* 81 [1964]:157–58)

It is Achebe's determination to regain the literary tradition of his people—the oral literature the Igbo all but lost with the introduction of Western education. His style has served as a model of cultural re-education for both his contemporaries and latter-day African writers. Achebe declares in "The Novelist as Teacher":

> I would be quite satisfied if my novels (especially the ones I set in the past) did no more than teach my readers that their past—with all its imperfections—was not one long night of savagery from which the first Europeans acting on God's behalf delivered them. Perhaps what I write is applied art as distinct from pure. But who cares? Art is important but so is education of the kind I have in mind. And I don't see that the two need be mutually exclusive. (*Morning Yet on Creation Day* 58)

His novels set in the past, *Things Fall Apart* and *Arrow of God*, dramatize the first Igbo encounter with Europe and its aftermath. While the literary war with Europe rages on, after reading *Things Fall Apart* no European critic could ever again say that Africans were savages and that their continent was "one long night of savagery from which the first Europeans acting on God's behalf delivered them."

FACTORS BEHIND ACHEBE'S SUCCESS

The documents that follow offer critical insight into why Achebe succeeded as a novelist and why *Things Fall Apart* is seen as the African novelists' novel. His preparation included listening to folktales, which he appropriates succinctly, especially in *Things Fall Apart* and *Arrow of God*—novels set in the village, the hub of Igbo morality and conscience; knowing the Igbo story-telling habits, including the use of proverbs; being born and raised "at the crossroads of cultures" as a result of British colonization of Nigeria; receiving a Western education and learning the art of novel-writing, which helped him to transform the oral literary tradition of his people into a written tradition; and assuming the self-imposed role of "the novelist as teacher" as a way of re-educating his readers on the true nature of African cultures and civilizations.

FROM C. L. INNES AND BERNTH LINDFORS, EDS., *CRITICAL PERSPECTIVES ON CHINUA ACHEBE* (1978)

Introduction

Born in Ogidi, in the eastern part of Nigeria in 1930, Achebe was, as he informs us in the autobiographical essay, "Named for Victoria, Queen of England,"[1] originally christened Albert Chinualumogu. His father was an evangelist and church teacher, although many of his relatives and neighbors adhered to the Ibo religion and customs. Thus, Achebe writes, he grew up "at the crossroads of cultures."

• • •

When the British assumed control of Nigeria in the late nineteenth century, they assumed, as other colonial powers have conveniently assumed, that they brought "history" and enlightenment and progress to a people which had no valid social, political and religious traditions of its own. Those religious beliefs which differed from their own they called superstition or fetishism, the differences in political and social structure they called chaos. In 1900, the British imposed a system of direct rule over the Ibos by dividing their territory into areas ruled by District Commissioners and appointing Ibos to act as warrant chiefs, clerks and messengers to assist them, a system resented by the Ibos not only because it was an alien imposition violating their own democratic structure, but also because those who accepted the appointments were men without status and without allegiance to their own communities. In modern terms, they were considered collaborators. In 1918, Lord Lugard introduced "indirect rule" as a policy for the whole of Nigeria, the District Commissioners were removed, and the warrant chiefs were given greater power, often resulting in greater abuse of power. These abuses led to further reorganization in 1930 to comply more closely with traditional Ibo groupings and institutions. This system survived until Independence in 1960.

The literature written about Africa during this time generally tended to reinforce those assumptions of the British and helped them defend colonial rule as an agent of enlightenment to primitive peoples without a valid civilization of their own. Hence Africa was seen as a dark continent, a symbol of the irrational, nourishing undifferentiated and childlike peoples governed by fear and superstition rather than reason, a people only too ready to welcome and, indeed, worship, the white man. Such is the picture sketched by Conrad in *Heart of Darkness* and Cary in *Mister Johnson*, whatever their doubts about the actual effectiveness of the colonial administrators. And such a picture is painted even more luridly and simplistically by Rider Haggard, Edgar Wallace, and a multitude of movie directors.

Chinua Achebe grew up at a time when Africans were not only opposing European rule through political action, but also beginning to question with increasing vigor and clarity the cultural assumptions used to justify that rule. Like many other young people of his generation, Achebe was given a British education, first at the local mission school, then at Government College in Umuahia, and finally at University College, Ibadan, where he had planned to study medicine. He soon switched to literature, however, and encountered a syllabus which included not only Shakespeare, Milton, Wordsworth, and others, but also the novels of Conrad, Greene and Cary on Africa. Although at Ibadan Achebe had written some short stories, essays and sketches for *The University Herald*, it was not until after his graduation in 1953 that he began his first novel, a novel whose impetus was the desire to "set the record straight" and to paint an African portrait of Mister Johnson. In an interview with Lewis Nkosi, Achebe said:

> I know around '51, '52, I was quite certain that I was going to try my hand at writing, and one of the things that set me thinking was Joyce Cary's novel, set in Nigeria, *Mister Johnson*, which was praised so much, and it was clear to me that it was a most superficial picture of—not only of the country—but even of the Nigerian character, and so I thought if this was famous, then perhaps someone ought to try and look at this from the inside.

Originally, Achebe had planned the story of Okonkwo and his grandson, Obi Okonkwo, who like Mr. Johnson worked for the colonial administration and was convicted of taking bribes, as one novel. But in the end, two novels emerged, *Things Fall Apart*, set at the turn of the century when the British first came to Iboland, and *No Longer at Ease*, set in the fifties as the British administration reluctantly prepared to hand over the running of the bureaucratic institutions it had established. *Arrow of God* returned to the past and to the early interaction between the Ibo and British cultures, while *A Man of the People* is set in contemporary Nigeria a few years after independence. As several critics have remarked, the novels can be seen as a tetralogy, documenting Nigerian history between 1890 and 1965.

• • •

Both as a creative writer and as a critic, Achebe has had a great influence, particularly on younger African writers. His novels have made an especially powerful impression upon young Ibo writers who first became acquainted with his works as high school or university students. By the early sixties many educational institutions in West Africa had adopted his first novel as a prescribed text in English courses, leading the *Times Literary Supplement* to suggest in 1965 that "Already *Things Fall Apart* is probably as big a factor in the formation of a young West African's picture of his past, and of his relation to it, as any of the still rather distorted teachings of the pulpit and the primary school."[2] Young Ibo readers who had grown up in villages and cities resembling those described in Achebe's novels were very excited to find their own world reflected in fiction; when they themselves turned to writing stories and novels they naturally tried to emulate what Achebe had done. By 1968 many new Ibo novelists—Nkem Nwankwo, Flora Nwapa, E.C.C. Uzodinma, John Munonye, Clement Agunwa—had broken into print, and it was no longer premature to generalize about the emergence of a "School of Achebe" in Nigerian fiction.

The master's influence was apparent in both theme and technique. Only one of the five writers set his novel in an Ibo city. The rest dealt with traditional Ibo society, two of them describing it as it was before the coming of the white man. Three, including the urban novelist, concerned themselves with aspects of the conflict between old and new values in Iboland, Achebe's favorite subject. And all five attempted to simulate vernacular expression by incorporating into dialogue and narration many proverbs, idioms and metaphors translated from their mother tongue. They were not slavish imitators. Each contributed something personal and unique to Nigerian fiction. But it is quite clear that they would not have written what they did or as they did had it not been for Achebe's example.

Notes

1. Published originally in *New Letters*, 40, 1 (1973), 15–22, and reprinted in Achebe's *Morning Yet on Creation Day: Essays* (London: Heinemann, 1975), pp. 65–70.

2. "Finding Their Voices," *TLS*, 16 September 1965, p. 791.

Washington, D.C.: Three Continents Press, pp. 1, 3–6.

FROM ERNEST N. EMENYONU, *THE RISE OF THE IGBO NOVEL* (1978)

Introduction

When Nigeria attained her independence in 1960 there were only two nationally well-known novelists and fewer than half a dozen Nigerian novels in English. Of the two novelists, Chinua Achebe had published two novels, *Things Fall Apart* (1958) and *No Longer at Ease* (1960), while Cyprian Ekwensi had published one major novel, *People of the City* (1954), two short novels—*The Passport of Mallam Illia* (1960) and *The Drummer Boy* (1960)—and some collections of short stories. Although Amos Tutuola had published *The Palm Wine Drinkard* (1952) two years before Cyprian Ekwensi's *People of the City* (acclaimed as the first modern Nigerian novel), and Timothy M. Aluko had published *One Man, One Wife* (1959), the year following Achebe's *Things Fall Apart*, it was to take some years before Tutuola and Aluko could enjoy the wide attention and acceptance which had greeted Achebe and Ekwensi on the publication of their first novels.

In the few years that followed Nigerian Independence, several other Nigerian novelists emerged who were read not only in Nigeria and other parts of Africa but also in Europe, the United States, and other parts of the world. Before the outbreak of the Nigerian civil war in 1967, a woman, Flora Nwapa, had joined the major Nigerian novelists with the publication of *Efuru* (1966). Recent studies[1] show that about eighty novels were published in English by West Africans at the end of the first decade of Nigerian Independence. Of this number, about fifty were by Nigerians, and furthermore, about thirty of the Nigerian titles were by Igbo writers. There is justification, therefore, in saying that the Igbo are among the most prolific writers in West Africa today, and probably in Africa as a whole. The two Nigerian pioneer authors, Achebe and Ekwensi, as well as the woman novelist, Flora Nwapa, are all Igbo.

Why are most contemporary Nigerian novelists Igbo? Here Joseph D. Kight asks this question:

Why They Are Igbo

A question which I have often heard asked is: Why are Nigerian leading novelists Ibo? Some have even narrowed it down to why do they come from the same district? Achebe, Ekwensi and Nzekwu come from Ogidi, Nkwele and Onitsha respectively—all within a radius of seven miles.

Recently some students of African Literature in the University of Ibadan gave as an answer to this question the presence of a great many printing presses in Onitsha. To my mind this is too cheap an answer, for printing presses do not produce authors. The suggestion becomes even more ridiculous when one takes into consideration the background of the various authors. Cyprian Ekwensi was born and bred in Jos and did not go home to Nkwele until he was about thirty-five. Onuora Nzekwu spent his first eleven years at Kafanchan and except for the four years he spent at St. Charles' College, Onitsha, was either away in the North or Lagos. Chinua Achebe is perhaps the only one who spent all his formative years in Ogidi and Umuahia.

One would have thought that these students should have investigated these authors' backgrounds before hazarding the guess that printing presses constituted a formative influence in their lives.[2]

This study recognizes the generous contribution made by the Igbo to Nigerian (and African) creative writing; but it does not attempt to answer the question, "Why are the leading Nigerian novelists Igbo?" Igbo writers have produced a relatively large number of novels, so that a study of Igbo literary development may have pertinent reflections on the modern African novel as a whole. An investigation of an essential aspect of an ethnic literary tradition and its continuity may provide one useful approach to the study of African literature characterized as it is now by its diffusion and cultural diversity. "In a multi-ethnic nation like Nigeria, it is imperative that the culture and life-ways of the component units should be given full airing so that national sentiments are built upon the firm foundation of understanding."[3] This is equally true of all African literature which should be considered in terms of the ethnic and national literatures of which it is made up.

Several years ago Chinua Achebe called for an end to the energy and efforts being spent over the rhetorical definition of African literature, and offered a new and challenging approach to it:

You cannot cram African literature into a small, neat definition. I do not see African literature as one unit but as a group of associated units—in fact the sum total of all the national and ethnic literatures of Africa. . . . An attempt to define African literature in terms which overlook the complexities of the African scene and the material of time is doomed to failure. After the elimination of white rule shall have been completed, the single most important fact in Africa, in the second half of the twentieth century will appear to be the rise of individual nation states. I believe that African literature will follow the same pattern. . . . Of course, you may group them together on the basis of anything you choose—the colour of their hair, for instance. Or you may group them on the basis of the language they will speak or the religion of their fathers. Those would all be valid distinctions; but they could not begin to account fully for each individual person carrying, as it were, his own little lodestar of genes.[4]

This call by Chinua Achebe for more knowledge of "the ethnic and national literatures of Africa" was one of my incentives in writing this book.

The first Igbo to write about Igbo life were Igbo expatriates. By the accident of the slave trade they found themselves in foreign lands but their thoughts were often about home. Having learnt the mystery of the written word, they were able to give utterance to their deepest yearnings by recreating with tender care aspects of Igbo life they could still recall.[5]

The first of these "expatriates" to write was Olaudah Equiano, and his autobiography, *The Interesting Narrative of the Life of Olaudah Equiano or Gustavus Vassa the African* (London, 1789), was the first literary work to be published by an Igbo in English and possibly in any language. Equiano writes nostalgically about his Igbo heritage when he says:

Our land is uncommonly rich and fruitful, and produces all kinds of vegetables in great abundance. We have plenty of Indian corn, and vast quantities of cotton and tobacco. Our pineapples grow without culture; they are about the size of the largest sugar-loaf and finely flavoured. We have also spices of different kinds, particularly pepper, and a variety of delicious fruits which I have never seen in Europe, together with gums of various kinds and honey in abundance. All our industry is exerted to improve those blessings of nature. Agriculture is our chief employment, and everyone, even the children and women, are engaged in it. Thus we are all habituated to labour from our earliest years. Everyone contributes something to the common stock, and as we are unacquainted with idleness we have no beggars. . . . Deformity is indeed unknown amongst us, I mean that of shape. . . . Our women too were in my eyes at least uncommonly graceful, alert, and modest to a degree of bashfulness; nor do I remember to have ever heard of an instance of incontinence amongst them before marriage. They are also remarkably cheerful. Indeed cheerfulness and affability are two of the leading characteristics of our nation.[6]

The abolition of the slave trade (in which Equiano played no small role) led to direct European contact with and penetration of the African continent for reasons of commerce, evangelization and colonization, and ushered in the era of Christian missionaries in Africa. The most important missionary group that settled among the Igbo was the Church Missionary Society (C.M.S.). The C.M.S. missionaries arrived and settled in Onitsha in 1857 and until the middle of the twentieth century, were engaged in the work of education, evangelization and westernization of the Igbo. They studied the Igbo language and adapted it to the Western alphabetic script. Using this script, they produced, and encouraged the Igbo to produce, a "literature." But the missionary writings were biased in their reporting of Igbo traditional mores and customs, and in their assessment of the relevance of Igbo traditional institutions to contemporary Igbo social and political behaviour.

> Perhaps one ought to give the missionaries the benefit of the doubt. They were not out to propagate the native institutions but to justify the eventual overthrow of them by the new missionary-oriented order. They may be excused therefore, if in their attempt to discredit the old order they did not devote adequate time and attention to a detailed study of them. Again, because a fair number of early studies of Igbo life and culture were by missionary writers, the image of the Igbo that emerged from them was debauched and grotesquely primitive.[7]

Probably, the single most enduring contribution of the Christian missionaries was that they provided the Igbo with the tool for preserving their literature in writing, and thus helped decisively to bring about the emergence of written Igbo literature.

Notes

1. Based on entries in Hans Zell and Helene Silver, *A Reader's Guide to African Literature* (London, Heinemann, 1972).

2. *Nigeria Magazine*, 18 (June 1964).

3. *The Conch*, III, 2 (September 1971), p. 15.

4. Chinua Achebe, "English and the African Writer," *Transition* IV, 18 (1965).

5. *The Conch*, III, 2 (September 1971), p. 11.

6. Paul Edwards (ed.), *Equiano's Travels* (London, 1967), pp. 7–8. This is an abridged edition of the original.

7. *The Conch*, III, 2 (September 1971), p. 7.

Ibadan, Nigeria: Oxford University Press, pp. ix–xiii, xxii–xxiii.

FROM EUSTACE PALMER, *THE GROWTH OF THE AFRICAN NOVEL* (1979)

Chinua Achebe's *Things Fall Apart* (1957) demonstrates a mastery of plot and structure, strength of characterization, competence in the manipulation of language and consistency and depth of thematic exploration which is rarely found in a first novel. Although he has never quite been able to sustain this exceptionally high standard in subsequent novels, the general level of performance remains consistently impressive and he assuredly deserves his place as one of the most accomplished African writers. In the history of the anglophone novel Achebe comes next to Ekwensi in chronological importance, but his work is much more comprehensive in scope than that of the latter who confines himself almost entirely to contemporary situations. All the shaping forces which combined to stimulate the growth of modern African literature in the 1950s are discernible in Achebe's work. Broadly speaking, the African novel is a response to and a record of the traumatic consequences of the impact of western capitalist colonialism on the traditional values and institutions of the African peoples. This largely explains the African writers' initial preoccupation with the past. While recognizing the need for a redefinition and reordering of values in modern Africa in the wake of the disruptive effects of colonial administration, writers like Achebe and Soyinka also realize that before this reordering can take place there must be a confrontation with the past. In the article "The novelist as teacher" Achebe talks interestingly of how he sees his role as a writer in society.[1] One of the consequences of the impact of western civilization on Africa, he says, is "the disaster brought upon the African psyche in the period of subjection to alien races." Africans were induced to prefer western culture and to regard their own with contempt. It is part of the African writer's business to teach his fellow-Africans that there is nothing shameful in African culture and tradition.

> Here then is an adequate revolution for me to espouse—to help my society regain belief in itself and put away the complexes of the years of denigration and self-abasement. And it is essentially a question of education, in the best sense of the word. . . . I would be quite satisfied if my novels (especially the ones I set in the past) did no more than teach my readers that their past—with all its imper-

fections—was not one long night of savagery from which the first Europeans acting on God's behalf delivered them.[2]

In another article, "The role of the writer in a new nation," Achebe consequently suggests that the African writer must primarily concern himself with the past in an effort to help his fellow-Africans regain that lost dignity "by showing them in human terms what happened to them, what they lost."[3] He goes on:

> There is a saying in Ibo that a man who can't tell where the rain began to beat him cannot know where he dried his body. The writer can tell the people where the rain began to beat them. After all the writer's duty is not to beat this morning's headlines in topicality, it is to explore in depth the human condition. In Africa he cannot perform this task unless he has a proper sense of history.[4]

The history of the colonialist impact on Africa proceeded in three phases: first there was the stage of actual conquest when the white man by sheer force of arms introduced an alien form of administration, education and religion and taught the African to look down on his own indigenous systems; the second was the period of resistance when the now-awakened masses struggled to shake off the imperialist yoke; finally there is the present post-independence stage with African society seeking to reorder itself, having thrown off imperialist oppression. The exploration of these three phases is the motive force behind the African novel, and Achebe is central to this concern. He deals with the first phase since in two of his novels he attempts to demonstrate the destructive impact of westernization on indigenous culture and to attest to the beauty of that culture; he touches on the second phase although he is not as concerned as Ngugi with the struggle to shake off the imperialist yoke, but he certainly shows the beginnings of the rumblings of discontent; and he is very much involved with the attempt at the reordering of values.

The theme of Achebe's four novels, then, all of which he had planned as a tetralogy from the very first, is that of tradition versus change; he gives a powerful presentation of the beauty, strength and validity of traditional life and values and the disruptiveness of change. It may be that Achebe's presentation of traditional life is not an accurate reproduction of the historical truth. However, what we shall be concerned with here, in an attempt to see the picture of his Ibo society that emerges, is not a faithful anthropological documentation but the way in which Achebe sees it.

Notes

1. Chinua Achebe, "The novelist as teacher," *African Writers on African Writing*, ed. G. D. Killam (Heinemann, London, 1973), pp. 1–4.
   2. Ibid., pp. 3–4.

3. Chinua Achebe, "The role of the writer in a new nation," in *African Writers on African Writing*, op. cit., p. 8.

4. Ibid., p. 8.

London: Heinemann, pp. 63–65.

FROM LEWIS NKOSI, *TASKS AND MASKS: THEMES AND STYLES OF AFRICAN LITERATURE* (1981)

History as the "Hero" of the African Novel

1

"To make the past present, to bring the distant near." It seems a modest enough task; it is what we have come to expect of any novelist with a pronounced sense of history: "to invest," as Macaulay put it, "with the reality of human flesh and blood beings whom we are too much inclined to consider as personified qualities in an allegory."[1] In defining the duties of the historical novelist which were once those of the historian, the English essayist uses a language which would surely find immediate emotional responses from those of our writers haunted by the African past and who are trying to develop strategies for "bringing the distant near." They must try

> to call up our ancestors before us with the peculiarities of language, manners, and garb, to show us over their houses, to sit at their tables, to rummage their old fashioned wardrobes, to explain the uses of their ponderous furniture.[2]

This is a task that very few of our writers have seemed ready or capable of performing; and when they have tried very few have performed it with as much success as the Nigerian novelist, Chinua Achebe, who has made day-to-day Ibo life a vivid experience for readers who have never set foot in West Africa. Part of the relative success of the West African novelist can be attributed to the fact that the traditional "past" is not really that "distant": it is still very much alive. But surely there is much that has also vanished; certain patterns of daily life and forms of belief in societies which were then effectively sealed off from many contacts with the outside world, social forms and patterns of behaviour which can now only be reconstructed through an intensive effort of a creative imagining.

• • •

2

Chinua Achebe's two novels of Ibo village life (*Things Fall Apart* and *Arrow of God*) provide fine examples of the good uses to which the

African past can be put by an imaginative writer acting both as an inventor of "fictions" and a recorder of "social history." Though Achebe is not an "historical novelist" in any ordinary sense of that word, Gerald Moore is right, it seems to me, to call attention to the historical dimension in Achebe's fiction.[3] Moore pays tribute to Achebe's "piety" toward the past and sees in the novelist's passion for reconstructing Ibo village life a necessary "act of restitution" the result of which is both "a piece of social history" as well as "offering ground for some degree of cultural continuity."

> Thus his first novel, *Things Fall Apart*, has made a deeper impression upon the literary sensibility of Africa than all the valued labours of historians and archaeologists put together.[4]

This is praise indeed but it is by no means excessive or unjustified praise. We have the novels themselves to substantiate these claims. Nor does it seem from what we know of the author's stated intentions that Achebe is unaware of what he meant to achieve by his labours; he has stated unequivocally that he considers the restoration of African "dignity" and "self-respect" as his, as well as what ought to be every African writer's responsibility.[5] According to Achebe a more fundamental theme than the "politics of 1964" is that reclamation of the past which surely can only come to us through novels as social history:

> This theme put quite simply—is that African people did not hear of culture for the first time from Europeans; that their societies were not mindless but frequently had a philosophy of great depth and value and beauty, that they had poetry, and, above all, they had dignity. It is this dignity that many African people all but lost during the colonial period and it is this that they must now regain.[6]

From Achebe's point of view nothing can happen to a people which is worse than a loss of dignity and self-respect. Accordingly, part of a writer's duty in Africa is helping his people, former colonial subjects, to regain their lost dignity. And here we must note that the terms which Achebe is using put the emphasis firmly, if by implication, on the historical dimension; a novelist must explain "what happened" and must show his people "what they lost": but being a creative writer himself Achebe insists that a novelist must do this "by showing in human terms what happened to them," by which he means through a social reconstruction of the past in novels which deal with recognisable people in recognisable human situations.

In this Achebe has already blazed a trail large enough to be followed by other writers; due to his painstaking fidelity in the representation of Ibo life his writing achieves the exact precision of the documentary; and yet the narrative is always illuminated at strategic points by the writer's skill in the creation of character, by his success in so ordering his materials that a dramatic interplay between characters and situation is achieved which lifts even a so-called anthropological novel like *Things Fall Apart* way above the documentary humdrumness of everyday truth. After all, however, devoted to the past, a novelist is not merely an auditor of his people's past habits and traditions; he is also a creator of "fictions," a fabulist beguiling us with half-truths and saucy "inventions." He does more; he illuminates that inner life in his characters without which the novel is flat and without much interest.

Here we are doing no more than recognise certain features in Achebe's approach to the past, his skill and precision in the documentation of that traditional African past; of greater interest to us, however, should be his treatment of two interrelated themes of fundamental, if not decisive, historical importance for the African society. The two themes form a backdrop to the action of his two novels about traditional Ibo life, *Things Fall Apart* and *Arrow of God*. Indeed, it is when Achebe explores the inner dynamics of the Ibo society as it comes increasingly under the external pressures of the twin movements of European colonialism and christianisation that he involves us more directly in matters of historical considerations as well as of interpretation.

What Achebe offers us in the two novels is a briefly encapsulated version of the nature of colonialism in Africa, its strategies, its effects on traditional society, and, in the face of this near total physical as well as psychological annexation of the African, the reactions of the indigenous population. Although, with his customary discretion, Achebe confines himself to a small Ibo clan rather than generalise about the whole of Africa, it is clear that the picture he gives us here of both colonialism and Christianity at work is intended to act as a paradigm for the whole of Africa.

Notes

1. Thomas Babington Macaulay, *Critical and Historical Essays*. Dent, London, 1961, p. 1.
2. *Ibid*.
3. Gerald Moore, *The Chosen Tongue*. Longman, London, 1969, p. 151.
4. *Ibid*.
5. See "The Role of the Writer in a New Nation" by Chinua Achebe, included in *African Writers on African Writing*, ed. by G. D. Killam. Heinemann, London, 1973, p. 8.
6. Achebe, "The Role of the Writer."

Harlow, Essex: Longman, pp. 30, 32–34.

FROM JONATHAN COTT, "CHINUA ACHEBE AT THE
CROSSROADS: AN INTERVIEW WITH THE NIGERIAN WRITER"
(1981)

J. C. As a person who grew up with the values of village and who
now lives in a country that is rapidly being modernized, you seem
to be in the position of someone who has found himself standing
at the crossroads.

C. A. Those who live at the crossroads are very lucky, and it seems
to me that there will never be this kind of opportunity again. My
generation belongs to a group whose fathers . . . my father, for instance, although a converted Christian, was really a member of the
traditional society—he was already full-grown in the traditions of
Igbo life when he decided to become a Christian; so he knew all
about our culture. My children, however, belong to the world culture to which American children belong. They went to school in
America for several years and liked the same kind of music that
children in America and England enjoy. But I'm in between these
two. And we can talk about "transitions"—it's a cliché, since every
day's a transition—but I think that I'm much more a part of a transitional generation than any other. And this is very exciting. Of
course it carries its penalties, since you're in no-man's land, you're
like the bat in the folk tale—neither bird nor mammal—and one
can get lost, not being one or the other. This is what we are, we
can't do anything about it. But it does help if you have the kind of
temperament I have, which tries to recover something from our past.
So you have one foot in the past—my father's tradition—and also one
in the present—where you try to interpret the past for the present.

J. C. The sociologist Philip Slater has written about the difference
he sees between the "community" and the "network." By the former he means the people whom we live with, and by the latter he
is referring to the people we communicate with professionally
throughout our own particular country or even throughout the
world—just as you have a readership and attend conferences in
many different countries.

C. A. I think there's a certain strength in being able to have one foot
in the network and another foot in the community. But if one forgets
one's foot in the community—and that is quite possible—one can
get carried away into the network system. And this is a real problem
for us—for the African intellectual, the African writer. I've sometimes

complained about African writers who blindly follow Western fashions with regard to what an author should be writing, saying, or even looking like . . . what ideas he should be expressing, what attitudes he should be having towards his community, and so on—all taken from the West—while we forget about the other part of our nature which has its roots in the community. So I think we have the responsibility to be both in the community and in the network. This is a challenge—it's very exciting and also very perilous.

J. C. You yourself are at the crossroads on many levels—spiritual, political, intellectual—and you have chosen to write for both adults and children. It's as if you've decided to balance and integrate all of these levels and activities.

C. A. Yes, I do that consciously, I think this is the most important and fascinating thing about our life—the crossroad. This is where the spirits meet the humans, the water meets the land, the child meets the adult—these are the zones of power, and I think this is really where stories are created. The middle of the day is a very potent hour in our folklore—noon. This is the time when morning merges into afternoon, and that is the moment when spirits are abroad. When the adults go to the farm and leave the children at home, then the spirits can come into the village.

I've talked about the "crossroad hour" in one of my poems—this hour when the spirits appear—and it is this transitional period that manifests, I think, the great creative potential. It's an area of tension and conflict. So I deliberately go out of my way to cultivate the crossroad mythology, if you like, because I think it's full of power and possibility.

J. C. In *Things Fall Apart*, Okonkwo tells his son Nwoye "masculine" stories of violence and bloodshed, but the boy prefers the tales his mother tells him about Tortoise the trickster, about the bird who challenged the whole world to a wrestling contest and was finally thrown by a cat, and about the quarrel between Earth and Sky— stories for "foolish women and children," as Okonkwo thinks of them. But in *No Longer at Ease*, Nwoye—now the father of the protagonist Obi—forbids the telling of folk tales to his son because he has become a Christian and doesn't want to disseminate what he now thinks of as "heathen" stories. All of this reminds me of the constant attacks against fairy stories in Europe by Enlightenment spokesmen and by any number of rigid moralists and educators during the past few centuries.

C. A. I think that stories are the very center, the very heart of our civilization and culture. And to me it's interesting that the man who thinks he's strong wants to forbid stories, whether it's Okonkwo forbidding the stories of gentleness, or whether, later on, it's a Christian who, so self-satisfied in the rightness and superiority of his faith, would forbid the pagan stories. It is there in those despised areas that the strength of the civilization resides—not in the masculine strength of Okonkwo, not in the self-righteous strength of the Christian faith. The stone which the builders reject becomes a cornerstone of the house. So I think a writer instinctively gravitates towards that "weakness," if you like; he will leave the "masculine" military strength and go for love, for gentleness. Because unless we cultivate gentleness, we will be destroyed. And this is why you have poets and story-tellers, this is their function.

J. C. The psychologist James Hillman has talked of the importance of "restorying the adult."

C. A. This is what I've been trying to say when I talk about weakness and strength. You see, "restorying the adult" is a very interesting phrase because what, in fact, is the adult as distinct from the child? The adult is someone who has seen it all, nothing is new to him. Such a man is to be pitied. The child, on the other hand, is new in the world, and everything is possible to him. The imagination hasn't been dulled by use and experience. Therefore, when you restory the adult, what you do is you give him back some of that energy and optimism of the child, that ability to be open and to expect anything. The adult has become dull and routine, mechanical, he can't be lifted. It's as if he's weighted down by his experience and his possessions, all the junk he's assembled and accumulated. And the child can still fly, you see. Therefore the story belongs to the child because the story's about flying.

J. C. In your autobiographical essay "Named for Victoria," you've mentioned that, like Nwoye, you were told stories by your mother and older sister. So you were lucky enough to be "storied" at an early age.

C. A. I was very lucky, but I would say that that was traditional. Any child growing up at that time, unless he was particularly unlucky, would as part of his education be told stories. It doesn't happen anymore. The stories are now read in books, and very rarely is there a situation in which the mother will sit down night after night with her family and tell stories, with the young children falling asleep to them. The pace of life has altered. Again, this is what I meant by saying that our generation is unique. And I was lucky to have been part of the very tail-end of that older tradition. Perhaps we may not be able to revive it, but at least we can make sure that the kind of

stories that our children read carry something of the aura of the
tales our mothers and sisters told us.

J. C. In traditional oral stories, the storyteller would employ into-
nation, gestures, eye contact, pantomime, acrobatics, and occasionally costumes, masks, and props in his or her dramatic presentation.

C. A. Yes, that's right and the loss is enormous. And all I'm saying
is that, rather than lose everything, we should value the written
story, which is certainly better than no story at all. It's impossible
in the modern world to have the traditional storytelling. But I think
that perhaps in the home we should not give up so quickly. I find,
for instance, that when I write a new children's story the best thing
I can do is to tell it to my children, and I get remarkable feedback
that way. My youngest child, incidentally, writes stories of her own!
. . . But the storyteller today has to find a new medium rather than
regret the passing of the past. Television is there, we can't do anything about it, so some of us should use this medium, we should
do stories for television.

J. C. You've often stated that stories impart important messages to
us and that they are repositories of human experience and wisdom.
Your children's stories are, of course, excellent examples of this
notion.

C. A. I realize that this is an area where there is some kind of un-
easiness between us and the Western reader concerning just how
much of a "message" is suitable for a story. I'm not talking about
"preaching," which isn't the same thing as telling a story. But to
say that a good story is weakened because it conveys a moral point
of view is absurd because in my view all the great stories do convey
such a point of view. A tale may be fascinating, amusing—creating
laughter and delight and so forth—but at its base is a sustaining
morality, and I think this is very important.

Going back to the Igbo culture, the relationship between art and
morality is very close, and there's no embarrassment at all in linking
the two, as there would be in Western culture. The earth goddess
Ala—the most powerful deity of the Igbo pantheon—is also the
goddess of the arts and of morality. I would say that Ala is even
more powerful than the supreme god because of her closeness to
us; the earth is where our crops lie, where we live, and where we
die. And any very serious offense is called an abomination—the literal translation of "abomination" in Igbo is *nso ani (nso = taboo,
ani = earth)—that which the earth forbids*. That's what you say
for the worst kinds of crimes like murder and rape. But Ala is also,
as I said, the goddess of art.

My concern is that stories are not only retrieved and kept alive but also added to, just as they always were, and I think this is really what a living traditional storyteller would do. I loved the stories my mother and elder sister told me, but there were always little changes here and there. And this was part of the entertainment—you hear a tale a hundred times, but each day there was one additional little twist, which was expected.

There's that combination of stability and change. You mustn't change it so much that you don't recognize it—that would be unacceptable. The child wouldn't accept tinkering with the folk tale to the extent that it becomes something else. But little twists now and then . . . yes.

J. C. It's right but obvious that it is children—the seemingly least significant members of society—who are given stories about the most important matters—selfishness, pride, greed, the meaning of life and death.

C. A. That's right, and this is wonderful for children. I think the adult sometimes loses sight of the nature of stories. But these great fundamental issues have never changed and never will. I mean, children always ask the same questions: Who made the world? How come some people are suffering? Who made death? And to think that we have somehow moved on to more "adult" subject matters is simply self-deception. What we do, of course, is quite often get trapped in trivia . . . we get carried way. But the basic questions are still the same, and this is what children's stories particularly deal with.

I think that mankind's greatest blessing is language. And this is why the storyteller is a high priest and why he is so concerned about language and about using it with respect. Language is under great stress in the modern world, it's under siege. All kinds of people—advertisers, politicians, priests, technocrats—these are the strong people today, while the storyteller represents the weakness we were talking about. But of course every poet is aware of this problem. . . . And this is where children come into it, too, because you can't fool around with children—you have to be honest with language: cleverness won't do.

We lose belief at our cost. Lines from an Eskimo poem called "Magic Words": "That was the time when words were like magic. / The human mind had mysterious powers. / A word spoken by chance / might have strange consequences. / It would suddenly come alive / and what people wanted to happen could happen— / all you have to do was say it," take you right back to the beginning of things. "And God said: 'Let there be light' "—he didn't do anything, he just said it. And you can also look at the Aborigines in Australia who are somehow closer to the beginning than ourselves; you have the same feeling there that the word has power.

J. C. I wanted to ask you about your first children's book, *Chike and the River*. The name Chike has *chi* in it, and so does your first name, Chinua. About *chi*, you've written: "There are two clearly distinct meanings of the word *chi* in Igbo. The first is often translated as god, guardian angel, personal spirit, soul, spirit double, etc. The second meaning is day, or daylight, but is most commonly used for those transitional periods between day and night or night and day. . . . In a general way we may visualize a person's *chi* as his other identity in spiritland—his spirit being complementing his terrestrial human being; for nothing can stand alone, there must always be another thing standing beside it."

C. A. When we talk about *chi*, we're talking about the individual spirit, and so you find the word in all kinds of combinations. Chinwe, which is my wife's name, means "*Chi* owns me"; mine is Chinua, which is a shortened form of an expression that means "May a *chi* fight for me." Chike is a shortened form of Chinweike, which means "She has the strength or the power." And that's what that little character has—he has the power.

Parabola: Myth and the Quest for Meaning 6, no. 2 (May 1981): 33–37.

CONCLUSION

The local color that Achebe gave to the standard aspects of the novel in *Things Fall Apart* became a model for other Nigerian and African novelists who wrote about their own particular countries and ethnic groups. Collectively, these novelists became known as the Achebe school of writers. The tradition that began with the publication of *Things Fall Apart* explored new issues in African literature. The examination of them is the subject of the next chapter.

TOPICS FOR WRITTEN OR ORAL EXPLORATION

1. Compare two aspects of the European or American novels with those of *Things Fall Apart*.

2. In what respects is the African novel different from other English-language novels?

3. Why did Chinua Achebe find Joyce Cary's *Mister Johnson* and Joseph Conrad's *Heart of Darkness* appalling?

4. Compare Cary's depiction of Fada with Achebe's depiction of Umu-ofia.

5. Why was it necessary for Achebe to set *Things Fall Apart* in the historical past?

6. Why is Achebe more successful in creating realistic African characters in *Things Fall Apart* than Cary was in *Mister Johnson*?

7. What do you enjoy and what do you find difficult in the language of narration that Achebe employs in *Things Fall Apart*?

8. Could Achebe have been successful in delineating Igbo culture and civilization in *Things Fall Apart* without using proverbs and other Igbo sentential expressions?

9. What is the Achebe school of writers?

10. What is the Achebe tradition in African fiction?

11. What nationalistic, political, and/or literary purposes did *Things Fall Apart* achieve for Africans?

12. Identify and comment on a work in your own literature that achieved the same purposes for your people that *Things Fall Apart* did for Africans.

13. What is a social critic? Does what Achebe did in *Things Fall Apart* qualify him as one?

SUGGESTED READINGS

Achebe, Chinua. *Arrow of God*. New York: Anchor/Doubleday, 1989.

Ackley, Donald G. "The Past and the Present in Chinua Achebe's Novels." *Ife African Studies* 1, no. 1 (1974): 66–84.

Brown, Lloyd W. "Cultural Norms and Modes of Perception in Achebe's Fiction." In *Critical Perspectives on Nigerian Literatures*, ed. Bernth Lindfors. Washington, D.C.: Three Continents Press, 1976.

Brown, Raymond. "Aspects of *Things Fall Apart*." In *Mambo Review of*

Contemporary African Literature (Salisbury), November 1, 1974, 11–13.

Carroll, David. *Chinua Achebe*. New York: Twayne, 1970.

Cary, Joyce. *Mister Johnson*. (1st American Edn). New York: Harper, 1920.

Champion, Ernest A. "The Story of a Man and His People: Chinua Achebe's *Things Fall Apart*." *Negro American Literature Forum* 8 (1974): 272–77.

Conrad, Joseph. *Heart of Darkness*. London: Penguin, 1983.

Griffiths, Gareth. "Language and Action in the Novels of Chinua Achebe." *African Literature Today* 5 (1971): 88–105.

Obiechina, Emmanuel. "Structure and Significance in Achebe's *Things Fall Apart*." *English in Africa* 2, no. 2 (1975): 39–44.

Wren, Robert M. *Those Magical Years: The Making of Nigerian Literature at Ibadan, 1948–1966*. Washington, D.C: Three Continents, 1991.

8

Things Fall Apart and the Language Choice Debate

> In the final analysis, however, the main problem remains a linguistic one, that is, how a writer can render vernacular experience into English and still retain a valid and convincing degree of vernacular authenticity. It is futile to pretend that this problem does not exist for West African writers or to give the impression that it disappears once the West African writer has mastered English.
> —Emmanuel N. Obiechina, *Language and Theme: Essays on African Literature*

A writer is a conscious, skilled artist who engages in critical thinking and *doing*, which constitute a creative activity that remains intangible until given oral or textual expression in a known language, the chosen tongue of the writer. That is why language is the most important element of fiction. Like God, the creative writer uses language to create and control his fictive world, its people, and their destinies as well as events, and to convey a message to his audience. In fact, the quality of a fictional work often is judged by how successfully the author uses language to unify the elements of fiction and by whether or not the style makes readers to want to read it time and time again.

Before we get into the debate on whether African literature

should be written exclusively in indigenous languages or in European ones—the languages of the colonizers—it should be noted that writers, like other craftspeople, are free to choose whatever medium gives full expression to their crafts. That free choice of an expressive medium is, however, predicated upon many factors. Novelists must have mastered the language, learned the art of story-telling (orally and in writing), and understood their target audience, their thematic material, and the message they want to convey.

Also, it should be noted that being born into a particular language community does not mean that a writer is automatically competent in the use of an indigenous language. In other words, writers may understand their native language, but that does not guarantee that they can use it in formal discourse. Furthermore, the writing of a novel implies more than translating one's native thematic material into another language for a foreign audience. It requires a creative effort that, when effective, results in the production of an artifact that can be appreciated in any language, including the indigenous one.

In writing *Things Fall Apart*, Achebe needed a medium through which to communicate with those who misjudged Igbo culture, apparently because they did not understand the Igbo language. So he chose the English language, a medium as international as his audience. That selection of a suitable medium increased his readership, even within his native land, Nigeria. Thus Achebe could speak to the colonized and the colonizers as well as to the non-participants in the tragic encounter between Africa and Europe. As a responsible literary emissary, Achebe would have failed his Igbo and African ancestors had he delivered their message in the language of the oppressors—conventional British English—without manipulating it to accommodate Igbo thought-patterns, idioms, aphorisms, proverbs, metaphors, and the Igbo philosophy of life in general. His peculiar use of English as a novelistic medium required that he first learn "how to write with his right hand"—the art of Igbo conversation and the appropriation of their proverbs, which are "the palm-oil with which words are eaten," and then learn "how to write with his left hand"—the art of writing fiction, which is a part of his colonial heritage. The two forms of creative writing education constitute the double heritage that he used to advantage. He underscores the importance of acquiring both skills, recommending them to any African writer using the English language as a chosen tongue:

> For an African, writing in English is not without its serious setbacks. He often finds himself describing situations or modes of thought which have no direct equivalent in the English way of life. Caught in that situation he can do one of two things. He can try and contain what he wants to say within the limits of conventional English or he can try to push back those limits to accommodate his ideas. The first method produces competent, uninspired and rather flat work. The second method can produce something new and valuable to the English language as well as to the new material he is trying to put over. But it can also get out of hand. It can lead to bad English being accepted and defended as African or Nigerian. I submit that those who can do the work of extending the frontiers of English so as to accommodate African thought-patterns must do it through their mastery of English and not out of innocence. (Achebe 160)

Indeed, the language of *Things Fall Apart* attests to Achebe's mastery of English and to the ingenious exploitation of it to address issues of great concern to him and to his people.

Achebe's successful language experiment, so to speak, in *Things Fall Apart* and *Arrow of God* opened a new thoroughfare where hitherto there was a wilderness for subsequent Igbo authors such as Onuora Nzekwu, John Munonye, and Elechi Amadi, who appear to have been influenced by "Achebe's sensitive sociological approach to the novel, with all its vision of history" (Emenyonu 164–85). They too became good writers, but their style and use of English did not rise to the standard that one finds in *Things Fall Apart*. Soon lesser African novelists began imitating the Achebe tradition of fiction, but in a way that led to their "bad English being accepted and defended as African or Nigerian" (Achebe 160). The situation gave great concern to African writers, critics, and researchers—a concern that triggered a debate on whether Africans were better off writing literature in indigenous languages or in European languages such as English, French, and Portuguese.

Following the publication of *Things Fall Apart* and *No Longer at Ease*, the question of language choice was so intense that African writers who wrote in English held a conference to deliberate the issue at Makerere College in Kampala in June 1962. At the end of their deliberations, the writers made a statement, which reads in part: "It was generally agreed that it is better for an African writer to think and feel in his own language and then look for English transliteration approximating the original." Many African scholars and critics were very sympathetic to that statement, because it was the way many of them learned to write, following the Western education they received. Yet a few critics disagreed. For example, Obiajunwa Wali dismissed the conference's recommendation as "naïve and misguided" in his article "The Dead End of African Literature." As more and more African writers published their works in foreign languages despite the decolonization movements from 1957 through the 1970s, writers and critics expressed their divergent opinions on language choice ever more vehemently.

Ngugi wa Thiong'o, a renowned East African writer, states: "The African writer who emerged after the Second World War has gone through three decisive decades which also mark three modal stages in his growth. He has gone, as it were, through three ages within only the last thirty years or so: the age of the anticolonial struggle; the age of independence; and the age of neocolonialism" (*Writing Against Colonialism* 1). Achebe's *Things Fall Apart* was published during the age of anticolonial struggle against the British; so were *Arrow of God* and *No Longer at Ease*. That is why he expressed his literary anticolonial struggle in English, the language the colonizers of his country understood. When Nigeria became an independent country and later a republic, the struggle was turned against neocolonialism in *A Man of the People*; and so Achebe chose to write in Pidgin or broken English, the language of less educated politicians and their electorates. Finally, when Nigeria and other West African countries came under military regimes, the struggle became revolutionary in *Anthills of the Savannah*. Again Achebe adjusted the form of his expressive medium; he used a brand of English that was capable of carrying the weight of the ideological tenets of his literary revolutionary struggles, which the African intelligentsia could easily appreciate.

In every case, Achebe was able to "do the work of extending the frontiers of English so as to accommodate African thought-patterns . . . through . . . mastery of English and not out of innocence." Had he chosen to write in his native Igbo, he may have had some success, but his audience and readership would have been limited even within his native Nigeria, which has about 400 ethnic languages. In a word, Achebe's choice of English as the language of expression in *Things Fall Apart* and in his other novels made them easy for literate Nigerians to read and perhaps to appreciate their messages; after all, English is Nigeria's national, administrative, legal, and (along with the vernaculars) literary language. That makes every literate Nigerian bilingual.

Commenting on the choice of English as a language in which to write African literature, Achebe said in 1964: "Is it right that a man should abandon his mother tongue for someone else's? It looks like a dreadful betrayal and produces a guilty feeling. But for me there is no other choice. I have been given the language and I intend to use it" (quoted in Ngugi, *Decolonising the Mind* 7). To that Ngugi says: "See the paradox: the possibility of using mother-tongue provokes a tone of levity in phrases like 'a dreadful betrayal' and 'a guilty feeling'; but that of foreign languages produces a categorical positive embrace, what Achebe himself, ten years later, was to describe as this 'fatalistic logic of the unassailable position of English in our literature' "(7).

Even though the position Achebe took in 1964 regarding language choice did not then (and does not now) sit well with many patriotic Nigerians and some pan-Africanists, it accurately expresses the dilemma of all Western-educated Africans and the paradox of their education. For educated Africans acquire Western languages, culture, and civilization at variance with their own. This not only creates conflicts in them but also makes them constantly aware of the centuries of denigration and dehumanization of Africans by Europeans. That is why they want to correct the mistaken ideas Europeans have spread about Africa. However, they can only do so effectively in a language that Europeans can understand. The process also helps educated Africans themselves to learn about the various cultures and civilizations of continental Africa recorded and portrayed in European languages acquired by the African writers and critics as part of their colonial heritage. In other words, although European languages constantly remind Africans of the sting and scourge of colonialism—especially slave trade and slave raid— they have helped the countries adopting them as *lingua francas* to forge national and regional unity. For example, Nigeria, a country of over 100 million people, comprised of about 400 ethnic groups with individual languages, is able to conduct its affairs nationally in English, the language of its creator and colonizer.

Unfortunately, despite their utilitarian value and their usefulness in unifying Africa, European languages have continued to be regarded by Africans, even the writers who use them, as tools of oppression wielded by the ex-colonizers. Therefore, their continued use in the literature of independent Africa is considered tantamount to linguistic dependency. Opposition to their use peaked between the 1970s and 1980s when many writers and critics, chief among them Ngugi wa Thiong'o, embraced Marxism as a sociopolitical and literary ideology.

In *Decolonising the Mind: The Politics of Language in African Literature*, Ngugi asserts:

> The oppressed and the exploited of the earth maintain their defiance: liberty from theft. But the biggest weapon wielded and actually daily unleashed by imperialism against that collective defiance is the cultural bomb. The effect of a cultural bomb is to annihilate a people's belief in their names, in their languages, in their environment, in their heritage of struggle, in their unity, in their capacities and ultimately in themselves. It makes them see their past as one wasteland of non-achievement and it makes them want to distance themselves from that wasteland. It makes them want to identify with that which is furthest removed from themselves; for instance, with other peoples' languages rather than their own. (3)

In agreement with this assertion, many African writers and critics have called for the adoption of Swahili, a language spoken daily in East Africa, as a continental language in which to express African literature and its continuing resistance to Western colonial traditions.

In his *Art, Dialogue and Outrage* (1988), "Meeting Point (Interview)" in *The Courier* (January/February 1987), and "We Africans Must Speak With One Tongue" in *Afrika* 20 (1979), Nobel laureate Wole Soyinka made the case for a continental language, favoring Swahili. His supporters include such writers and scholars as Ayi Kwei Armah, Jan Knapperts, and David Westley. But other writers oppose the adoption of a continental African language because of the problems it would create in the development of African literature and its potential audience. They include B. Hofer, R. Heyman, Ali Mazrui, Lewis Nkosi, and John Reed, all of whom make a case for the continued use of European languages, especially English, along lines similar to Achebe's argument, briefly touched upon early in this chapter. David Westley's *Choice of Language and African Literature: A Bibliographic Essay* is a good source to consult for the opinions of those on both sides of the issue.

In the final analysis, most African writers, critics, and scholars prefer simultaneous development and expression of their continental literature in both European and ethnic languages. In fact, this is what Ngugi has been doing beautifully in his writing career. His works are written both in English and Gikuyu (his native language), and Heinemann publishes many of his works in Gikuyu while simultaneously translating them into English. Chinua Achebe writes mostly in English, but he has also edited *Uwa Ndigbo*, a journal of the Igbo world and culture. Since educated Africans are bilingual, they already have the opportunity to write in both indigenous and foreign languages. But as Achebe has taught African writers, those who prefer English must strive to extend its frontiers to accommodate African thought-patterns. The same goes for Swahili, Igbo, Yoruba, Hausa, and other African languages.

FRAMING THE ARGUMENTS IN THE LANGUAGE CHOICE DEBATE

The following excerpts, one by Ngugi wa Thiong'o and one by Emmanuel N. Obiechina, frame the general argument of the language choice debate. Ngugi makes a radical demand for African writers to express their writings in indigenous African languages instead of English, insisting that his own early choice of the latter was based on European cultural imposition. Ironically, however, without adequate training in English he could not have received his high school education in Nairobi, Kenya, and his college education in Makerere and Leeds, respectively, because none of the institutions he attended there offered instruction in his native Gikuyu language.

Obiechina, a renowned Nigerian (Igbo) scholar and literary critic, concerns himself with writers maintaining the balance between African literary aesthetics and European ones. For that reason his literary studies stress the importance of mastering the English language as well as ethnic vernacular verbal arts, which, expertly married, can enable a writer to produce a good hybrid novel like *Things Fall Apart*, which evidences Achebe's mastery of the English language as well as Igbo story-telling techniques.

FROM NGUGI WA THIONG'O, *DECOLONISING THE MIND: THE POLITICS OF LANGUAGE IN AFRICAN LITERATURE* (1986)

The Language of African Literature

I started writing in Gikuyu language in 1977 after seventeen years of involvement in Afro-European literature, in my case Afro-English literature. It was then that I collaborated with Ngugi wa Mirii in the drafting of the playscript, *Ngaahika Ndeenda* (the English translation was *I Will Marry When I Want*). I have since published a novel in Gikuyu, *Caitaani Mutharabaini* (English translation: *Devil on the Cross*) and completed a musical drama, *Maitu Njugira*, (English translation: *Mother Sing for Me*); three books for children, *Njamba Nene na Mbaathi i Mathagu, Bathitoora ya Njamba Nene, Njamba Nene na Cibu King'ang'i*, as well as another novel manuscript: *Matigari Ma Njiruungi*. Wherever I have gone, particularly in Europe, I have been confronted with the question: why are you now writing in Gikuyu? Why do you now write in an African language? In some academic quarters I have been confronted with the rebuke, "Why have you abandoned us?" It was almost as if, in choosing to write in Gikuyu, I was doing something abnormal. But Gikuyu is my mother tongue! The very fact that what common sense dictates in the literary practice of other cultures is being questioned in an African writer is a measure of how far imperialism has distorted the view of African realities. It has turned reality upside down: the abnormal is viewed as normal and the normal is viewed as abnormal. Africa actually enriches Europe: but Africa is made to believe that it needs Europe to rescue it from poverty. Africa's natural and human resources continue to develop Europe and America: but Africa is made to feel grateful for aid from the same quarters that still sit on the back of the continent. Africa even produces intellectuals who now rationalise this upside-down way of looking at Africa.

I believe that my writing in Gikuyu language, a Kenyan language, an African language, is part and parcel of the anti-imperialist struggles of Kenyan and African peoples. In schools and universities our Kenyan languages—that is the languages of the many nationalities which make up Kenya—were associated with negative qualities of backwardness, under-development, humiliation and punishment. We who went through that school system were meant to graduate with a hatred of the people and the culture and the values of the language of our daily humiliation and punishment. I do not want Kenyan children growing up in that imperialist-imposed tradition of contempt for the tools of communication developed by their communities and their history. I want them to transcend colonial alienation.

Colonial alienation takes two interlinked forms: an active (or passive) distancing of oneself from the reality around; and an active (or passive) identification with that which is most external to one's environment. It starts with a deliberate disassociation of the language of conceptualisation, of thinking, of formal education, of mental development, from the language of daily interaction in the home and in the community. It is like separating the mind from the body so that they are occupying two unrelated linguistic spheres in the same person. On a larger social scale it is like producing a society of bodiless heads and headless bodies.

So I would like to contribute towards the restoration of the harmony between all the aspects and divisions of language so as to restore the Kenyan child to his environment, understand it fully so as to be in a position to change it for his collective good. I would like to see Kenya peoples' mother-tongues (our national languages!) carry a literature reflecting not only the rhythms of a child's spoken expression, but also his struggle with nature and his social nature. With that harmony between himself, his language and his environment as his starting point, he can learn other languages and even enjoy the positive humanistic, democratic and revolutionary elements in other people's literatures and cultures without any complexes about his own language, his own self, his environment. The all-Kenya national language (i.e., Kiswahili); the other national languages (i.e. the languages of the nationalities like Luo, Gikuyu, Maasai, Luhya, Kallenjin, Kamba, Mijikenda, Somali, Galla, Turkana, Arabic-speaking people, etc.); other African languages like Hausa, Wolof, Yoruba, Ibo, Zulu, Nyanja, Lingala, Kimbundu; and foreign languages— that is foreign to Africa—like English, French, German, Russian, Chinese, Japanese, Portuguese, Spanish will fall into their proper perspective in the lives of Kenyan children.

Chinua Achebe once decried the tendency of African intellectuals to escape into abstract universalism in words that apply even more to the issue of the language of African literature:

> Africa has had such a fate in the world that the very adjective *African* can call up hideous fears of rejection. Better then to cut all the links with this homeland, this liability, and become in one giant leap the universal man. Indeed I understand this anxiety. *But running away from oneself seems to me a very inadequate way of dealing with an anxiety* [emphasis added]. And if writers should opt for such escapism, who is to meet the challenge?[1]

Who indeed?

We African writers are bound by our calling to do for our languages what Spenser, Milton and Shakespeare did for English; what Pushkin and Tolstoy did for Russian; indeed what all writers in world history have done for their languages by meeting the challenge of creating a literature in them, which process later opens the languages for philosophy, science, technology and all the other areas of human creative endeavours.

But writing in our languages per se—although a necessary first step in the correct direction—will not itself bring about the renaissance in African cultures if that literature does not carry the content of our people's anti-imperialist struggles to liberate their productive forces from foreign control; the content of the need for unity among the workers and peasants of all the nationalities in their struggle to control the wealth they produce and to free it from internal and external parasites.

In other words writers in African languages should reconnect themselves to the revolutionary traditions of an organised peasantry and working class in Africa in their struggle to defeat imperialism and create a higher system of democracy and socialism in alliance with all the other peoples of the world. Unity in that struggle would ensure unity in our multi-lingual diversity. It would also reveal the real links that bind the people of Africa to the peoples of Asia, South America, Europe, Australia and New Zealand, Canada and the U.S.A.

But it is precisely when writers open out African languages to the real links in the struggles of peasants and workers that they will meet their biggest challenge. For to the comprador-ruling regimes, their real enemy is an awakened peasantry and working class. A writer who tries to communicate the message of revolutionary unity and hope in the languages of the people becomes a subversive character. It is then that writing in African languages becomes a subversive or treasonable offence with such a writer facing possibilities of prison, exile or even death. For him there are no "national" accolades, no new year honours, only abuse and slander and innumerable lies from the mouths of the armed power of a ruling minority—ruling, that is, on behalf of U.S.-led imperialism—and who see in democracy a real threat. A democratic participation of the people in the shaping of their own lives or in discussing their own lives in languages that allow for mutual comprehension is seen as being dangerous to the good governments of a country and its institutions. African languages addressing themselves to the lives of the people become the enemy of a neo-colonial state.

Note

1. Chinua Achebe, "Africa and her Writers" in *Morning Yet on Creation Day*, p. 27.

London: Heinemann, pp. 27–30

FROM EMMANUEL N. OBIECHINA, *LANGUAGE AND THEME: ESSAYS ON AFRICAN LITERATURE* (1990)

Language and the African Novel

Writing in English presents the West African writer with a problem the English writer does not have. Stated simply, it is how to express the African experience in a language that was originally evolved to embody a different kind of experience and to convey a different kind of sensibility? How can the novelist render his characters' words, feelings, and attitudes in English and still retain their idiomatic quality and authenticity?

This, in a way, is the problem of all translations; but, for the West African writer, the problem is more immediate and acute than in ordinary cases of translation. To the West African living in one of the ex-British colonies, English is the national, administrative, legal, and (along with the vernaculars), literary language. The writer using the English language is therefore bilingual and expected to be "at home" both in English and in his own language.

Whereas the literary reputation of European novelists translated into English has been made in the language in which they originally wrote, West African novelists, by an ironic twist of history, have to make their literary reputation in a language that traces its development as a literary language to King Alfred and his Anglo-Saxons in the sixth century A.D. In other words, if an English translation of *Crime and Punishment*, or *Mastro-don Gesualdo* fails to convey the idiom of the Russian or Italian original, or the setting, experience, and inner atmosphere and vision the writer intended to convey, there is some consolation that the original is still there, to be translated at any future time by someone more competent. With West Africans writing in English, the process of translation is part and parcel of the process of creation and determines summarily whether the completed book is a success or a failure.

The problem for the West African writer is that bilingualism in Africa, that is, the situation in which people speak one of the European "colonial" languages with as much ease and fluency as they speak their native tongues, is a phenomenon associated with a small (if continually growing) minority. In spite of the strides made in education since the early fifties, less than one-quarter of the population of any of the West African countries in the sixties and perhaps the seventies, is truly bilingual in English and the vernaculars. This means that a large section of the West African population still thinks, feels, and reacts in the vernaculars and is more deeply affected by the oral tradition than by the introduced literary tradition. The writers, because of their peculiar privilege of belonging to "both worlds," are in a position to use their literary gifts and to exploit the advantages of their bilingual knowledge to make available to the world at large the culture, traditions, and heritage of their people. Their knowledge of a "world" language, coupled with their background of African life, qualifies them to interpret this life through fiction. It is a fact that West African writers using the English language are conveying the West African experience that has distinguished West African literature from English literature proper.

There is common ground in the writings of West Africans and their English counterparts in the same genre, since West African writers base their writing on Western models; but there are also significant differences that derive from differences in culture, experience, language, outlook, and so on. Thus, because the social and cultural background of the West African novel and the major impulses that bring it about differ from those of the English novel, we notice obvious differences between them.

English writers convey their English experience in a language that has evolved specifically to bear the full weight of this experience. Their stylistic efforts do not demand fundamental changes in the pattern of their language to fit it into a new structure of thought, feeling, and expression. The West African writer has to recast his material in a fundamental way if his West African experience is to remain West African, while at the same time making sure that the English in which it is expressed remains intelligible to users of the English language all over the world. This problem has been identified by Ngugi wa Thiong'o in respect of all African writers using English. Contrasting their position with that of native English writers and even West Indian writers in English, he observes:

> The African writer in fact, has got his added problem . . . [that] . . . whereas people like George Lamming or an English writer can get narrative value from "slang" from twisting of language from his community, we have got to get the slang and the twists of language in a different language and then try to put that into English. . . . not many Africans speak English . . . and even those who speak it don't use it as their normal language. It is not what they use every day, at breakfast, lunch, when they make jokes and so you're getting nourishment, linguistic nourishment in a different medium and then trying to use the English medium to create.[1]

Indeed, the comparison between West African writers in English, and American and West Indian writers is quite instructive. People have often, erroneously it would appear, compared West African writing in English or French with American, Caribbean, and Latin American writing; for, in each of these cases, the writers are using the language of a former colonial master for literary purposes. Leaving aside the Indians in the Americas and the Caribbean Islands and the West Indies, neither the American nor the Latin American writer, nor even the West Indian is bilingual or multilingual. The American has his American English, the Brazilian has Portuguese, the Chilean or Cuban has Spanish, and the Jamaican or Martiniquan has his own local variations of English or French. In West Africa, we have vernaculars spoken by large sections of the populations of individual nation-states. In Nigeria alone, six major language groups—Hausa, Yoruba, Igbo, Kanuri, Fulani, and Efik-Ibibio—account for 85 percent of the population, but more than fifty other language groups account for the remaining 15 percent. Of the whole Nigerian population of around one hundred million people, not more than 25 percent speak English at all. To the preponderant majority of West Africans, the vernaculars are the first language and English (French, Portuguese, and other metropolitan languages) a mere second. West Africa is in the same position, as far as language is concerned, as India, Pakistan, Ceylon, and Burma, which are multilingual, combining a number of vernaculars with one or more metropolitan European languages that function as "link" languages.

For the West African writer, the problem of translation from the vernacular into English is a crucial matter. In an article, "Problems of Linguistic Inequivalence in Communication," L. F. Brosnahan throws light on some of the main differences between English and West African languages, like Yoruba and Bini, and emphasizes the kinds of problems involved in translation from the vernaculars into English.[2] For the professional translator, these problems probably have more obvious as well as specialized answers worked out for them. For example, Malinowski, speaking from the point of view of a trained ethnographer, puts forward this broad blueprint for translators:

> The object of a scientific translation of a word is not to give its rough equivalent, sufficient for practical purposes, but to state exactly whether a native word corresponds to an idea at least partially existing for English speakers, or whether it covers an entirely foreign conception. That such foreign conceptions do exist for native languages and in a great number, is clear. All words which describe the native social order, all expressions, referring to native beliefs, to specific customs, ceremonies, magic rites—all such words are obviously absent from English as from any European language. Such words can only be translated into English, not by giving their imaginary equivalent—a real one obviously cannot be found—but by explaining the meaning of each of them through an exact ethnographic account of the sociology, culture and tradition of that native community.[3]

Such a blueprint is of little practical use to the creative writer, even if it may prove valuable to the ethnographer or professional translator. The creative writer's medium requires a greater subtlety of procedure than that suggested here. Indeed, experience has shown that where the writer has adopted the ethnographic approach suggested by Malinowski, as Nzekwu has done in his novels, the result has proved less than happy. The social scientist's interest in surface factuality could easily become a crippling weakness in the creative writer who, in addition to being expected to be faithful to surface truths about society and people, is also under the pressures of art and form. These demands on the creative writer's loyalties ought not to clash, but sometimes they do, as in this matter of fidelity to sociological fact and the exigencies of art. The similar conflict confronting the Marxist writer, between the maintaining of the Marxist ideological line and artistic integrity, has been defined by Mao Tse-tung in his famous "Talks at the Yenan Forum on Art and Literature":

What we demand is unity of politics and art, of content and form, and of the revolutionary political content and the highest possible degree of perfection in artistic form. Works of art, however politically progressive, are powerless if they lack artistic quality. Therefore we are equally opposed to works with wrong political approaches and to the tendency towards so-called "poster and slogan style" which is correct only in political approach but lacks artistic power.[4]

The advice is pertinent to the West African writer in his need to render cultural effects, ideas, thoughts, feelings, and sensibilities from the vernacular culture into English, but the other oversimplified suggestion that the artist maintain his artistic integrity at the expense of social realism has also to be rejected because the African writer's artistic purpose in this context includes the ability to transfer sets of realities from the vernacular into the operative linguistic medium, which in this case is English.

Translation itself is an art. We talk of the art of translation, which determines the ends as well as the means for reaching them. Certain clearly discernible techniques dictated by an intuitive, and imaginative grouping are adopted in translation in order to attain ends that include transference of "meaning" from one autonomous language to another. What confers the quality of art on the operation is not the ordinary mechanical aspect of the activity but the bringing to bear on it of the powers of the imagination. Calling the imagination into play is necessary because the definition of "meaning" in translation transcends the direct, symbol-referent structure and includes structures of feeling and association. The good translator not only achieves literal transference of meaning, but evokes equivalent feelings and associations. There is another reason why the matter of fidelity to social and cultural fact in transferring meaning from the vernacular into English is critical for the African writer. One of the major impulses in African writing is the desire to portray African life and experience realistically in order to refute formally the centuries of slander and misrepresentation by European and American commentators. Writers are directly or indirectly influenced by this consideration when they represent African traditional life in literature. Therefore, the least that will be expected of them by their African audience is truth to cultural life. Earlier, when many of them wrote with a largely European and foreign audience in mind, the need to justify the African way of life was a strong pressure for a projection of traditional realities, but even now that a home audience has come more and more to be assumed, the need to represent faithfully realities of which vast numbers of people have intimate knowledge remains very strong, to obviate a writer's being accused of misrepresenting these realities. This is not just a hypothetical fear: books can be given a hostile reception by readers and reviewers, as was

Aluko's *One Man One Wife*, which was condemned for distorting traditional life.

Notes

1. Dennis Duerden and Cosmo Pieters, eds., *African Writers Talking: A Collection of Interviews* (London, 1972), 130–31.

2. *Ibadan* 13 (November 1961).

3. C. K. Ogden and I. A. Richards, *The Meaning of Meaning* (London, 1923), 299–300.

4. Anne Fremantle, ed., *Mao Tse-Tung: An Anthology of His Writings* (London, 1971), 259.

Washington, D.C.: Howard University Press, pp. 53–57.

ARGUMENTS FOR AND AGAINST
CONTINUED USE OF EUROPEAN LANGUAGES

The following excerpts, one by Lewis Nkosi, and the other by David Westley, make arguments for and against the continued use of European languages by African writers to express modern African literature. Both Nkosi and Westley adopt a historical approach in making their cases.

Nkosi urges African writers and critics to acknowledge the language crisis in modern African literature, and he traces its origin to the politics of anticolonial struggle, which required that the writers' messages be expressed in European languages that the colonizers understood. The process created a dialogue between an educated African elite and European colonial masters who excluded the ordinary peoples of Africa, the masses, from participation in literature and politics. As a result, 80 percent of the peoples of Africa became lost as a potential audience of their literature. The situation remained the same even after independence, and that is why Nkosi does not support the continued use of European languages in the expression of modern African literature. Nevertheless, he concedes that some partial answers to the language problem have already been suggested by writers, chief among them Achebe and Tutuola.

Westley asserts that because Europeans introduced literature as a means of promoting literacy in African schools, the influence of European traditions on African literary genres is undeniable. He buttresses his point by explaining how the European literary influence helped Africans, especially Nigerians, to become great writers who produced great literature, and to form literary clubs for the promotion of continental and national literatures of Africa. Furthermore, modern African literature written in European languages is now studied in American and European universities. If written in non-European languages, its study in such venues would have been unthinkable without the prerequisites of African ethnic language studies and oral literature. Overall, Westley recommends the continued development of African literature in English and French simultaneously with that written in indigenous African languages.

FROM LEWIS NKOSI, *TASKS AND MASKS: THEMES AND STYLES OF AFRICAN LITERATURE* (1981)

The Language Crisis

African literature as a university discipline, as a subject of numerous textual exegeses, or simply as an object of serious critical comment, has only come into its own during the last twenty years or so. Though some writing by Africans, chiefly memoirs of ex-slaves, dates as far back as the eighteenth century, and though there is some evidence of literary production by African "exiles" in Renaissance Europe,[1] modern African literature as such can be said to have achieved its present status concomitantly with the maturation of the long struggle for political independence and the achievement of the modern state in Africa.

The point needs emphasising because modern African writing has its origins in the politics of anti-colonial struggle and still bears the marks of that struggle. That observation alone yields another more astounding recollection, that in asserting their right to self-determination Africans had to employ the languages of their colonial masters; that the rhetoric of political demands they adopted was better understood in Europe among both rulers and the common people, than among the African masses for whom, presumably, the demands were being made.

That fact alone has been responsible for a considerable weakness in the political institutions of African societies and finally suggests the limits to the kind of support African leaders can reasonably expect from ordinary people who, after all, were largely excluded from the dialogue between the *evolués* [Westernized Africans] and their masters. In literature, at least, that historical development has planted the seeds of the present crisis.

Let me state at once that to speak of a crisis in this connection is not to be unduly alarmist. It is now an open secret that much of African literature written in the European languages—by far the most influential from the perspective of developing national consciousness—has been, and continues to be, created in a barely concealed state of profound anxiety, even panic. The anxiety stems in large measure from an uncomfortable feeling that this literature, however deeply conscious of its responsibilities, somehow lacks relevance for 80 per cent of the African people who enjoy no literacy. Quite conceivably, the majority of those who can read could easily handle vernacular literature but cannot be expected to deal with the complex forms of modern fiction and contemporary verse, written in the European languages.

Already, one can anticipate an immediate objection to this line of argument. A retort could be made, and quite rightly, that even in European societies people who read serious books form a depressingly small minority; that the majority, for lack of intellectual training or through choice, confine themselves to the world of the newspaper, radio and television. What ordinary people in Europe, however, share with their educated elite is a common tongue, which does mean that a great deal of information, usually a whole set of assumptions which form the common currency of the educated classes, do filter down, in whatever debased form, to the ordinary man in the street. Listen to working people talk in any European city, listen to individuals who have never struggled through the psychoanalytical theories of Freud: you will be amazed to hear how so-and-so is "fixated" on one or other of the parents, or how this or that person is supposed to have made a "Freudian slip." Language then becomes a living organism, forever changing to accommodate concepts and ideas which, in time, become the common heritage of all those who grow up speaking the same language, whatever their class or educational background.

In Africa, quite the contrary is true. The masses are effectively sealed off from the educated elite who, through training and the constant use of an official language in creative and intellectual discourse, constitute an objectification on African soil of another culture and its values. "The effect of the colonial presence (in Africa)," writes the Kenyan novelist, Ngugi wa Thiong'o, "was to create an elite who took on the tongue and adopted the style of the conquerors."[2] This presents the writer with something of a dilemma. If in trying to rehabilitate their smashed-up cultures African writers are forced to write in foreign languages their task must obviously remain incomplete: for it is one of the bitterest ironies that even when an assault had to be made on those opposing values which the masters used to control their colonial subjects, values which constituted the very underpinning of the colonial system, that war had to be waged by Africans in the same languages that were used to enslave them: in French, English and Portuguese, as such, if not in mental attitude, at least in the tool of its production, the best of African literature reflects a former colonial dependency. Similarly, even at its most complex and formally competent level, this literature presents to us the aspect of a cultural hybrid in which African and European concerns are inextricably mixed through the twine and woof of a common language.

• • •

The feelings of dislocation that reading certain African novels induces finally leads one to question the very *appropriateness* of the novel in recapturing the true feel of traditional African society; the anxiety is caused by the knowledge that inherent in the novelistic form itself, as it has come to us from the European tradition, is a view of life that is essentially hostile to African traditional society. Consequently, when we read a novel about African traditional society we are looking, as it were, through a mirror which continually refracts African experience according to its own optical "illusions"—if not actual delusions. The prisms of that mirror impose their own shape on the reality they try to view; the judgements on African values are therefore already inherent or built-in in the form itself.

For instance, the novel—the traditional novel at any rate—proposes the "individual" as its centre. To be truly dynamic, to have progression, the novel further proposes as one of its essential mechanisms "conflict" between "individuals" or between an individual and a group, between the individual and his environment. Its main characteristic is the exploration of individual character and as such it is an art form that best serves bourgeois society or manifestations of incipient bourgeois society. The novel, it has often seemed to me, must distort the African past and tradition in order to contain it within its framework. At this stage no one needs to be told that certain notions inherent in bourgeois society, in particular the greater regard for individual rights over those of the community as a whole, would have been considered a perversion and an evil in a traditional African society; also that competition between individuals was regarded with a great deal of unease as a basis for considerable disharmony in African traditional society. Naturally, the art forms that any society develops are intimately related to the kind of social structures which it has built up. Thus the kind of art which was prized above all others in the Old Africa was the one which promoted *harmonisation* of the potential areas of conflict within the community by psychological projection or the externalisation of opposing forces of good and evil through ritual and communal forms of art. The novel, much more than drama, represents therefore a radical departure from natural art forms.

So far as I know, only one critic of African literature has recognised the anomalous character of the novel in the face of a social system such as I have been elaborating. In *Transition*, Number 18, the Nigerian critic, Obi Wali, wrote:

In a real sense, the chief obstruction to the three characters [discussed in his essay] is the community, with its tyranny and incomprehensibility, the community where the individual does not exist in his own right but is compelled to lose his identity for the sake of social cohesion. In a certain technical sense then, we say that the character in traditional African society does not exist, yet the African novelist in order to make his craft possible is forced to hammer out characters from this social block which is amorphous in many ways.

All this may lead the reader to suspect that the situation of the African writer using English or French is necessarily a hopeless one. The reader may further suppose that given the complexity of his linguistic situation this kind of African writer has insurmountable obstacles placed in the way toward full expression, and that therefore he could only falsify African experience or at best create something that falls short of the genuine article. In a way, any writer always falls short of his true ideal: his struggle with his materials, the attempt to wrestle from language the true meaning of the world he seeks to depict, is always endless and incomplete. Incomplete, because in describing the true lineaments of what the writer sees with his inner eye language can only approximate the shapes and figures of his imagination. In this respect, therefore, the situation of the African writer is not unique. It is the same struggle with language. But clearly what the African writer lacks in this enterprise is the silent *complicity* of his people, the majority of whom still use African languages to express their most intimate thoughts and emotions; in writing in a European language the African writer is alone, operating outside the boundaries of either his own society or that of his adopted language, therefore always on the outside, looking, increasingly in need of some more specific corroboration of his vision through language that can be consented to, or the authenticity of which can be attested to, by his people. The fact that the people about whom he makes up these stories cannot corroborate the truth of what he is saying is finally what makes his situation intolerable. Certainly, it is an ambiguous one; it may even be said to be critical: at the same time it imposes upon the truly creative writer the kind of discipline which is quite beneficial: his search for form, his straining for the sort of distillation of language which will accurately reflect the movement of African society, will be even more relentless, just because in some hopelessly tragic way it cannot be truly fulfilled: and this search can only be steadily reinforced by good criticism and the writer's own sense of what is fitting.

Technically, some partial answers to the problem of language have already been suggested by several writers, two of whom are quite outstanding in their own ways. The two writers I have in mind are Chinua Achebe and Amos Tutuola, both Nigerians, each of whom starts from the opposite end of the scale: Chinua Achebe, because his sense of responsibility to African material has led him to put his Western training and reading of English fiction at the service of a rigorously selective intelligence which is forever trying to widen the possibilities of what the structure of the English language can support of the African experience; Tutuola, because his lack of self-conscious sophistication and training has permitted him to take the kind of liberties with the English language which no sophisticated African writer could have allowed himself.

Notes

1. Janheinz Jahn, *A History of Neo-African Literature*, Faber, 1968, p. 30–1.
2. Ngugi wa Thiong'o, *Homecoming*, London, Heinemann, 1972, p. 10.

Harlow, Essex: Longmans, pp. 1–6.

FROM DAVID WESTLEY, *CHOICE OF LANGUAGE AND AFRICAN LITERATURE: A BIBLIOGRAPHIC ESSAY* (1990)

The influence of European traditions is undeniable, since schools brought literary models to those able to pursue English studies beyond the primary grades. Black Africa's first doctorate B. W. Vilakazi wrote Zulu poetry in the 1930s strongly reminiscent of nineteenth-century Romantic poetry, as in "Impophoma ye Victoria" ("Victoria Falls") and "We Moya" ("Oh Wind") in which he experimented with rhyme. Both the obsession with "nature," a term which even in English has undergone vast changes of meaning, and the use of rhyme are totally foreign to traditional Zulu poetry but so is the genre of fiction. This did not prevent Vilakazi from writing not only traditionally oriented Zulu verse but the powerful "Ezinkomponi" ("In the Mines"), an indictment of the dehumanization and victimization of the gold mines of Johannesburg which, like Victoria Falls, he had never visited. Despite editorial control, then, much of literature in African languages was surprisingly vital despite the necessarily amateur status of its authors. The emergence of African literature in European languages may be dated from sources from West to South Africa depending on definitions . . . but certainly it goes back a long way. Still, it was the Francophone writers such as Senghor who emerged as early as the 1940s, long before most Anglophone writers, perhaps for the very reason that no literature in African languages existed for speakers of French (or Portuguese, for whom literary chronology is even more difficult).

The development of Anglophone literature can be imagined from a number of vantage points. Nigeria provides one such starting place since this country has produced not only the greatest number of African writers but the best-known Igbo language literature, as Emenyonu . . . points out, was crippled by problems of finding a standard form with an orthography acceptable to all members of a loosely federated, linguistically diverse amalgamation of peoples. The birth of "Onitsha Market Literature," privately printed pamphlets in an approximation of English in every conceivable genre, covering topics from amorous advice to an account of the death of Patrice Lumumba tallies vaguely with the end of Igbo language literature. Onitsha literature could still be found when I visited the famed market in 1976, but the genre was clearly dying out. Oozing "sophistication" it was a literature of the Igbo for the Igbo. Why, then, was it written in English? The answer surely has less to do with orthographic problems and more to do with the prestige of English and everything associated it, a cliche about the Igbo, perhaps, but one that is surely related to the phenomenal success of Igbo writers like Cyprian Ekwensi, Chinua Achebe, Christopher Okigbo, and many others who are well known in their own country. Thus Igbo literature became Anglophone, but not as a result of the failure of the literature in the Igbo language.

It was in Western Nigeria that such writers as Achebe from the East, John Pepper Clark and Gabriel Okara from the Delta, and Wole Soyinka from the West met to form the literary group known as the Mbari Club, which published materials mostly in English: poetry, myths, stories and studies on African themes. Among them were South African exiles Dennis Brutus and Ezekiel Mphahlele and expatriates such as Ulli Beier and Janheinz Jahn. There is little wonder that English, Nigeria's official language, became the language of literature at this point for of these only Soyinka knew Yoruba. Yoruba had one of the richest literary traditions in all of Africa, but this master of English could hardly be blamed for wanting to reach fellow Nigerians as well as the rest of the English-speaking world. This was hardly an abandonment of Yoruba since his work, whether in poetry or drama, breathes the culture not only of Yoruba tradition but the modern world of lorry divers and mangled roadside spectacles with Ogun in spectral attendance. The Muslim Hausa have for the most part continued to gaze east. Prizing centuries-old forms of poetry but also composing drama, a form especially popular in Niger, they have composed novels since a colonial officer named R. M. East insisted on their creation in 1934 as part of a bid to increase literacy in the *boko* or Roman script. Since most pious mallams [Muslim teachers] found fiction an affront to their religion, this form has taken off only recently though Nigeria's first prime minister, Abubakar Tafawa Balewa, wrote a moving work of historical fiction, *Shaihu Umar*, in 1934, that has been translated into English while several other works of the 1930s continue to be read in schools. Nigeria, then, is a typical example of diverse responses to the language problem in African literature, the Igbo abandoning their language, the Yoruba keeping it alive alongside English, while the Hausa, though influenced by colonialism, maintain a stolid loyalty to their native tongue especially through poetic genres meant to be performed publicly rather than experienced as a solitary literary experience.

Achebe and Soyinka were soon followed by Ghanaians Ayi Kwei Armah and Kofi Awoonor and other writers from southern West Africa but it was in a literary journal published in Kampala that the language question was first seriously raised. In the most-quoted (and most often mis-cited) article in African literary criticism Obiajunwa Wali . . . then a graduate student at Northwestern University, asked how a literature that called itself African could be written in colonial languages. The storm which ensued is ably documented in Benson. . . . But in the years which followed African literature made a name for itself worldwide, courses on African literature were offered in American and European universities, and in this context African literature became almost by definition literature in English or French (Lusophone literature being more esoteric). Those of us who studied literatures in African languages were a snooty minority and of course many of us only took that path through language studies on the way to hopeful competence in studies of oral tradition (still a wayward child in the early 1970s when it was most often called "oral literature," a contradiction in terms replaced eventually by the even more ghastly "orature"). Again, the language problem seemed to fade.

• • •

South African exiled writer Lewis Nkosi once showered Ngugi at a conference with a burst of Zulu as the Kenyan harangued his audience to write in their own languages. The point, of course, was that Ngugi could not understand him. Even more importantly, as an exile then living in London, he could hardly write in Zulu when even his English works were banned in his native land. Years earlier, Nkosi had written off South African "vernacular" literature as a government controlled, childish spinoff of the despised "Bantu Education," literature for inferiority. . . . His sentiments were shared by many other South African writers, notably Ezekiel Mphahlele who as early as the 1950s had noted Afrikaaner publishers' interests in African language manuscripts forced to adhere to urban nightmare/retreat to the homelands plots as a handy advert for influx control. . . . Apartheid seeks, of course, not only to separate races but ethnic groups whose potential combined power is formidable. Language divisions, given added emphasis by official sponsorship and textbook requirements in ethnically segregated schools, are merely another facet of "separate development." Furthermore, as Sipho Sepamla notes . . . English provides access to black authors beyond Africa, whether in America or the Carribean. Though African language literature has continued and many of her writers have gone well beyond the plots that Mphahlele describes and found increasing sophistication, the language protest in South Africa has been English. In addition, the literature that began in African language newspapers and continued with magazines like *Drum* in the 1950s has invented new forms to outwit the censor and to stimulate political awareness. Since Soweto the art form is not the printed book, subject to confiscation and destruction, but mobile spare theater without fixed texts or the usual theatrical trappings. Using a variety of languages, reflecting merely the reality of township life, the medium is English not so much as a political statement in itself but as a practical matter where so many of such diverse background are bound together.

Boston: African Studies Center at Boston University, pp. 2–5.

ACHEBE'S POSITION ON THE LANGUAGE CHOICE DEBATE

Achebe's own choice of English instead of his native Igbo in which to write *Things Fall Apart* and other novels is one of the factors that began the language choice debate. He has succeeded tremendously in romanticizing Igbo culture and civilization in fiction not only within Nigeria and Africa, but also in America and Europe. That success is measured by the number of copies (over 8 million) *Things Fall Apart* has sold and the number of languages (fifty-two worldwide) into which it has been translated. In the following excerpt, Achebe discusses and defends his use of English.

FROM CHINUA ACHEBE, *MORNING YET ON CREATION DAY*
(1976)

The African Writer and the English Language

You cannot cram African literature into a small, neat definition. I do not see African literature as one unit but as a group of associated units—in fact the sum total of all the *national* and *ethnic* literatures of Africa.

A national literature is one that takes the whole nation for its province and has a realized or potential audience throughout its territory. In other words a literature that is written in the *national* language. An ethnic literature is one which is available only to one ethnic group within the nation. If you take Nigeria as an example, the national literature, as I see it, is the literature written in English; and the ethnic literatures are in Hausa, Ibo, Yoruba, Efik, Edo, Ijaw, etc., etc.

Any attempt to define African literature in terms which overlook the complexities of the African scene at the material time is doomed to failure. After the elimination of white rule shall have been completed, the single most important fact in Africa in the second half of the twentieth century will appear to be the rise of individual nation-states. I believe that African literature will follow the same pattern.

What we tend to do today is to think of African literature as a newborn infant. But in fact what we have is a whole generation of newborn infants. Of course, if you only look cursorily, one infant is pretty much like another; but in reality each is already set on its own separate journey. Of course, you may group them together on the basis of anything you choose—the color of their hair, for instance. Or you may group them together on the basis of the language they will speak or the religion of their fathers. Those would all be valid distinctions; but they could not begin to account fully for each individual person carrying, as it were, his own little, unique lodestar of genes.

Those who in talking about African literature want to exclude North Africa because it belongs to a different tradition surely do not suggest that Black Africa is anything like homogeneous. What does Shabaan Robert have in common with Christopher Okigbo or Awoonor-Williams? Or Mongo Beti or Cameroun and Paris with Nzekwu of Nigeria? What does the champagne-drinking upper-class Creole society described by Easmon of Sierra Leone have in common with the rural folk and fishermen of J. P. Clark's plays? Of course, some of these differences could be accounted for on individual rather than national grounds, but a good deal of it is also environmental.

I have indicated somewhat offhandedly that the national literature of Nigeria and of many other countries of Africa is, or will be, written in English. This may sound like a controversial statement, but it isn't. All I have done has been to look at the reality of present-day Africa. This "reality" may change as a result of deliberate, e.g., political, action. If it does, an entirely new situation will arise, and there will be plenty of time to examine it. At present it may be more profitable to look at the scene as it is. What are the factors which have conspired to place English in the position of national language in many parts of Africa? Quite simply the reason is that these nations were created in the first place by the intervention of the British which, I hasten to add, is not saying that the peoples comprising these nations were invented by the British.

The country which we know as Nigeria today began not so very long ago as the arbitrary creation of the British. It is true, as William Fagg says in his excellent new book, *Nigerian Images*, that this arbitrary action has proved as lucky in terms of African art history as any enterprise of the fortunate Princess of Serendip. And I believe that in political and economic terms too this arbitrary creation called Nigeria holds out great prospects. Yet the fact remains that Nigeria was created by the British— for their own ends. Let us give the devil his due: colonialism in Africa disrupted many things, but it did create big political units where there were small, scattered ones before. Nigeria had hundreds of autonomous communities ranging in size from the vast Fulani Empire founded by Usman dan Fodio in the north to tiny village entities in the east. Today it is one country.

Of course there are areas of Africa where colonialism divided up a single ethnic group among two or even three powers. But on the whole it did bring together many peoples that had hitherto gone their several ways. And it gave them a language with which to talk to one another. If it failed to give them a song, it at least gave them a tongue, for sighing. There are not many countries in Africa today where you could abolish the language of the erstwhile colonial powers and still retain the facility for mutual communication. Therefore those African writers who have chosen to write in English or French are not unpatriotic smart alecks with an eye on the main chance—outside their own countries. They are by-products of the same process that made the new nation-states of Africa.

You can take this argument a stage further to include other countries of Africa. The only reason why we can even talk about African unity is that when we get together we can have a manageable number of languages to talk in—English, French, Arabic.

. . . And there are scores of languages I would want to learn if it were possible. Where am I to find the time to learn the half dozen or so Nigerian languages, each of which can sustain a literature? I am afraid it cannot be done. These languages will just have to develop as tributaries to feed the one central language enjoying nationwide currency. Today, for good or ill, that language is English. Tomorrow it may be something else, although I very much doubt it.

Those of us who have inherited the English language may not be in a position to appreciate the value of the inheritance. Or we may go on resenting it because it came as part of a package deal which included many other items of doubtful value and the positive atrocity of racial arrogance and prejudice which may yet set the world on fire. But let us not in rejecting the evil throw out the good with it.

. . . I think I have said enough to give an indication of my thinking on the importance of the world language which history has forced down our throats. Now let us look at some of the most serious handicaps. And let me say straightaway that one of the most serious handicaps is *not* the one people talk about most often, namely, that it is impossible for anyone ever to use a second language as effectively as his first. This assertion is compounded of half truth and half bogus mystique. Of course, it is true that the vast majority of people are happier with their first language than with any other. But then the majority of people are not writers. We do have enough examples of writers who have performed the feat of writing effectively in a second language. And I am not thinking of the obvious names like Conrad. It would be more germane to our subject to choose African examples.

The first name that comes to my mind is Olauda Equiano, better known as Gustavus Vassa, the African. Equiano was an Ibo, I believe from the village of Iseke in the Orlu division of Eastern Nigeria. He was sold as a slave at a very early age and transported to America. Later he bought his freedom and lived in England. In 1789 he published his life story, a beautifully written document which, among other things, set down for the Europe of his time something of the life and habits of his people in Africa, in an attempt to counteract the lies and slander invented by some Europeans to justify the slave trade.

Coming nearer to our times, we may recall the attempts in the first quarter of this century by West African nationalists to come together and press for a greater say in the management of their own affairs. One of the most eloquent of that band was the Honorable Casely Hayford of the Gold Coast. His presidential address to the National congress of British West Africa in 1925 was memorable not only for its sound common sense but as a fine example of elegant prose. The governor of Nigeria at the time was compelled to take notice and he did so in characteristic style: he called Hayford's Congress "a self-selected and self-appointed congregation of educated African gentlemen." We may derive some amusement from the fact that British colonial administrators learned very little in the following quarter of a century. But at least they *did* learn in the end—which is more than one can say for some others.

. . . I do not see any signs of sterility anywhere here. What I do see is a new voice coming out of Africa, speaking of African experience in a world-wide language. So, my answer to the question *Can an African ever learn English well enough to be able to use it effectively in creative writing?* is certainly yes. If on the other hand you ask: *Can he ever learn to use it like a native speaker?* I should say, I hope not. It is neither necessary nor desirable for him to be able to do so. The price a world language must be prepared to pay is submission to many different kinds of use. The African writer should aim to use English in a way that brings out his message best without altering the language to the extent that its value as a medium of international exchange will be lost. He should aim at fashioning out an English which is at once universal and able to carry his peculiar experience. I have in mind here the writer who has something new, something different to say. The nondescript writer has little to tell us, anyway, so he might as well tell it in conventional language and get it over with.

New York: Anchor/Doubleday, pp. 75–82.

CONCLUSION

In this language choice debate, we have seen the various positions taken by African writers and critics, ranging from continued use of foreign languages—English, French, and Portuguese—to advocacy of the national and ethnic languages of Africa. In making their choice, writers must take into consideration such factors as ethnicity, nationalism, pan-Africanism, literary independence and, above all, audience. Some have even characterized the issue of language choice as a crisis to underscore its complex nature and the need for urgent solutions. In evaluating writers' opinions on this complex issue, bear in mind Achebe's caution: "Nothing is absolute. *I am the truth, the way and the life* would be called blasphemous or simply absurd, for is it not well known that a man may worship Ogwugwu to perfection and yet be killed by Udo?" (*Morning Yet on Creation Day* 223). Budding writers may want to adopt Achebe's own choice of African themes and that brand of English and hybrid style in which he expressed them, for his marriage of themes to language and style resulted in the worship of both Ogwugwu and Udo to perfection, so to speak. So far, neither of the gods has had any reason to kill him.

TOPICS FOR WRITTEN OR ORAL EXPLORATION

1. What is the language choice debate in modern African literature?

2. Evaluate the arguments for and against continuing to write African literature in European languages.

3. Chinua Achebe and Ngugi wa Thiong'o are two famous African writers who have taken different sides in the language debate. Evaluate the position of each and state your own position on the issue.

4. Considering the arguments made against the continued use of European languages as "tools of oppression," do you think Africans are better off writing in their national and ethnic languages?

5. What are the benefits of and impediments to writing African literature in a single adopted continental African language, say Swahili?

6. What advantages and/or disadvantages does Nigeria have in adopting English as its official language?

7. Do you think *Things Fall Apart* could have attracted the type of national and international audience it has if it had been written originally in Igbo, Achebe's native language?

8. Do the Igbo phrases and proverbs in *Things Fall Apart* hinder the narrative activity of the novel?

9. Could Achebe have achieved the same language realism in *Things Fall Apart* had he written it in so-called Queen's English?

10. Based on your understanding of the language choice debate in African literature, do you find any language crisis in *Things Fall Apart*?

SUGGESTED READINGS

Achebe, Chinua. *Morning Yet on Creation Day*. New York: Anchor/Doubleday, 1976.

Emenyonu, Ernest N. *The Rise of the Igbo Novel*. Ibadan, Nigeria: University Press plc, 1978.

Ngugi wa Thiong'o. *Decolonising the Mind: The Politics of Language in African Literature*. London: Heinemann, 1986.

———. *Writing Against Colonialism*. Trenton, N.J.: Red Sea, 1986.

Nkosi, Lewis. *Tasks and Masks: Themes and Styles of African Literature*. Harlow, Essex: Longman, 1981.

Obiechina, Emmanuel N. *Language and Theme: Essays on African Literature*. Washington, D.C.: Howard University Press, 1990.

Westley, David. *Choice of Language and African Literature: A Bibliographic Essay*. Boston: African Studies Center at Boston University, 1990.

Glossary

Afo fourth Igbo weekday in Umuofia

Agalaba ji Igwe pillar that holds the heavenly dome: God

agbala woman; also used to characterize a man who has taken no title

agbara devil or evil spirit

aja sacrifice

Ala (Ani) earth goddess

ala (ani) land or earth

ala mmuo spiritworld

alu (aru) taboo or abominable act

Amadioha god of thunder and war

Anyanwu sun god

Bekee English (language); *ndi bekee*: English people

chi guardian angel, personal god or spirit, soul, or spirit double

Chi-na-Eke creation and destiny of man; also Chi-Okike: creator god

Chineke Christian god

Chukwu Igbo high god

dibia traditional medicine man, healer, or diviner

dike brave man

ede cocoyam, queen of Igbo crops

efulefu   worthless man; also the dregs of society collectively

Egbe   Kite

egwugwu   masked spirits, the personified dead-living ancestors

Ejula   Snail

Eke   Python

Eke   second Igbo weekday in Umuofia

ekwe   talking drum

iba   malarial fever

igba afa (igba aja)   divination

Igbo (Ibo)   the Igbo people; the Igbo language

igbu ichi   facial scarification of titled men and women

Igwe ka Ala   Heaven that is greater/higher than Earth: praise name for the Igbo high god, Chukwu

Ijiji   fly

ilo   the village green; open space for sports, meetings, weddings, and other village assemblies

Ilu Igbo   Igbo proverb

ji   yam, king of Igbo crops

Mbe   Tortoise, the trickster in Igbo folktales

mmanwu (mmuo)   masquerader; masked spirit

mmanya ngwuo   palm wine

mmuo   spirit

ndichie   clan or village elders

Nfijoku   yam god

Ngwere   Lizard

Nkita   Dog, Igbo man's best friend

nkwá   statue

nkwa   dance, as in *nkwa umuagbogho* (dance of the maidens)

Nkwo   first Igbo weekday in Umuofia

nso-ala   taboo or abominable act against the earth goddess, Ala

nwanyi   female

nwoke   male

nza   a small sun bird

obodo dike   land of the brave

ochu   murder or manslaughter

ogbanje   a changeling: a child who repeatedly dies and returns to its mother to be reborn

ogene   gong

Ogwugwu   a river god

oja (opi)   flute

oji   kola nut

omenala   custom

Orie (Oye)   third Igbo weekday in Umuofia

osu   outcast; having been dedicated to a god, the *osu* was taboo and was not allowed to mix with the freeborn in any way

ozo   one of the titles and ranks Igbo men take

ugo   eagle

uke (ogbo)   age-grade

uri (uli)   a dye used by women for drawing ornamental patterns on the skin

Index

Achebe, Chinua: colonialism and, 56–57; criticisms of British novelists, 157, 159–63, 170; "crossroads" analogy of, 181–82; education of, 56, 158–59, 170; influence of, 1–2, 171–72; on language, 185–86; overall theme of, 177; personal chronology of, 157–58; problem of literary language and, 211; on stories and storytelling, 182–86; technical style of, 16; as writer-teacher, 2, 12, 82, 106, 176–77

Achebe school of writers, 163–64, 171–72

Adventures of an African Slaver (Canot), 36–38, 42–44

Africa: Achebe's authentic historical view of, 2; British novelists' accounts of, 2–3, 159–63, 170; Christian missionary efforts in, 103–4, 175; chronology of, 21–22; distorted and stereotypical images of, 22, 159–63, 164; European colonial rule in, 51–55, 58–60, 169–70; European scramble for, 24–26; geography of, 28–31; partition of, 27; Portuguese navigators in, 24, 32–34; pre-colonial European contacts with, 22–24. *See also* Slave raids and trade

African literature: Anglophone, 212–13; appropriateness of novelistic form in, 209–10; definition of, 173–74; elements of modern novel and, 3–16, 16; in Gikuyu (Kenyan) language, 198–200; as hybrid genre, 163–64; Nigerian and Igbo writers of, 171, 172–75; Onitsha market literature in, 212–13; preoccupation with history in, 176–80; West African writers in, 201–6. *See also* Language choice debate

About the Author

KALU OGBAA, an Igboman scholar, is professor of English at Southern Connecticut State University, where he teaches Africana (African, African American, and Afro-Caribbean) and American literatures. He is the editor of *The Gong and the Flute: African Literary Development and Celebration* (Greenwood, 1994), and the author of *Gods, Oracles and Divination: Folkways in Chinua Achebe's Novels* (1992), *Igbo* (1965), as well as numerous articles on African and Commonwealth literatures.